THE 1999
CRICKET
WORLD CUP

Essential Stats
and Facts

D1355502

THE 1999
CRICKET
WORLD CUP

Essential Stats and Facts

STEVE PEARCE & BILL DAY

ACKNOWLEDGEMENTS

The authors would like to thank the following
for their valuable help in producing this book — Tony
Graham and Mark Goldsmith at Allsport, all at
Final Score, Chris Lane, Lawrence Booth, Graeme
Wright, Ian Piercy, Cara Sloman and especially Jean
Day and Ruth Pearce.

All Wisden World Cup Verdicts by Steven Lynch,
managing editor of Wisden Cricket Monthly.

First published in 1999 by Boxtree, an imprint of Macmillan Publishers Ltd, 25 Eccleston
Place, London, SW1W 9NF and Basingstoke.

Associated companies throughout the world.

ISBN 0 7522 1736 4

Copyright © 1999 ECB ™

A CIP catalogue record for this book is available from the British Library

Design by Colin Halliday Design (01322 527034)
Repro by Final Score, Fairview House, Blind Lane, Billericay, Essex. CM12 9SN.

All photographs supplied by Allsport UK.

Printed by Mackays of Chatham plc, Kent

CONTENTS

PART 1: ENGLAND 99

PART TWO: THE TEAMS
GROUP A

GROUP B

PART THREE: MEMORIES

INDEX

* All statistics correct as at January 24, 1999 unless stated.

PART ONE: ENGLAND 99

A CARNIVAL OF CRICKET

Cricket is coming home! The World Cup, the greatest festival of one-day cricket on earth, is returning to England in 1999 for the first time in 16 years.

As the Football Association dispatch emissaries overseas on a regular basis to test the prospects of hosting the 2006 World Cup, and the feasibility of Britain holding an Olympic Games remains an impossible dream for the British Olympic Association, so their cricket and rugby union counterparts have stolen the show and walked off with sport's two other crown jewels — the cricket and rugby World Cups.

Cricket's 'Mardi Gras' begins at Lord's on Friday, May 14 and ends there 37 days later on June 20, unless it rains, when the captain of one of the 12 competing countries will raise the new £27,000 crafted sterling silver and gilt World Cup trophy above his head to celebrate the ultimate in cricket achievement.

Not since India's captain Kapil Dev kissed the Prudential Assurance trophy, in one of those famous balcony scenes reserved for one-day winners back in 1983, has Lord's had the opportunity to stage the final of the tournament.

In those days, the commercial possibilities created by the World Cup were in their infancy. Today, some fear that the cricket has become secondary to commercialism, a complaint that is rejected by the England Cricket Board as it prepares to exploit, not the pound or the dollar, but a national passion for the game that has lain dormant since English crowds warmed to the runs that flowed from the bats of Len Hutton, Denis Compton, Peter May, Colin Cowdrey and Ian Botham.

Terry Blake, the England 99 Tournament Director and a mere university student when the first World Cup was held here in 1975, wants to generate a 'carnival' atmosphere, selling tickets to those who would not normally attend a cricket match.

"We want to attract a new audience. We want families. We want primary and secondary schools to run World Cup theme events. We want to encourage street parties close to the grounds where matches will be played," he says.

"On any visit to India (they co-hosted the 1987 and 1996 World Cups) you notice that cricket, in terms of popularity, is right up there with films and music. A lot of people feel passionately about cricket in the United Kingdom, but it is not a national passion.

"When England beat Australia at Edgbaston in 1997, five million people were watching. If England's football team reaches the World Cup semi-finals, 25 million will watch it. We must aspire to those figures. I believe it is not a hopeless task."

Ground regulations, so strictly adhered to since hooliganism desecrated sport's image as family entertainment in Britain, will be relaxed in an effort to generate the right mood inside cricket grounds. Trumpets, banners, flags and the other trappings of spectator worship will be pulled out of cupboards as the barriers come down.

As the England Cricket Board's chief executive Tim Lamb points out: "The ECB will take the game to the people. The 1999 World Cup will attract a whole new audience to the game."

Terrestrial and satellite television channels will share the tournament; large profits are guaranteed; the format for the 12 competing countries is designed to maintain public interest from start to finish; and the promotion of a 'cricket carnival' remains paramount, seeking to ensure that all the commercial wheeler-dealing is kept firmly where it should be — behind closed doors, well away from the punter carrying his ice-box and sandwich tin.

The big difference between World Cup 99 and the last tournament, hosted by India, Pakistan and Sri Lanka, is that all the countries will share the financial risks involved and profit will be distributed evenly among the competing countries.

Sky Sports and the BBC will share television coverage of the 42-match tournament. The World Cup final, on June 20, will be shown live on both Sky Sports and BBC TV — shared coverage in an £8 million television agreement that demonstrates Blake's negotiating skills. "A great deal for cricket, a great deal for viewers," is his explanation.

The cumulative global reach of the World Cup is expected to exceed two billion residents in some 80 to 100 countries. The sponsorship is huge and half a million ticket application forms were released in May 1998 for matches to be held in England, Ireland, Scotland, Wales and Holland. Costs range from £14 for some group matches to £100 for the best seats at the final.

Package deals, priced £160-465, are being encouraged. Marquee restaurants will be set up in and around the grounds. Hostesses will serve champagne in private viewing boxes; and the junketing promises to go on long after stumps.

But the rising mood of anticipation felt by your average punter for this blue riband event suggests that for all the multi-million pound deals, the explosion of media interest and free-loading, the cricket itself and the carnival played out in the public seating areas on grounds from Dublin's fair city to Amsterdam, and from Edinburgh to Southampton, will have held sway when the spectators have gone home and ECB officials hold their debriefing inquest.

Teams from the nine International Cricket Council Full Member countries, plus Bangladesh, Kenya and Scotland, who came first, second and third in the 1997 ICC Trophy, will compete in England 99.

The squads represent a 'Who's Who' of cricketing talent from all corners of the globe. For many players World Cup 99 will represent their last World Cup appearance.

As Imran Khan bade farewell to the game in spectacular fashion at Melbourne after leading Pakistan to triumph in the 1992 tournament and Australia's captain Allan Border also made that his last World Cup, so several more of the game's great players will leave the stage this time as the unique physical demands of one-day cricket take their toll on the bodies of those aged more than 30.

World Cup captains Alec Stewart (England), Steve Waugh (Australia), Hansie Cronje (South Africa), Wasim Akram (Pakistan), Arjuna Ranatunga (Sri Lanka) and Kenya's vice skipper Maurice Odumbe will all probably be playing in their last tournament.

And how much more cricket can the West Indies expect from Curtly Ambrose and Courtney Walsh?

Each and everyone of them can expect to receive generous ovations wherever they play come May and June, win or lose.

When the first World Cup was played in England 24 years ago, limited-overs cricket was in its infancy worldwide but becoming increasingly popular in the English domestic game at the beginning of that World Cup season in which Lancashire would win the Gillette Cup and Hampshire the Sunday League.

In those days everyone played cricket in cream shirts, flannels and white buckskin boots, and not until the 1992 World Cup would coloured 'pyjamas' appear at the finals, and then to the obvious disgust of cricket's traditionalists and old buffers.

Today, cricket's often-maligned visionaries have somehow managed to encourage the onslaught of limited-overs cricket in order to protect the game's future, whilst also managing to covet and preserve all its Test Match traditions. Nowhere will this clever juggling act become more spectacularly poignant than at Lord's on Sunday, June 20, 1999 — the World Cup final.

Dust down your sun hats, dig out your T-shirts and shorts, grab your flip-flops and sun cream and prepare to enjoy the greatest cricket carnival on earth.

Let's hope it's a classic!

WHO, WHERE AND WHEN

The 12 World Cup teams have been seeded and are divided up into two groups. They each play the other five countries in their section with the top three teams in each group progressing to the Super Six Round, taking with them the points scored against the other successful teams in their group. They then each play the three teams left in the tournament that they haven't already met, adding to their points tally. The top four at the end of the Super Six phase compete in the semi-finals with the winners meeting at Lord's on June 20.

GROUP A	GROUP B
England	Australia
India	Bangladesh
Kenya	New Zealand
South Africa	Pakistan
Sri Lanka	Scotland
Zimbabwe	West Indies

Date	Match	Venue	TV Broadcaster
May 14	England v Sri Lanka	Lord's	SKY
May 15	India v South Africa	Hove	SKY
May 15	Zimbabwe v Kenya	Taunton	SKY
May 16	Australia v Scotland	Worcester	BBC
May 16	West Indies v Pakistan	Bristol	BBC
May 17	Bangladesh v New Zealand	Chelmsford	SKY

SUPER SIX

June 4	Runner-up A v Runner-up B	The Oval	SKY
June 5	Winner A v Winner B	Trent Bridge	BBC
June 6	Third in A v Third in B	Headingley	SKY
June 8	Runner-up A v Winner B	Old Trafford	SKY
June 9	Third in A v Runner-up B	Lord's	BBC
June 10	Winner A v Third in B	Edgbaston	SKY
June 11	Third in A v Winner B	The Oval	BBC
June 12	Runner-up A v Third in B	Trent Bridge	BBC
June 13	Winner A v Runner-up B	Headingley	SKY

May 18	England v Kenya	Canterbury	BBC
May 19	Sri Lanka v South Africa	Northampton	SKY
May 19	India v Zimbabwe	Leicester	SKY
May 20	Australia v New Zealand	Cardiff	BBC
May 20	Pakistan v Scotland	Chester-le-Street	BBC
May 21	West Indies v Bangladesh	Dublin	SKY
May 22	England v South Africa	The Oval	BBC
May 22	Zimbabwe v Sri Lanka	Worcester	BBC
May 23	Kenya v India	Bristol	SKY
May 23	Australia v Pakistan	Headingley	SKY
May 24	West Indies v New Zealand	Southampton	BBC
May 24	Scotland v Bangladesh	Edinburgh	BBC
May 25	England v Zimbabwe	Trent Bridge	SKY
May 26	Sri Lanka v India	Taunton	BBC
May 26	South Africa v Kenya	Amsterdam	BBC
May 27	West Indies v Scotland	Leicester	SKY
May 27	Australia v Bangladesh	Chester-le-Street	SKY
May 28	New Zealand v Pakistan	Derby	SKY
May 29	England v India	Edgbaston	SKY
May 29	Zimbabwe v South Africa	Chelmsford	SKY
May 30	Sri Lanka v Kenya	Southampton	BBC
May 30	West Indies v Australia	Old Trafford	BBC
May 31	Scotland v New Zealand	Edinburgh	SKY
May 31	Pakistan v Bangladesh	Northampton	SKY

SEMI-FINALS

June 16		Old Trafford	TBA
June 17		Edgbaston	TBA

FINAL

June 20		Lord's	SKY/BBC

·BBC and SKY will each cover one semi-final.

ON THE SCREEN

Every ball, every shot, every catch, every controversial decision will be captured by the cameras of BBC and Sky during the World Cup.

With an estimated cumulative global television audience of approaching two billion, the battle for honours on the screen is sure to be as intense as the one for the trophy.

The group matches and coverage of the Super Six stage will be shared between the two channels, with both covering one semi-final each. The final at Lord's will be screened by BBC and Sky.

And there is plenty of cricketing talent in the commentary box, each expert no doubt ready to air their views on everything from a catch at short leg to a mini-skirted beauty with long legs.

Here are the men behind the voices you will be hearing a lot from during this summer's extravaganza.

DAVID GOWER
PRESENTER AND COMMENTATOR ... SKY

David Gower will present and commentate on Sky Sports' live international cricket, making his debut with the 1999 Cricket World Cup.

One of the most gifted batsmen of his generation, he made 117 Test appearances for England, scoring 8231 runs at an average of 44.25.

His stylish play took him to 18 Test match centuries and he was awarded the captaincy of his country for 32 Tests.

In 1992 he overtook Geoff Boycott as England's most prolific Test batsman and the country's most capped cricketer, records since overtaken only by Graham Gooch.

In domestic cricket he played for Leicestershire for 14 seasons from 1975 — five as captain — before ending his career with Hampshire.

He hit a total of 26,339 runs in first class cricket, averaging 40.08 with 53 centuries to his name. In that time he took 280 catches — and even one stumping to prove his all-round talent.

The stylish left-handed batsman retired from first-class and international cricket in November 1993 and elected to pursue a career in the media world.

He worked for Sky Sports on England's overseas tour to India (1992-93), West Indies (1993-94) and Australia (1994-95), has commentated for Channel 9 in Australia and has been contracted to BBC Television as a presenter and commentator since 1995.

He is also a captain on the popular sports quiz show *They Think It's All Over*, opposite his great friend from their days together in the city

of Leicester, Gary Lineker — Gower the idol of the cricket half of Leicester, Lineker the football half.
WORLD CUPS PLAYED IN: 1979,1983

IAN BOTHAM OBE
COMMENTATOR ... SKY

The English cricket legend has been with Sky since 1995 when he covered the tour to South Africa, as well as the trips to Zimbabwe and New Zealand in 1996-97 and the Caribbean a year later.

Botham was a massive hit from day one of his Test career, taking five wickets on his debut in 1977, at the age of just 21. He played over 100 times for his country, scoring 5,200 runs and included 14 centuries in that tally.

But 'Beefy' will be most remembered for one memorable performance above all back in July 1981. In a seemingly hopeless position for England, he blasted his way to an 87-ball century against Australia at Headingley, eventually finishing unbeaten on 149, to give Mike Brearley's side a fighting chance. He then helped a wind-assisted Bob Willis blow away the stunned Australians and take the match by 18 runs.

It was one of the most amazing Test Matches of all time and Fred Trueman described Botham's match haul of 199 runs and seven wickets as: "the greatest all-round display I have ever seen in a Test Match."

Somerset, Worcester and Durham all had the luxury of watching the master craftsman at work and the Leukaemia Research Fund benefited from his long-distance walks up and down Britain that raised millions for the charity.

Botham also became a TV favourite when he joined former England rugby captain Bill Beaumont as skippers in the popular BBC quiz game, *A Question of Sport*.

Now he is at the wicket for the other side.
WORLD CUPS PLAYED IN: 1979, 1983, 1992

BOB WILLIS MBE
COMMENTATOR ... SKY

A seasoned campaigner with Sky Sports, he covered both the 1992 and 1996 World Cups, as well as England tours of Australia, New Zealand, South Africa, Zimbabwe and the West Indies, and many domestic seasons.

Willis is arguably the most successful bowler in English Test Match history, playing in 90 Tests in an international career that spanned 13 years.

A captain in 18 Tests, he took a total of 325 Test wickets after making his debut against Australia in Sydney in 1971, and like Botham, enjoyed an amazing match against the Australians in 1981, when his second innings figures of eight for 43 gave England victory.

His county career began at Surrey in 1969. He moved to Warwickshire three years later and stayed there until his retirement in 1984, captaining the side over the final five years of his career.

He is a co-author of several books, was on the editorial board of Wisden Cricket Monthly for 16 years and toured the West Indies with England in 1986-87 as assistant manager.

WORLD CUPS PLAYED IN: 1979, 1983

PAUL ALLOTT
COMMENTATOR ... SKY

Retired from first-class cricket in 1992 and has developed a career in broadcasting and journalism since then, working for both the BBC and now Sky.

Was part of the Test Match Special team before joining Sky Sports as a commentator for the Ashes series in 1994-95.

Allott played 13 times for England after starting his county career with Lancashire in 1978. His first international cap came in the Old Trafford win over the Australians in 1981, when he took four for 88 in the match and made 52 not out as England retained the Ashes.

As well as his Sky TV work, Paul is a contributor to both the *Observer* and *Guardian* newspapers and is a director of *The Cricketer Magazine*.

WORLD CUPS PLAYED IN: 1983

MICHAEL HOLDING
COMMENTATOR ... SKY

The former West Indian great will commentate on Sky Sports' live coverage of the 1999 Cricket World Cup, as well as Sky Sports' live domestic and international cricket.

In his playing career he was one of the most feared fast bowlers in the game, and formed a famous pace attack with Andy Roberts, Joel Garner and Malcolm Marshall.

Playing in the same era as fellow Sky commentators Ian Botham, Bob Willis and David Gower, he made 60 Test appearances for the West Indies, taking 249 wickets at 23.68 apiece.

His best Test performance brought 14 for 149 against England at The Oval in 1976 on his second tour with West Indies. He finished that trip with 55 victims, 28 of them in Test Matches, taking five batsmen for just 17 runs as England were dismissed for 71 at Old Trafford.

Born in 1954, Holding made his first class debut for Jamaica in 1972-73, and also went on to play domestic cricket for Lancashire and Derbyshire in the English county Championship, and Tasmania and Canterbury.

He finished his first-class career with a total of 778 wickets at an average of 23.43 and tasted glory in the World Cup in 1979, when he helped West Indies to victory over England in the final at Lord's.

As a commentator, his voice has been heard on Sky's winter tours to the West Indies in 1989-90, 1993-94 and 1997-98 and Sky Sports' domestic cricket in the summers of 1995, '97 and '98.

WORLD CUPS PLAYED IN: 1979, 1983

RICHIE BENAUD OBE
PRESENTER AND COMMENTATOR ... BBC

One of the greatest captains in Test cricket, and now regarded as one of the best – if not the best – commentator in the world.

The silky voice of the Australian legend has been heard in every cricket-loving family's living room around the world for over 35 years.

Benaud was primarily a leg-spin bowler when he took over the captaincy of Australia in the late-fifties, following an era in which England were the dominating force in the Ashes clashes.

The New South Wales player turned the tide in Australia's favour with his shrewd leadership skills, allied to his imaginative bowling, helping his side beat England in two series wins, as well as successes against Pakistan, India and West Indies.

He proved he should be considered an all-rounder on the tour to South Africa in 1957-58 when he scored four centuries in his total of 817 runs as an attacking lower middle-order bat.

Benaud was at his best again in 1958-59, taking 31 wickets as Australia regained the Ashes. In 1961, he brought his team to England for one final time and blitzed his rivals again in the Fourth Test at Old Trafford.

With England standing at 150 for one and needing only another 106 for victory, Richie turned on the magic with the ball to skittle his opponents out for 201 with figures of six for 70.

Born on October 6, 1930, he is as popular in England as he is in Australia and with 63 Tests under his belt, 2201 runs at an average of 24.45 and 248 wickets at 27.03 apiece before a shoulder injury forced his retirement in 1964, he can truly be considered as one of cricket's greats.

WORLD CUPS PLAYED IN: None

• At the time of going to press, the BBC had not finalised the rest of their team for the World Cup.

THE VENUES

The 42 matches will be shared between the 18 first-class counties with Scotland, Ireland and Holland all hosting games as well.

AMSTERDAM VRA GROUND, AMSTELVEEN

TEL: 0031 20 6418525/6459816

CAPACITY: 3000

HOSTS: MAY 26 ... SOUTH AFRICA v KENYA

Based on the outskirts of Amsterdam and is also home to the Dutch Cricket Board. South Africa have already played here, with Gary Kirsten scoring an unbeaten 123 in a limited overs match against Holland last year. The host club side, VRA, are the reigning Dutch League champions. Holland crashed out of the ICC Trophy at the quarter-finals after reaching the World Cup in 1996 and although plans are in motion to erect seating area at the ground, the Dutch Cricket Board are not expecting a big attendance for their one group match.

HOW TO GET THERE

By Rail: Amsterdam Central.

By Road: Follow Amstelveen signs to Amstelveen Centre exit. Turn right at lights into Keizer Karelweg. After just over a mile, turn left into Nieuwe Kalfjeslaan. Follow signs to the ground from there.

BRISTOL SUN ALLIANCE COUNTY GROUND

TEL: 0117 9108000

CAPACITY: 8383

HOSTS: MAY 16 ... WEST INDIES v PAKISTAN; MAY 23 ... KENYA v INDIA

Former Gloucestershire favourite Courtney Walsh will be back at his old hunting ground for West Indies' clash with Pakistan, the pick of the two matches at a ground that celebrates its centenary this year.

HOW TO GET THERE

By Rail: Bristol Temple Meads or Bristol Parkway.

By Road: Come off at Junction 2 on the M32 and follow signs for Fishponds. Join Muller Road and then left into Ralph Road. Turn left at end into Ashley Down Road, then right into Kennington Avenue. Then turn left, ground is on the left.

CANTERBURY ST LAWRENCE GROUND

TEL: 01227 456886

CAPACITY: 9000-9500

HOSTS: MAY 18 ... ENGLAND v KENYA

One of the most attractive grounds in the country, made famous by the lime tree that stands within the boundary and guarantees a four should you hit it.

HOW TO GET THERE

By Rail: Canterbury East.

By Road: From M2 take A2, pass first Canterbury turn, then turn off for Bridge. Turn right, then right and follow right again to follow signs for Canterbury (A290). Ground is on left. Approaching from the city centre, take the Old Dover Road (a continuation of the A290) at the roundabout by the bus station.

CARDIFF SOPHIA GARDENS

TEL: 01222 343478

CAPACITY: 6500

HOSTS: MAY 20 ... AUSTRALIA v NEW ZEALAND

Major building work has gone on through the winter at Sophia Gardens, home of Glamorgan since they played their first match there against India in 1967. Should house a big crowd for the clash between big rivals Australia and New Zealand.

HOW TO GET THERE

By Rail: Cardiff Central.

By Road: From M4 come off at junction 29 and follow A48, then A4161 towards the city centre. Follow signs over the Taff Bridge and turn right into Cathedral Road. Ground is on right.

CHELMSFORD THE COUNTY GROUND

TEL: 01245 252420

CAPACITY: 5200

HOSTS: MAY 17... BANGLADESH v NEW ZEALAND;
MAY 29 ... ZIMBABWE v SOUTH AFRICA

Hosted India's victory over Australia in 1983 that took Kapil Dev and co into the semi-finals and is regarded as one of the most modern grounds outside the Test arenas. Not the biggest World Cup venue so expect a few sixes to land in the nearby river.

HOW TO GET THERE

By Rail: Chelmsford.

By Road: Coming from London via A12 or M25, head for Chelmsford. In city centre near junction of A138, take New London Road then turn into New Writtle Street. Ground is 50 yards along on right.

CHESTER-LE-STREET THE RIVERSIDE

TEL: 0191 387 1717

CAPACITY: 6840

HOSTS: MAY 20 ... PAKISTAN v SCOTLAND;
MAY 27... AUSTRALIA v BANGLADESH

Home of English cricket's new boys, Durham, and one of the most impressive. Designed with the aim of becoming a Test Match venue, the extensive site will be the venue of a variety of other sports including tennis, hockey, rugby, athletics and American Football amongst others, and there are also plans for a nature reserve and family housing. Locals should see plenty of runs with two of the minnows in action.

HOW TO GET THERE

By rail: Chester-le-Street.

By Road: From A1 take junction 63, then A167 (Shields Road) south from roundabout. Stay on A167 as it becomes Park Road North then Park Road Central. Turn left at roundabout into Ropery Lane, then right into the Riverside complex.

DERBY THE COUNTY CRICKET GROUND

TEL: 01332 383211

CAPACITY: 3000

HOSTS: MAY 28 ... NEW ZEALAND v PAKISTAN

A ground steeped in history. Formerly a racecourse until 1939, it also housed
the FA Cup Final replay between Blackburn Rovers and West Bromwich Albion
in 1886. A new pavilion and scoreboard as well as stands have been introduced
over the last few years with Derbyshire taking out a 125-year lease on the
ground in the early 1980s.

HOW TO GET THERE

By Rail: Derby.

By Road: The ground is well signposted from Derby ring road, the A61 (Sir
Frank Whittle Road) and A52.

DUBLIN CLONTARF CRICKET CLUB, CASTLE AVENUE

TEL: 003531 8332621

CAPACITY: 3500

HOSTS: MAY 21 ... WEST INDIES v BANGLADESH

One of the smallest venues for World Cup action, but the ground is sure to be
packed for the visit of the West Indies against the underdogs from Bangladesh.
Ireland beat Middlesex at the ground in the Benson and Hedges Cup in 1997
thanks to 94 not out by South African import, Hansie Cronje. A Bangladesh win
in Dublin would put that result very much in the shade.

HOW TO GET THERE

By Rail: Killester (DART).

By Road: From the city centre follow signs to Howth and Clontarf. When you
reach Fairview Park, continue down right fork along Clontarf Road. Castle
Avenue is on left after about half a mile.

EDGBASTON COUNTY GROUND

TEL: 0121 4464422

CAPACITY: 20,744

HOSTS: MAY 29 ... ENGLAND v INDIA; JUNE 10 ... SUPER SIX MATCH;
JUNE 17 ... SEMI-FINAL

One of the premier grounds in England and awarded the accolade of hosting
one of the two semi-finals as well as England's clash with India. Australia were
bowled out for 36 when the ground was used for Test cricket for the first time
in 1902.

HOW TO GET THERE

By Rail: Birmingham New Street.

By Road: From city centre take A441 south, then turn left into Edgbaston
Road (B4217), ground on right. The ground is well signposted from the M6 and
use the ring road to link up with the A441 from other directions.

EDINBURGH GRANGE CRICKET CLUB, RAEBURN PLACE

TEL: 0131 332 2148

CAPACITY: 5231

HOSTS: MAY 24 ... SCOTLAND v BANGLADESH;
MAY 31... SCOTLAND v NEW ZEALAND

Grange Cricket Club have used the facilities as their home for 126 years and the Scots are sure to get plenty of support for their group matches against Bangladesh and New Zealand. The Australians, West Indies and Pakistan all have experience of Raeburn Place and Worcestershire came unstuck there in the NatWest Trophy last season.

HOW TO GET THERE

By Rail: Edinburgh Waverley.

By Road: From city centre, take Princes Street then turn into Frederick Street. After half a mile turn left into South East Circus Place. Continue until the road splits at the end of Deanhaugh Street. Raeburn Place is the middle option and the ground is seen easily on the right of there.

HEADINGLEY HEADINGLEY CRICKET GROUND

TEL: 0113 278 7394

CAPACITY: 14,500

HOSTS: MAY 23 ... AUSTRALIA v PAKISTAN;
JUNE 6 ... SUPER SIX; JUNE 13 ... SUPER SIX MATCH

Leeds Rugby League club backs onto the main stand and while Headingley had its critics in the past with some unsavoury incidents involving the crowds, it is also the venue of so many amazing matches. Botham's heroics in the Ashes of 1981, Winston Davis' seven for 51, including a spell of six for 14, in the World Cup demolition of Australia in 1983 and one of Yorkshire's favourite sons, Geoff Boycott, completing his century of centuries in the 1977 Ashes Test just three of some magic memories the ground holds.

HOW TO GET THERE

By Rail: Headingley.

By Road: From the M1, take junction 47, then M621 and A643 towards city centre. Join A58M and follow signs on to the A660 (Otley, Skipton). The road then becomes Headingley Lane. Turn left into North Lane and the ground is on the left. From M62, take junction 27, then M621 to junction 2, then as described.

HOVE COUNTY GROUND

TEL: 01273 827100

CAPACITY: 6000

HOSTS: MAY 15 ... INDIA v SOUTH AFRICA

Based on the South Coast, only a mile from Brighton. Has some good surrounding vantage points with a nearby block of flats offering the best view of the mouthwatering clash between Allan Donald and Sachin Tendulkar.

HOW TO GET THERE

By Rail: Pick up a connection from Brighton to Hove.

By Road: Take A23 into Brighton then follow signs for A27 Hove. At roundabout take second exit to Brighton. Right into Woodland Drive, left into Shirley Drive, left into Eaton Avenue. Ground is on left.

LEICESTER COUNTY GROUND, GRACE ROAD
TEL: 0116 283 2128/1880

CAPACITY: 4500

HOSTS: MAY 19 ... INDIA v ZIMBABWE: MAY 27 ... WEST INDIES v SCOTLAND

Home of the English county Champions in two of the last three years, Grace Road sees a repeat of the 1983 World Cup clash between India and Zimbabwe which was played at Tunbridge Wells. But locals will have their eye on the West Indies and Brian Lara's side can expect massive support if they include Leicester favourite, Phil Simmons.

HOW TO GET THERE

By Rail: Leicester.

By Road: Take junction 21 off the M1, then A563 in the direction of the city centre. Pick up the A426, then turn right into Grace Road. From city centre, take A426 from inner ring road, Grace Road is a left turn.

LORD'S CRICKET GROUND ST JOHN'S WOOD, LONDON
TEL: 0171 289 1611

CAPACITY: 29,500

HOSTS: MAY 14 ... ENGLAND v SRI LANKA; JUNE 9 ... SUPER SIX MATCH; JUNE 20 ... FINAL

The home of cricket. Has changed completely since the last final there in 1983 with the introduction of a plush new media centre at the Nursery End and a new Grand Stand. The Victorian Pavilion still remains. England and Sri Lanka start the event with their May 14 showdown and just over a month later the eyes of the cricket world will once more be directed at St John's Wood.

HOW TO GET THERE

By Rail: St John's Wood (Underground)

By Road: From central London take inner ring road A501, turn north into A41 at Gloucester Place. From the A41, on right going south just before junction with St John's Wood Road (A5205). From M1 turn left on to North Circular (A406) then follow signs to A41.

NORTHAMPTON COUNTY CRICKET GROUND
TEL: 01604 514455

CAPACITY: 7000

HOSTS: MAY 19 ... SRI LANKA v SOUTH AFRICA; MAY 31 ... PAKISTAN v BANGLADESH

So easy to miss amongst the terrace housing, the County Ground was shared by Northampton Town Football Club and the cricket side. The football pitch was even used as car parking on occasions with no home games allowed in August as cricket took preference. But the cricketers are the lone tenants now after Town's move to Sixfields in 1996.

HOW TO GET THERE

By Rail: Northampton.

By Road: From A45 take A5095 (Rushmere Road) then left into Wellingborough Road (A4500). Then right into Wantage Road which takes you to the ground. From town centre pick up the A4500 Wellingborough Road. Ground is situated north-east of town.

OLD TRAFFORD MANCHESTER
TEL: 0161 282 4000

CAPACITY: 22,000

HOSTS: MAY 30 ... WEST INDIES v AUSTRALIA; JUNE 8 ... SUPER SIX MATCH;
JUNE 16 ... SEMI-FINAL

Home of the one-day kings Lancashire, whose NatWest triumph over Derbyshire last year was their 15th limited-overs triumph in 30 seasons. Old Trafford holds British cricket's all-time crowd record at 38,600 for the 1926 Roses match and is also the second longest-standing English Test venue, staging 63 Test Matches.

HOW TO GET THERE

Rail: Manchester Piccadily then Metrolink to Old Trafford.

By Road: From city centre take A56 south, then left onto A5067. From M60, exit junction 7, take A56 towards Manchester. Turn right onto A5067 (Talbot Road) and ground on right.

THE OVAL KENNINGTON, LONDON
TEL: 0171 582 6660

CAPACITY: 17,500

HOSTS: MAY 22 ... ENGLAND v SOUTH AFRICA; JUNE 4 ... SUPER SIX MATCH;
JUNE 11 SUPER SIX MATCH

North London has Lord's, South London has The Oval. Made famous by the gasholders that dominate the skyline, and a pitch that always seems to bring results. The track is fast and Allan Donald is sure to want revenge for that Test series defeat by England last summer. Dramatic redevelopment at the Pavilion End will provide a spectacular backdrop to the action on the pitch.

HOW TO GET THERE

By Rail: Vauxhall, Oval (Underground).

By Road: Ground is just south of Vauxhall Bridge on the A202 Vauxhall Road, close to the junction of the A3 and A23.

SOUTHAMPTON COUNTY CRICKET GROUND
TEL: 01703 333788

CAPACITY: 4697

HOSTS: MAY 24 ... WEST INDIES v NEW ZEALAND;
MAY 30 ... SRI LANKA v KENYA

Likely to see its last World Cup action as Hampshire prepare to develop new premises at West End, Southampton ready for 2001. A new cricket ground with a capacity of up to 10,000 will be one of the main facilities in a multi sports arena for the area.

HOW TO GET THERE

By Rail: Southampton Central.

By Road: Take A33 into Southampton from M3, then follow yellow AA signs. Ground is one and a half miles north of city centre, take the turning on the right at the end of Southampton Common.

TAUNTON THE CLERICAL MEDICAL COUNTY GROUND

TEL: 01823 272946

CAPACITY: 7500

HOSTS: MAY 15 ... ZIMBABWE v KENYA; MAY 26 ... SRI LANKA v INDIA

Arjuna Ranatunga will return to the scene of his World Cup meeting with England in 1983 when his 12 overs for Sri Lanka cost him 65 runs as David Gower hit a superb 130 in the home side's 47 run victory. This picturesque ground , that played host to Viv Richards and Ian Botham in a glorious period in English county cricket, may see one of the games of the first round when India and Sri Lanka go head to head.

HOW TO GET THERE

Rail: Taunton.

Road: From M5 take junction 25, A358, then A38 towards town centre. At roundabout take Priory Avenue, straight over next roundabout into Priory Bridge Road. Ground is on the left.

TRENT BRIDGE NOTTINGHAM

TEL: 0115 982 1525

CAPACITY: 15,000

HOSTS: MAY 25 ... ENGLAND v ZIMBABWE; JUNE 5 ... SUPER SIX MATCH;
JUNE 12 ... SUPER SIX MATCH

Trent Bridge celebrates the centenary of its first Test in June of this year and England will be hoping that Zimbabwe won't be celebrating another World Cup victory in Nottingham to follow their shock win against the Australians back in 1983 in their first ever World Cup match.

HOW TO GET THERE

By Rail: Nottingham.

By Road: Well signposted if you leave M1 at junction 25. Near junction of A60 and A52, across Trent Bridge from city centre.

WORCESTER COUNTY GROUND, NEW ROAD

TEL: 01905 748474

CAPACITY: 5200

HOSTS: MAY 16 ... AUSTRALIA v SCOTLAND;
MAY 22 ... ZIMBABWE v SRI LANKA

The 14th century cathedral highlights New Road, generally regarded as the prettiest ground in England. Another that celebrates its centenary this year but how many balls will the Australians attempt to put in the Severn, a river that left the ground totally under water during flooding that affected the area last year.

HOW TO GET THERE

By Rail: Worcester Foregate

By Road: Follow AA signs for Worcester Races towards city centre. Take Bridge Street (A38) and go left over Bridge, continue down New Road (A44. Ground is on left.

PART TWO: THE TEAMS

ENGLAND

> GROUP A • **England** • India • Kenya
> • South Africa • Sri Lanka • Zimbabwe

England have come so close to winning the World Cup on three occasions that they advance on the 1999 tournament as host nation with realistic hopes of lifting the trophy for the first time.

Three times they have reached the World Cup final since the tournament was launched in 1975 and three times England captains have seen one-day international cricket's ultimate prize slip from their grasp.

In the 1979 final, in front of a capacity crowd at Lord's, Viv Richards scored a brilliant 138 not out against England to steer the West Indies to victory by 92 runs.

In 1987, Graham Gooch scored a century in England's semi-final win against host nation India in Bombay to set up a dream clash with Australia in the final held before 70,000 spectators packed into Eden Gardens, Calcutta.

Australia clinched the trophy in a seven-run win, but England looked capable of overhauling the Aussies' total of 253 for five, needing 46 runs off the last five overs. They finished seven runs short on 246 for eight from 50 overs.

England beat South Africa in a rain affected semi-final to reach the 1992 World Cup final. Pakistan reached 249 for six, thanks largely to Wasim Akram's vital quickfire 33 from 19 deliveries, and the former Lancashire skipper demonstrated his superb talents as an all-rounder to take three for 49 as England slumped to 227 all out.

So, England approach their opening group match of World Cup 99, scheduled for May 14 against Sri Lanka at Lord's, with a reputation for making an impact on the tournament without ever truly fulfilling their potential as prospective world champions.

The difference this time is that the England Cricket Board covered every eventuality to give Alec Stewart's team the best possible chance to win the tournament for the first time.

They broke new ground in late 1997 by divorcing the selection of their limited-overs squad from the Test side. The new policy was unveiled when Adam Hollioake led England to victory in the Sharjah tournament, a competition they had shunned for a decade.

England reverted to the old system by choosing Mike Atherton as captain for the one-day international tournament in the West Indies in 1998, but when he resigned as leader at the end of the Test series, Hollioake stepped into the breach for the five matches.

The selectors policy to encourage one-day specialists has led to the promotion of players such as the dynamic Matthew Fleming (Kent) and Dougie Brown (Warwickshire), both highly proficient exponents of the short-form game.

The lottery of one-day limited-overs cricket means that the final 15 England players chosen for the tournament will stand as good a chance as any of winning the trophy at Lord's on June 20.

More than three years will have elapsed since England's ignominious exit from the 1996 tournament when they play their opening game of the 1999 tournament. They need no reminding that Sri Lanka condemned them to quarter-final defeat by five wickets in Faisalabad in March that year, and it is the defending world champions who provide the opposition when England kick off the tournament at what is sure to be a packed Lord's.

Sri Lanka's famous Test victory over England at The Oval in 'Muralitharan's Match' last summer gives an edge to this initial encounter between one of Test cricket's oldest nations and the international circuit's new kids on the block from Colombo.

In the previous World Cup encounter, the England side included Robin Smith, Phil DeFreitas, Jack Russell, Dermot Reeve and Richard Illingworth. Since then a bright new crop of exponents of the cut and thrust of limited-overs cricket have emerged.

Ben Hollioake, picked for England's Ashes squad for the 1998-99 tour to Australia, is a typical example of this new specialist force. A naturally gifted all-rounder, the Surrey man marked his international debut by scoring 63 off 48 balls in the Texaco Trophy against Australia at Lord's in 1997.

Kent's Mark Ealham is another two-in-one player. Belligerent and reliable with the bat, tight and economical with the ball, and lethal in the field given a run-out opportunity.

Both have played Test cricket, but that is not the prerequisite of selection for England's one-day squad under the new system, which has seen Fleming bring his flamboyance with the bat to the limited-overs scene, if not England's Test dressing-room.

Fleming has the same impudence and audacity to destroy an attack as that of Neil Fairbrother, still a destructive force with the bat at 35.

Warwickshire's Nick Knight is another dynamic England performer at the short game with aspirations to becoming a Test regular.

But truly gifted batsmen can embrace both codes as demonstrated by England captain Alec Stewart, his predecessor Atherton, a master at playing the anchor role in the construction of a formidable total, Graham Thorpe, Graeme Hick and Nasser Hussain.

Adam Hollioake's credentials for higher status were obvious from the moment he scored a century on his Championship debut for Surrey in 1993 and struck the fastest ever one-day 50 from 15 balls in a Sunday League game the following season.

Imaginative captaincy, quick scoring and the ability to remove dangerous batsmen with the ball have been properly rewarded by the selectors at a time when Hollioake senior has not always been blessed with the best of luck.

A stress-fracture of the foot after taking 20 wickets in three Tests on the 1994-95 Ashes tour and a series of other injuries have blunted Darren Gough's progress, but that extra pace he generates, topped up with a devastating yorker, gives the attack a potent warhead.

Angus Fraser, Alan Mullally, Dean Headley, Peter Martin, Ian Austin and new discovery Alex Tudor provide England with a wealth of penetration, and spinners Robert Croft and Ashley Giles can bowl a mean line and length when the run chase hots up.

England's group contains reigning World Cup champions Sri Lanka, 1983 winners India, South Africa, plus Zimbabwe and Kenya.

But a strong squad, passionate home support and a distinguished World Cup record stretching back 24 years could yet land England that ultimate, but hitherto elusive prize in their own backyard.

WORLD CUP HIGHLIGHT

Graham Gooch's brilliant 115 for England in their score of 254 for six against India in the semi-final in 1987. A knock that silenced the Bombay crowd and set up Mike Gatting's side for a victory by 35 runs.

WORLD CUP RECORD

1975	Lost to Australia in semi-final
1979	Lost to West Indies in final
1983	Lost to India in semi-final
1987	Lost to Australia in final
1992	Lost to Pakistan in final
1996	Lost to Sri Lanka in quarter-finals

WORLD CUP ODDS: 10-1

CAPTAIN **ALEC STEWART**
Born 8.4.63 ... **right-hand bat** ... wicket-keeper

Few players in cricket history have undertaken the awesome burden of responsibility that separates Alec Stewart from lesser mortals on the world cricket circuit.

Here is the ultimate professional. Captain of his country, prolific run-getter in the top-order, and agile wicket-keeper. A rare species, the three-in-one cricketer.

The two best wicket-keeper-batsmen England have ever produced are Les Ames and Alan Knott. Neither was ever asked to take on the additional stress of captaincy. Yet when Mike Atherton resigned at the end of England's winter tour to the West Indies in 1997-98, Stewart stepped smartly into the breach as if he was born to the role.

England's subsequent Cornhill Test series defeat of South Africa not only silenced critics prepared to question his sanity in taking the job in a particularly unsuccessful era for England, but also proved beyond measure that Surrey's favourite son was more than capable of absorbing all the pressure that came with the prestigious title.

Alec Stewart was destined to earn his living from sport from the moment he was born in leafy Surrey suburbia. The son of former England and Surrey batsman Micky Stewart, who played football for Charlton, West Ham, Hendon and Corinthian Casuals, he grew up in a house often full of celebrity players from both codes. Ex-England football manager Bobby Robson was a frequent visitor, and the famous cricketing Bedser twins, Alec and Eric, would pop in for a chat with his parents on regular occasions.

The young Stewart spent most of his childhood playing 'Test Matches' in the backgarden with his father and brother, Neil. And if it rained, the stumps were carried indoors for a resumption of play in the hallway. Few children have ever received the grounding in how best to play cricket than England's current captain.

A product of Tiffin Boys School, which to this day proudly exhibits photographs of teams containing one of its most famous old boys, he made his county debut in 1981, gaining experience on the first-class Championship circuit in the summer and flying off to Australia to play for the Midland-Guildford club in Perth.

If the county treadmill gave him a thorough grounding in how to score runs, the regular Aussie sojourns instilled in him a mental toughness that renders him a formidable opponent in the cauldron atmosphere of Test cricket.

He crossed swords with Desmond Haynes in his second Test appearance on England's tour to the West Indies in 1989-90, a spirited clash that cast doubts as to whether he would ever become captaincy material.

He was dropped after England's disastrous Ashes tour of 1990-91 but recalled for the final Test against the West Indies the following summer. The significance of that call up was the selectors' request that he should keep wicket, and so began a success story that has propelled him into the 1999 World Cup as one of England's most successful post-War players.

England gained a memorable victory in his comeback Test of 1991. Two weeks later he scored his first Test century – against Sri Lanka – and in the 17 Test innings after his return he scored 952 runs at an average of 68.

There have been times since when confusion over his multi-purpose role has affected his form, but he has managed to handle all the pressure and demands on him with a maturity that has stood the test of time in the England dressing-room for a decade.

He became the first England batsman to score a century in both innings against the West Indies in Barbados in 1993-94 and his 173 against New Zealand at Auckland in 1996-97 was the highest ever score by an England wicket-keeper. He was also the leading scorer in Test cricket in the 1996 calendar year, scoring 793 runs, some 92 runs clear of Pakistan's Saeed Anwar in second place.

Vice-captain first to Graham Gooch, then Mike Atherton, his no-nonsense style carries little of the finesse associated with former England captains such as Peter May and Mike Brearley, but his 'get-stuck-into-them' attitude has galvanised a healthy spirit and motivation within the England squad.

Named one of Wisden's Five Cricketers of the Year in the 1993 almanack, author, Mike Selvey, tells a story that illustrates the all-round brilliance of England's man for all seasons.

He writes: "It was at Lord's, midway through the morning session of the fourth one-day international last summer, that it was spotted. Alec Stewart, England captain for the day, opening batsman some days, floating middle-order batsman other days, infielder, outfielder, shake-it-all-about fielder and wicket-keeper, was standing behind the bowler's stumps, quietly buffing the ball on his flannels as, with a wave here and a flourish there, he set the field. 'Omigod' said someone, 'I think he's going to bowl'."

He didn't, of course, but it is testament to the image created that Alec James Stewart would open the bowling if requested ... and probably take a wicket in his first over!

Off the edge

- Alec's benefit for Surrey in 1994 netted £202,187.
- **His nickname for Surrey and England is Stewie or Ming.**
- Being the son of former England manager Micky Stewart led to unfounded cries of nepotism in his early Test days. Micky insisted, in cricketing terms, he never had a son, referring to Alec simply as 'Stewie'.
- **Alec's mother, Sheila, was a top netball and hockey player and his brother, Neil, has captained Malden Wanderers in the Surrey Cricket League.**
- Stewie led England for the first time in a Test Match against India in Madras, 1992-93.
- **He is a big Chelsea fan and loves watching Gianluca Vialli's side at Stamford Bridge on his days off.**
- Bernie Coleman OBE, stalwart Surrey supporter and close friend of Stewart, told a national newspaper after England's drawn Test in Brisbane last November: 'Don't they understand that no man can captain England and keep wicket and bat at number four. The strain is just too much!'
- **England v South Africa, Edgbaston June 4-8 1998 was his first Test as England's appointed skipper after Mike Atherton's resignation.**
- Among the cricketers he admires most are Graham Gooch, Alan Knott and Geoff Arnold, and he rates Surrey team-mate Ben Hollioake as a youngster to watch.
- **He has been quoted as saying that England players, especially bowlers, should be rested from county cricket whenever necessary.**

MARK ALLEYNE
Born 23.5.68 ... **right-hand bat** ... right-arm medium

Valuable one-day all-rounder. Youngest player to score a double century (256) for Gloucestershire in 1990. Graduate of Haringey Cricket College. Appointed Gloucestershire captain in 1997 and named England captain for subsequently cancelled World Super Max 8s tournament.

MICHAEL ATHERTON
Born 23.3.68 ... **right-hand bat**

His exhibition of monumental defiance against Allan Donald's withering fire on the fourth evening of the Nottingham Test last summer illustrates vividly the character of one of England finest post-War batsmen. If gallantry medals were awarded for sport, Atherton would have a chestfull. England's longest serving Test captain, he had led his country 52 times when he stood down at the end of the series against the West Indies in 1998.

He made his county debut in 1987 and two years later his Test debut against Australia. Since then he has established himself as a pillar of reliability at the helm of England's batting.

Typically, he went out and scored his first century in 13 Tests against South Africa last summer after resigning the England captaincy. Some critics suggested the responsibility of skippering the side affected his run-getting, but statistics show that he actually improved his batting average from 34 to 41 during his time in charge of England.

One of the eight Test centuries he scored during his reign includes the 185 not out against South Africa at Johannesburg in 1995-96. England had to bat for five sessions to save the match and 'Athers' was still there at the end, having resisted for a magnificent 10 hours and 43 minutes.

Voted England's Player of the Series against West Indies in 1995, he was also named Man of the Series against South Africa in 1998, scoring a century and three fifties.

IAN AUSTIN
Born 30.5.66 ... **left-hand bat** ... right arm medium

Scored the quickest first-class century in 1991 from 61 deliveries. A Lancashire regular since his debut in 1987, he is utterly dependable as a one-day specialist and was his county's Player of the Year in 1997. Member of England squad for the Wills International Cup in Bangladesh last autumn and picked also for cancelled World Super Max 8s tournament in Perth.

ALISTAIR BROWN
Born 11.2.70 ... **right-hand bat**

Exploded onto the county scene in 1992 when he hit three centuries in 79,71 and 78 balls. Was called up for England Texaco Trophy duty against India in 1996 and celebrated in style with a match-winning 118 at Old Trafford. A powerful batsman, he made the highest ever Sunday League score of 203 against Hampshire in 1997.

DOUGIE BROWN
Born 29.10.69 ... **right-hand bat ...** right arm medium

Ex-Scotland Under-18 footballer and member of Scotland's Benson and Hedges Cup squad in 1989, he made his Warwickshire county debut in 1992 after first playing for them on their 1991-92 trip to South Africa. Played for England in Hong Kong Sixes 1997 and in Sharjah for victorious England that same year. Called up for England 'A' tour to Kenya and Sri Lanka in 1997-98 after Chris Silverwood's promotion to senior tour. Outstanding summer for Warwickshire in 1998, taking 50 Championship wickets and averaging 29.91 with the bat.

JOHN CRAWLEY
Born 21.9.71 ... **right-hand bat**

A regular member of the England squad since making his Test debut against South Africa in 1994. Reliable middle-order batsman, at his best against Muttiah Muralitharan's magic in The Oval Test in 1998. He scored 156 not out. Occasional wicket-keeper for Lancashire and has covered for Alec Stewart behind the stumps.

ROBERT CROFT
Born 25.5.70 ... **right-hand bat ...** off-spin

Since making his Test debut against Pakistan in 1996, his guile and control has made him a Test regular. Toured Zimbabwe and New Zealand in 1996-97, West Indies 1997-98 and Ashes tour 1998-99. Fluent Welsh speaker, he can be a good bat on his day as well as his obvious off-spin talents.

MARK EALHAM
Born 27.8.69 ... **right-hand bat ...** right-arm medium

The Kent all-rounder is a formidable one-day opponent, with that rare ability to break a stand to change the game or thrash quick runs to snatch victory from defeat.

In 1995 he scored the fastest Sunday League century, from 44 balls, against Derbyshire and forced his way into England's one-day international side against India the following year.

He went on to play two Cornhill Tests that summer before injury sidelined him from the series against Pakistan. That loss of career momentum meant he had to settle for England 'A' cricket in the tour to Australia in 1996-97 but he returned to his best form to play a part in the three Texaco Trophy wins against the Aussies in 1997 and gained four Test caps in the home Ashes series later that summer.

He returned to 'A' team duty in Kenya and Sri Lanka in 1997-98 and played in the Sharjah tournament that same winter, before appearing in two Tests against South Africa in 1998 and the Wills International Cup in Bangladesh last autumn.

Selection for England's one-day squad for duty in Australia at the end of the Ashes series has brought him firmly into the reckoning for England recognition on all fronts.

Son of former Kent captain Alan Ealham, his brilliant fielding makes him a very useful all-round cricketer.

MATTHEW FLEMING
Born 12.12.64 ... **right-hand bat ...** right-arm medium

Appointed captain of Kent for 1999, his dashing, carefree batting style empties the bars and restaurants whenever he walks to the wicket.

A one-day specialist, he can cut a tight attack to ribbons, take a rest in the interval, and rip out a middle order with bowling that rarely receives the credit it merits.

Former officer in the Royal Green Jackets, he launched his career by hitting the first two balls he received for six on his county Championship debut in 1989.

He made his international breakthrough when picked for the Hong Kong Sixes at the end of the 1997 season and then reinforced England's attack in the Sharjah Cup later that winter when Darren Gough withdrew through injury.

He kept his place for the one-day international series in the West Indies in 1997-98 and flew out to Bangladesh as a member of the England squad for the Wills International mini-world cup held in Dhaka last autumn.

Chairman of the Professional Cricketers' Association, Fleming does not like being reminded of the day he was out twice before lunch batting three for Kent against the West Indies in 1995.

ANDREW FLINTOFF
Born 6.12.77 ... **right-hand bat ...** right-arm medium

Made Test debut at Nottingham in 1998 against South Africa and travelled with the England 'A' team to Zimbabwe and South Africa earlier this year. Struck 34 in one over off Alex Tudor in 1998 Championship match at Old Trafford.

ANGUS FRASER
Born 8.8.65 ... **right-arm medium**

The man they cannot write-off! Picked as a so-called makeweight role-model support for the younger bowlers chosen for England's West Indies' tour in 1997-98, he emerged as England's Man of the Series.

He took 27 wickets in the series to equal John Snow's record for an England bowler in the Caribbean and then claimed a further 24 victims in England's Cornhill Test series win against South Africa in 1998.

If skipper Alec Stewart's name was the first on the team sheet for selection for England's Ashes tour trip in 1998-99, Gus must have been second, chosen for courage in the face of adversity, reliability, and a warmth of character that renders him a popular member of any dressing-room.

Named Middlesex Player of the Year in 1988 and 1989, the deadly seam bowling that has made him an England regular for the past decade was evident from the moment he made his Test breakthrough against Australia in 1989.

A chronic hip condition developed in Australia in 1990-91 left him working for a living in the City, but he recovered to become one of the heroes of England's famous victory over the West Indies in Barbados in 1993-94, when he took eight for 75. Four years later he took eight for 53 in Trinidad. He claimed his 100th Test wicket against the West Indies in 1995. His victim? Brian Lara.

ASHLEY GILES
Born 19.3.73 ... **slow left-arm**

Made his Test debut against South Africa at Old Trafford in 1998 and his Texaco one-day debut against Australia a year earlier. Missed tour to West Indies in 1997-98 through injury.

DARREN GOUGH
Born 18.9.70 ... **right-hand bat** ... right-arm fast

Unfairly hailed as the new 'Ian Botham' when he launched his international career against New Zealand and South Africa in 1994. Injury and loss of promising early form with the bat enabled him to shed the association he inherited as Botham's heir apparent, allowing him to establish his own mark on the Test and one-day scene.

England Cornhill Player of the Year in 1994, he made his big breakthrough on the Ashes tour of 1994-95, taking 20 wickets in three Tests before suffering a stress fracture of the foot.

He recovered well enough to make the 1995-96 tour to South Africa only to be sidelined again with hamstring trouble. Toured Zimbabwe and New Zealand in 1996-97 but after spearheading England's attack in the first four Tests against Australia in 1997, he was crippled with an inflamed knee.

Surgery forced him to withdraw from England's tour to West Indies in 1997-98 but the venomous pace and the devastating inswinging yorker that has accounted for many of his victims since breaking into the Yorkshire side in 1989 returned last summer when he bagged 17 wickets in England's winning Test series against South Africa.

Selected for the 1998-99 Ashes tour, he joined the elite band of Englishmen to have taken a hat-trick against Australia when he achieved the feat in the Fifth Test. He remains England's main strike weapon but has failed to shine with the bat since making his debut. The big success on the Ashes tour.

DEAN HEADLEY
Born 27.1.70 ... **right-arm fast-medium**

Grandson of George Headley — the West Indies batsman nicknamed the 'Black Bradman' — and son of Ron Headley, the former Worcestershire and West Indies strokeplayer, he was destined to play Test cricket from birth. Left Middlesex for Kent in 1992 and emerged as major Test prospect on the 'A' tour to Pakistan in 1995-96, taking 25 wickets at 15 apiece. Equalled world record of three hat-tricks in a season in 1996 and enjoyed a fair share of success on the Ashes tour with England in 1998-99.

WARREN HEGG
Born 23.2.68 ... **right-hand bat** ... wicket-keeper

Youngest player for 30 years to score a century for Lancashire in his fourth first-class game. His eleven victims against Derbyshire equalled the world wicket-keeping record. Toured Pakistan and Sri Lanka with England 'A' in 1990-91 and chosen for 1998-99 Ashes tour where he came in for Alec Stewart in the latter stages of the Test series to take some weight away from the over-worked shoulders of the skipper.

A LOOK AT...
GRAHAM THORPE

There was no sadder sight in cricket on England's 1998-99 Ashes tour than 17 squad members flying from Melbourne to Adelaide last December, leaving Graham to make the long journey home by himself to Heathrow airport.

It was his second early return home in nine months from a tour due to a recurrence of pain in his lower back.

A product of four England 'A' tours, he had become England's most reliable batsman when back trouble forced him to withdraw from the one-day series in the West Indies after the first match in 1997-98.

The problem flared again in the Third Test against South Africa at Old Trafford last summer and this latest career blow in Australia has left him seriously short of match practise for the World Cup.

He scored a century on his Test debut against Australia in 1993, joining W.G. Grace and Ranji in an elite group who have made their first Test century in an Ashes series.

Following that landmark, Thorpe gained a reputation for becoming a nearly-man, raising his bat to celebrate half-centuries but rarely passing three figures. Since that maiden hundred, he took another 14 Tests before scoring his second century, in Australia in 1994-95, and a further 19 before his third.

Successive centuries in New Zealand in 1996-97 was the breakthrough he needed. He asked a press conference: "I didn't notice too much of a barrier today, did you?"

Polite, shy and sometimes reserved, Graham has been a naturally gifted sportsman since childhood. He played English Schools cricket at Under-15 and Under-19 level and English Schools football at Under-18. He might have been lost to Brentford Football Club as a 'nip your ankles midfielder' but fortunately the left-hander joined Surrey, making his county debut in 1988 as a teenager.

His early development was moulded by Micky Stewart and Geoff Arnold, and later he came under scrutiny from Keith Fletcher on the England 'A' tours. A willing student, he made himself English cricket's most dependable batsman on those trips.

Ironically, apart from a broken thumb, which kept him out of the last Test of the 1993 Ashes series, and a brief spell in 1994 when he was dropped, Thorpe was a constant factor in the England team for the next four years.

He left Australia in December to return home to face an uncertain future. But typically he bade farewell to his England colleagues with a promise full of optimism: "With time and effort, I can get it right."

But as Thorpe landed back in England after that long, lonely flight back from Australia, he immediately set out to prove his fitness for the World Cup.

"It has always been one of my main ambitions to play for England in the World Cup and I have been told that I will get a chance to prove my fitness," said the Surrey left-hander.

"I have suffered with the problem before and I'm looking for a long-term solution but time is precious at the moment."

And so is Thorpe's talent!

THE STATS

Full name: Graham Paul Thorpe

Born: August 1, 1969 in Farnham, Surrey

Role: Left-hand bat, occasional right-arm medium

Represents: Surrey, England

Test debut: For England v Australia, Third Test, Trent Bridge, 1993

One-day international debut: For England against Australia at Old Trafford in 1993.

Finest hour: Marking his Test debut with an unbeaten 114.

Extras: In that summer of 1993, Graham took four for 40 playing for Surrey against the Australians at The Oval.

NOW THAT'S A FACT

● Both of Graham's brothers play for Farnham, his Surrey birthplace. His father plays cricket also. His mother is a professional scorer.

● He played only seven Championship innings for Surrey in 1998 because of injury and England commitments.

● He admires West Indian legend Viv Richards, former Surrey batsman Graham Clinton and David Gower.

● Thorpe reckons his Surrey and England team-mate Ben Hollioake is a young player to look out for.

● He was England's Player of the Series and leading run-scorer in the 1997 Ashes campaign with 453 runs at an average of 50.

● He played midfield for the England Under-18 football team.

● After 19 Tests littered with half centuries, he scored successive hundreds in Tests against New Zealand in 1996-97.

● Graham gained 7 O-Levels and a PE diploma as a student.

● He is a big fan of Chelsea Football Club and watches them with Alec Stewart.

● To relax, he plays golf — and sleeps!

THE THINGS THEY SAY

THORPE ON

❝I don't have to shout it from the rooftops but my hundreds are getting bigger.❞ **On his batting in the 1997 season.**

❝Our dressing-room is easier to come into. There's no airs and graces.❞ **On a welcome a visitor receives when entering the England dressing-room.**

ON THORPE

❝The Australians have more respect for Thorpe than for almost any other Pom.❞ **Rob Steen writing for Wisden Cricket Monthly.**

GRAEME HICK
Born 23.5.66 ... **right-hand bat**

The most prolific batsman of his generation. Born in Zimbabwe, Hick scored his first century at the age of six for his school team.

He was the youngest player participating in the 1983 Prudential World Cup, when he represented Zimbabwe at 17. And at 20 he became the youngest player to score 2,000 runs in an England season (1986), being named as one of Wisden's Five Cricketers of the Year in the process.

Two years later he made 405 not out for Worcestershire against Somerset at Taunton, the highest individual score in England since 1895, and scored 1,000 first-class runs by the end of May that year. In 1990 he became the youngest batsman ever to make 50 first-class centuries.

Qualified as an English player in 1991, he scored his maiden Test century for his adopted country against India in Bombay in 1992-93.

He was overlooked for the Ashes tour 1998-99 but was sent out as cover for Michael Atherton, who had a bad back.

ADAM HOLLIOAKE
Born 5.9.71 ... **right-hand bat** ... right-arm medium

Appointed England captain for Texaco Trophy series against South Africa 1998. Led England to victory in Sharjah in December 1997 but suffered 4-1 series defeat as skipper in West Indies 1997-98. First impressed as England 'A' captain in Australia 1996-97 and lifted Benson and Hedges Cup in his first season as Surrey captain in 1997. Older brother of Ben.

BEN HOLLIOAKE
Born 11.11.77 ... **right-hand bat** ... right-arm fast medium

Gifted all-rounder, he became England's youngest Test cricketer for almost half a century when he won his first cap against Australia at Trent Bridge in 1997. Adam played in same match, making them the first brothers to appear in the same England side since Peter and Dick Richardson in 1957. Made 63 off 48 deliveries on his international Texaco Trophy debut at Lord's in 1997 and then hit 98 to lead Surrey to victory over Kent in the Benson and Hedges Cup Final the same year. Ashes tourist 1998-99.

NASSER HUSSAIN
Born 28.3.68 ... **right-hand bat**

Taken over from Paul Prichard as Essex captain for next season and is vice-skipper to Alec Stewart on England duty. Enjoyed a good Ashes series, averaging 45.22 in the Test Matches. He made his Test debut against the West Indies in 1989-90 though failed to hold down a regular place in the side for a while after that through doubts about his ability and temperament. But has regained the selectors' confidence at Test and one-day level.

NICK KNIGHT
Born 28.11.69 ... **left-hand bat**

One of the few opposing batsmen to gain Curtly Ambrose's admiration. The big

West Indian paceman had no option but to show approval after the England opener had massacred the Windies attack in Barbados in 1998 with a dazzling innings of 122 off 130 deliveries and 90 from 107 balls. He also scored 65 from 67 balls in the final match of the one-day series to establish his place as one of England's most dangerous batsmen in limited-overs internationals.

A century against Pakistan in the Headingley Test in 1996, two more centuries in the Texaco Trophy matches and a 96 in England's vain run-chase in the First Test against Zimbabwe the following winter, marked him out as an opening batsman of enormous potential.

He has found the competition tough and his best form elusive, not least because of a succession of broken fingers but was chosen for England's one-day series against Australia and Sri Lanka at the end of the recent Ashes tour.

DARREN MADDY
Born 23.5.74 ... **right-hand bat ...** right-arm medium

The Leicestershire opener scored his first double century in first-class cricket on the England 'A' tour to Kenya and Sri Lanka in 1997-98. Selected for the 1998 Texaco Trophy series against South Africa and England 'A' tour to Zimbabwe and South Africa this year.

PETER MARTIN
Born 15.11.68 ... **right-arm fast medium**

Made his Test debut in 1995 as England played host to West Indies. Reliable one-day bowler with deadly accuracy. Named in England squad for Wills International Cup in Bangladesh, 1998.

ALAN MULLALLY
Born 12.7.69 ... **left-arm fast**

Born in Southend but raised in Western Australia, for whom he made his first class debut in 1987-88. He tasted international action for the first time in the Australian Under-19 team but turned down a place in the famed Australian Cricket Academy to play for England. He made his England debut in 1996, the year he took 47 wickets in Leicestershire's Championship winning year. Ashes tourist 1998-99 and holder of another county Championship medal after Leicestershire's success last summer.

MARK RAMPRAKASH
Born 5.9.69 ... **right-hand bat ...** right-arm off-spin

Topped England's Test tour averages against West Indies with 266 runs at 66.50 in 1997-98. Repeated that success, scoring 379 runs at 47.38 to head the Ashes tour averages for 1998-99. England's most technically correct batsman, the Middlesex man made his Test debut against West Indies in 1991 aged 21. A brilliant fielder, he has taken wickets with his off-spin as well.

BEN SMITH
Born 3.4.72 ... **right-hand bat**

Finished top of Leicestershire's 1998 Championship winning averages with 1,165 runs at 64.72. Made his highest ever score in first-class cricket against Surrey last summer of 204. Made his county debut in 1990 and named as

Cricket Society Young Player of the Year in 1991. A useful tennis player, he represented Leicestershire aged 12.

VINCE WELLS
Born 6.8.75 ... **right-hand bat ...** right-arm medium

Considered by many to be to most underrated all-rounder on the English county circuit. Key player in Leicestershire's two Championship winning years in 1996 and 98, he was picked for England duty in the one-day internationals against Sri Lanka and Australia at the turn of the year.

❶ TO WATCH NEIL FAIRBROTHER
Born 9.9.63 ... **left-hand bat**

One of the most destructive batsmen in one-day cricket. Christened Neil Harvey Fairbrother after the great Australian batsman Neil Harvey, he was destined to play professional cricket from an early age.

Played for England YC against Australia in 1983 and was capped by Lancashire in 1985, soon becoming an Old Trafford favourite.

He made his England Test debut against Pakistan in 1987 but slipped from the Test scene after making 10 appearances. Since then has established himself as a dangerous exponent of the one-day game in over 65 England appearances.

His innings of 366 for Lancashire in 1990 is the fourth highest score ever made in the county Championship, the second highest first-class score by a Lancashire batsman and the best at The Oval.

Appointed Lancashire captain in 1992, he resigned in 1993 to concentrate on run-getting duties in the county's middle-order. Called up to join England tour party as a replacement in Australia in 1994-95, he was sidelined immediately after damaging shoulder ligaments as he dived for the ball in the field and was forced to return home. Represented England in the last World Cup and played in the one-day triangular series in Australia at the start of 1999.

Gavin Hamilton was selected for the initial England World Cup squad but is also available for Scotland. More information on the Yorkshire youngster can be found on page 142.

WISDEN WORLD CUP VERDICT
They have home advantage — but that wasn't much help in the first three tournaments. Actually England have done better away from home recently. All the allrounder-swapping in Australia didn't prove much, and the selectors may be best advised to stick with orthodox players like Atherton and Hussain for the tournament. The early matches are being played in England in May, after all. The pressure's on: anything less than a fourth final appearance will be a disappointment.

INDIA

India, winners of the third World Cup in 1983, are arguably the best equipped squad of all the 12 countries to exploit the English conditions that will confront them at World Cup 99.

They arrive on territory familiar for many of their players, possess arguably the best batsman in the world in Sachin Tendulkar; the most prolific current run-getter in the world in Rahul Dravid; three of the most dangerous bowlers in the world in Venkatesh Prasad, Javagal Srinath and Anil Kumble; all led by the most experienced captain in the world, Mohammad Azharuddin.

Add the flair of star performers such as Navjot Sidhu, Sourav Ganguly and wicket-keeper Nayan Mongia and it is difficult to make an argument against India having the firepower to mount their biggest challenge since that June day 16 years ago when Madan Lal and Mohinder Amarnath bowled out the West Indies cheaply at Lord's to allow their captain Kapil Dev to collect the Prudential sponsored trophy.

The Indians were blessed with plenty of world-class talent in those times but Gavaskar, Kapil Dev, Srikkanth and Amarnath were not expected to prevent the reigning world champions West Indies, led by Clive Lloyd, from completing a hat-trick of World Cup victories that year.

It is only three years since new stars Ganguly and Dravid emerged as batsmen of impressive technique and temperament on their first England Test tour and Srinath and Prasad impressed on that trip as one of the best new-ball attacks in the world.

The two new batsmen conquered the peculiar demands of English conditions, where the ball swings and can move alarmingly at times off the seam, as if they were born to the ever-changing weather they saw on the 1996 tour and the two bowlers picked up 26 wickets between them in the three Test series.

India did not take kindly to losing their recent series in New Zealand 1-0 but returned home from the drawn Third Test in Hamilton to prepare for the World Cup with several of their players the richer for their Southern Hemisphere excursion.

India have come a long way since they were comprehensively beaten by England in the opening batch of matches in the first World Cup of 1975. They found themselves on the wrong end of an innings of 137 by Dennis Amiss and after New Zealand's Glenn Turner had taken a century off their attack at Old Trafford, all hope of progressing to the later rounds had vanished.

Bracketed with West Indies, New Zealand and Sri Lanka at the tournament held again in England in 1979, India lost all three group matches. They were particularly stunned by Sri Lanka's victory, the first in the World Cup by a non-Test playing country.

Clear underdogs at the 1983 tournament with a record of modest achievement in previous World Cups, Yashpal Sharma struck 61 at Old Trafford to end England's semi-final dream.

For once the West Indies' big batting guns allowed the Indian attack to dominate the final and Kapil Dev's side duly walked off with the spoils.

India's 1987 campaign was enhanced by playing the tournament on home territory. Joint hosts with Pakistan, they reached the semi-final in Bombay only to lose to an England side boosted by a century from Man of the Match, Graham Gooch.

Five defeats in eight qualifying group matches led to India's exclusion from the sharp end of the 1992 World Cup, held in Australia and New Zealand, and their bid to halt Sri Lanka's audacious charge in the 1996 tournament led to a farcical exit from the competition at the semi-final stage.

India were 120 for eight, chasing Sri Lanka's formidable total of 251 for eight, at Calcutta, when some spectators in the 100,000 crowd began throwing bottles on the pitch.

Referee Clive Lloyd took the players off the pitch for a 15 minute cooling off period but the crowd was still hostile and more bottles were hurled when officials attempted to resume play.

Lloyd had no option but to award the match to Sri Lanka, who went on to win a famous victory over Australia in the final.

Tendulkar scored 523 runs, more than any other batsman in that tournament, and he prepares for the England challenge determined to show the world that he is still the world's master batsman, despite Brian Lara's bid to prove otherwise.

This time India are bracketed in Group A with holders Sri Lanka, South Africa, England, Zimbabwe and Kenya. They have three warm-up matches: against Leicestershire; Yorkshire, the county Tendulkar once served as their first overseas player; and Nottinghamshire on May 7, 9 and 11; before the tournament proper begins with their opening match against South Africa, at Hove, on Saturday, May 15.

They then face Zimbabwe and Kenya on the 19th and 23rd in two group matches they will be expected to win before meeting old rivals Sri Lanka, at Taunton, on May 26.

If India show a semblance of the form they are capable of producing in one-day competition, they could arrive to play host country England at Edgbaston, on Saturday, May 29 with a scalp or two in the locker and confidence high.

The lottery of World Cup action makes forecasting a precarious occupation. India's record in Test and one-day internationals enhances the belief that a punter can soon be parted from his money if he relies on hunch and formbook to second guess the team Mohammad Azharuddin leads.

On their day they can be world beaters. Unfortunately, cricket history reveals that India have tended to under-achieve when put to the ultimate test.

One-day internationals have become the staple diet of Indian cricket. No country competing at England 99 has more experience of the cut and thrust of this form of instant cricket, be it in daylight or under floodlights.

India have everything in their favour to win the World Cup a second time. But can they deliver?

WORLD CUP HIGHLIGHT

Lifting the trophy against the odds at Lord's in 1983. Their total of 183 didn't look anywhere near enough to stop the powerful West Indian battling line-up but tight bowling from Kapil Dev, one for 21 off 11 overs, Madan Lal, three for 31 off 12 and Man of the Match, Mohinder Amarnath, three for 12 off seven, reduced Clive Lloyd's all-conquering side to 140 all out.

WORLD CUP RECORD

1975	Eliminated at group stage
1979	Eliminated at group stage
1983	Beat West Indies in the final
1987	Lost to England in the semi-finals
1992	Eliminated at group stage
1996	Lost to Sri Lanka in semi-finals on default

WORLD CUP ODDS: 12-1

CAPTAIN **MOHAMMAD AZHARUDDIN**
Born 8.2.63 ... **right-hand bat**

India's captain follows a distinguished line of prolific run-makers blessed with wristy fluency that brings an oriental artistry to the crease every time they bat.

He launched his career spectacularly against David Gower's England team with three centuries in his first three Tests in 1984-85, and the 21-year-old Indian was hailed as the new Gavaskar.

Born in Hyderabad, he began as a medium pace swing bowler but by the time he was playing for Hyderabad Schools the artistic strokeplay was beginning to blossom. He made his first-class debut at 18 in the Ranji Trophy and international recognition followed with a place on the Young Indians tour to Zimbabwe in 1983-84.

He never maintained the staggering run-scoring start to his international career and had to wait until his first visit to Pakistan in 1989-90 before he scored his first century abroad, in the Faisalabad Test.

He was made captain of the tour to New Zealand in 1989-90 and celebrated by scoring a majestic 192 in the Auckland Test, the highest score by an Indian captain abroad.

By the time he led the tour to England later that year he had added a new dimension to his game, characterised by the ability to counter-attack and rarely allow bowlers to dictate terms. He was also using one of the lightest bats on the circuit.

Azharuddin's batting reached its zenith on that tour. He scored match-winning half-centuries in the two Texaco one-day internationals, a brilliant century in the Lord's Test, another in the Old Trafford Test, and completed a golden harvest of runs that summer with 78 in the final Oval Test.

He began this year having scored almost 6,000 runs in 94 Tests with 21 centuries but his career has been marred by the occasional loss of form, and by controversy.

Navjot Sidhu flew home in a huff after a bitter disagreement with his captain on the 1996 England tour and Azharuddin was accused in some quarters of being distant from the players on that tour.

Off the edge

- After 94 Tests he had scored more centuries (21) than 50s (19).
- **By the turn of the year Azhar had played in a world record 306 one-day internationals.**
- He made his one-day debut against England, at Bangalore in 1984-85.
- **The stylish bat was one of Wisden's Five Cricketers of the Year in 1991.**
- He broke the record for the fastest century in one-day internationals in December 1988, reaching his hundred in 62 deliveries against New Zealand at Baroda, although that record has since been beaten.
- **He was a late replacement for the injured Ian Bishop as Derbyshire's overseas player in 1994, having played for them in 1991.**
- Azharuddin once scored 226 for South Zone against Central Zone in 1983-84.
- **He averaged 55.40 for Derbyshire in 1991.**
- His education took place at Nizam College and Osmania University.
- **The Indian skipper started his career as a seam bowler who could make the ball move in a banana arc.**

There were also mutterings about his personal life. He had left his wife and two children a few months previously and his girlfriend, a glamorous product of the film industry, accompanied him for much of the tour. His form evaporated; he scored just 42 runs in five Test innings.

In October 1996, the selectors stripped him of the captaincy, handing the job to the new idol of Indian cricket lovers, Sachin Tendulkar, but the master batsman's subsequent loss of form led to 'Azhar's' re-instatement in 1998 and he led India on the 1998-99 tour to New Zealand.

A top-class close fielder, he has over 100 catches in Tests to his name, he also produces some audacious run-outs with that trademark flick-of-the-wrist return from gully and backward point.

He scored 2,016 runs for Derbyshire in 1991 and returned to top their averages in 1994. He marked his comeback by stepping into his first match, against Durham, straight from the airport and scored a quite wonderful 205 runs.

'Azhar' has made more than 300 one-day international appearances, including leading India in the 1992 and 1996 World Cups, as well as playing in the 1987 tournament and this summer's competition is likely to be his final farewell on the biggest one-day stage of them all.

AJIT AGARKAR
Born 4.12.77 ... **right-arm fast medium**

Made his Test debut against Zimbabwe in Harare in 1998-99. Played his first one-day international against Australia in Pepsi Triangular series in 1997-98 and by November 1998 had played 30 one-dayers with 58 wickets at 23.77. Deceptive bowler who generates pace off the pitch and swings the ball both ways.

SALIL ANKOLA
Born 1.3.68 ... **right-arm fast medium**

Made his Test and one-day international debuts on the 1989-90 tour to Pakistan. Since then unable to command regular place. Recalled for the 1996 World Cup. Bowls much tighter than he did and gains steep lift off the pitch. Born in Sholapur, he is a hard-hitting tailender.

SAIRAJ BAHUTULE
Born 6.1.73 ... **right-arm leg-spin**

Made his one-day international debut against Sri Lanka, at Guwahati in 1997-98. Toured Bangladesh with India for the Silver Jubilee Independence Cup in 1997-98. Born in Bombay.

RAJESH CHAUHAN
Born 19.12.66 ... **right-arm off-spin**

His career has been marred by allegations that his bowling action is suspect. Made his Test debut against England's 1992-93 touring team in Calcutta. Formed deadly spin triumvirate with Kumble and Raju but allegations that he 'chucked' led to a period in the wilderness. Took 55 wickets in the 1996-97 Ranji Trophy and had his action cleared to tour Sri Lanka in 1997-98.

NIKHIL CHOPRA
26.12.73 ... **right-arm off-spin**

Made his one-day international debut against Kenya at Gwalior in the Coca-Cola Triangular series in 1997-98. Played in the one-day international series against New Zealand in 1998-99.

RAHUL DRAVID
Born 11.1.73 ... **right-hand bat ...** wicket-keeper

He emulated the feats of Sunil Gavaskar and Vijay Hazare in becoming one of only three Indian batsmen in cricket history to score separate hundreds in the same match in January 1999.

Gavaskar performed the feat twice, against West Indies and Pakistan, and Hazare took on Australia's Ray Lindwall and Keith Miller in their prime in 1947-48 to score two tons.

Dravid joined the elite in January 1999, against New Zealand, at Hamilton, when he followed his first innings 190 with an unbeaten 103 in the drawn Third Test.

Light on his feet and with an immaculate range of strokes, this attacking middle-order batsman batted eight hours for his first innings 190, his highest score in Tests.

He was averaging a remarkable 57.46 after 25 Test appearances with an aggregate of 2,126 runs.

Made his Test debut against England, at Lord's in 1996 after scoring three half-centuries in three successive unofficial Tests against England 'A' in 1994-95.

The slick right-hander made his one-day international debut against Sri Lanka in the 1995-96 Singer Cup in Singapore and by January 19, 1999 had played 70 one-dayers with a batting average of 34.77.

Part of India's 1996 World Cup party, he acts as reserve wicket-keeper and is used very occasionally as an off-spinner in one-day internationals as well.

SOURAV GANGULY
Born 8.7.72 ... **left-hand bat ...** right-arm medium

Ganguly launched his Test career in spectacular fashion on India's 1996 tour to England with a maiden century at Lord's on his debut and shared the limelight with Dickie Bird, who was making his final Test appearance before retirement.

Born and brought up in Calcutta, he batted for more than seven hours and hit 20 fours in his knock of 131. His emergence as an outstanding batsman coincided with another departure as well — that of Vinod Kambli from the Test scene.

Ganguly toured Australia in 1991-92 but played in only two first-class matches and was subsequently overlooked by the selectors despite some high scoring performances for Bengal in the Ranji Trophy.

He hit a career best 200 not out, including a century before lunch at Calcutta in 1993-94, and then represented India 'A' against the touring England 'A' in 1994-95 but his breakthrough finally came in that debut at Lord's and he has been an automatic selection for Tests and one-day internationals for his country ever since.

He was averaging more than 50 with the bat after he played in his 23rd Test on India's tour to New Zealand in 1998-99 and by the start of this year he had played 86 one-day internationals with a batting average of 40.

His running between wickets is sometimes suspect and he is not one of India's best fielders but he is a useful medium pace bowler, with a career best five for 16 in one-day internationals.

Likely to be one of India's main weapons in this summer's tournament.

SUNIL JOSHI
Born 6.6.69 ... **left-hand bat ...** left-arm spin

Steady middle-order batsman who made his Test debut against England, at Edgbaston, in 1996. Appeared in a one-day international against Zimbabwe at Colombo, the fourth match of the 1996-97 Singer World series. Had played nine Tests and 34 one-day internationals by November 1998.

VINOD KAMBLI
Born 18.1.72 ... **left-hand bat**

Made his Test debut against England at Calcutta in 1992-93. He scored an unbeaten 100 in the first one-dayer in that series followed by a double century in the Bombay Test. Hit a double century against Zimbabwe and centuries against Sri Lanka in a brilliant start to his international Test career.

Confident against spin, occasionally suspect against pace, his form has not maintained that early promise. Averaging 54 after 17 Tests and had played 86 one-day internationals by the end of January 1999.

HRISHIKESH KANITKAR
Born 14.11.74 ... **left-hand bat ...** right-arm off spin

Has the makings of the quality all-rounder India so badly needs. Bats lower-order and bowls off-spin with a devastating quicker ball. One-day international debut against Sri Lanka, at Indore in 1997-98. Has 27 one-day international appearances to his name. Born in Pune.

AASHISH KAPOOR
Born 25.3.71 ... **right-hand bat ...** right-arm off spin

Seen as a foil for Anil Kumble, he is an economical one-day bowler who hails from Punjab. A useful batsman, he made his Test debut against West Indies at Mohali, in 1994-95 and had played four Tests and 15 one-day internationals by the turn of the year.

SABA KARIM
Born 14.11.67 ... **right-hand bat ...** wicket-keeper

Toured West Indies as reserve wicket-keeper in 1988-89. Returned from the wilderness to tour South Africa in 1996 as reserve `keeper. Capitalised on first choice Nayan Mongia's injury to score 55 runs from 48 deliveries on his one-day international debut against South Africa at Bloemfontein in 1996-97. Made 26 one-day appearances for India and is a more than capable batsman/wicket-keeper.

A LOOK AT...
SACHIN TENDULKAR

The world's greatest batsman, as he is acclaimed by many, with an average of more than 50 in Tests. He is also set to become the richest cricketer in the world after signing a contract worth £5 million with the American company WorldTel.

Sachin was only 16 when he became India's youngest Test player, in Pakistan in 1989-90, and just 17 years and 112 days when he won the hearts of the Old Trafford crowd by saving his side from defeat in the Second Test of 1990 with his first century.

At 19, he became the youngest player to complete 1,000 runs in Tests and, a month before his 21st birthday, he had passed 2,000 runs in only his 32nd Test for his country, again the youngest to reach this milestone.

Yorkshire made him their first overseas player in 1992 and he happily posed with a cloth cap and a pint of bitter to keep the public relations people smiling. But the massive responsibility placed upon the teenager became an albatross and he scored only one century, barely scraping past 1,000 runs in his only season.

He returned to England in 1996 as a seasoned cricketer, scoring two centuries in three Tests – the first of them, at Edgbaston, a score of 122 not out in an Indian innings of only 219.

At 23, Tendulkar succeeded Mohammad Azharuddin as India's captain, a job that had been almost held in abeyance for him until the time was right for him to take control. He made 10 and nought in his first Test in charge against Australia and has since relinquished the captaincy to concentrate on his batting.

The genius was evident from childhood in Bombay. He made unbeaten scores of 207, 329 and 346 in the space of five innings at school and scored a century on his first-class debut, at 15.

At first glance he appears to lack the stature expected of a cricketing god. He is stout with bandy legs, his voice is thin, and he shows a decent respect for opponents until he straps on the pads.

His batting pedigree indicates that he will eclipse most of the Indian batting records held by Sunil Gavaskar, and even though the mantle of captaincy rests uncomfortably on his strong shoulders, there is no denying the value of his cricket wisdom to the team.

A point emphasised by one of his former team-mates, Ravi Shastri, who says: "Sachin spots things in opponents no one else can see. Even when he was a teenager we were learning from him.

"He has a great cricketing brain and you could see that he would go on to become one of the best players in the world in no time at all."

Shastri was proved correct of course and although Tendulkar has stepped down from his role as captain of his country, he is still very much the man India will look at to lead them to World Cup glory again — just like another young genius, Kapil Dev, inspired his men to success in England 16 years ago.

THE STATS

Full name: Sachin Ramesh Tendulkar

Born: April 24, 1973 in Bombay

Role: Right-hand bat, occasional right-arm medium pace

Represents: Mumbai, India

Test debut: For India against Pakistan at Karachi, First Test, 1989-90

One-day international debut: For India against Pakistan at Gujranwala, 1989-90

Finest hour: Becoming the youngest player to represent India at Test level.

Extras: In 1995, Tendulkar turned down £350,000 to have his wedding televised live.

NOW THAT'S A FACT

● Tendulkar shared an unbeaten stand of 664 with Vinod Kambli in a schoolboy match.

● In that game, both players topped 300.

● He played for Yorkshire on a one-year contract in 1992 and scored 1070 runs in first-class cricket in that time.

● Aged 19, he became the youngest player to score 1,000 runs in Tests during India's tour to South Africa 1992-93.

● He scored only one first-class century in his season with Yorkshire, helping his side to victory over Durham.

● After 97 Test innings he was averaging 54.77.

● He scored 4820 runs in 64 Tests.

● His first one-day international century came against Australia in Colombo in 1994-95.

● Sachin put on 231 with Sidhu against Pakistan in Sharjah in 1995-96 to record the second highest one-day partnership in international cricket.

THE THINGS THEY SAY

TENDULKAR ON

❝My season as Yorkshire's overseas player was a great experience and I made many friends.❞ **On leaving Headingley for Bombay.**

❝I have never ruled out the possibility of returning to English cricket.❞ **Comment during India's tour to England in 1996.**

ON TENDULKAR

❝The boy genius is set to become the richest cricketer in the world.❞ **England souvenir programme for the 1996 series against India.**

GAGAN KHODA
Born 24.10.74 ... **right-hand bat**

Opening batsman from Rajasthan with an outstanding record as a schoolboy talent. Made a century on his Ranji Trophy debut in 1991-92 and scored 237 not out in the Ranji quarter-finals in 1994-95. His one-day international debut came against Bangladesh, at Mohali, in Coca-Cola Triangular series in the 1997-98 season.

NILESH KULKARNI
Born 3.4.73 ... **left-arm spin**

At 6ft 4ins, one of India's tallest spinners. Needs 10 victims to reach 100 wickets in Ranji Trophy matches for Bombay but has suffered a series of back problems during his career. Made his Test debut against Sri Lanka in the First Test, at Colombo, 1997-98. Played in Coca-Cola Triangular series at Gwalior the same year.

ANIL KUMBLE
Born 17.10.70 ... **right-arm leg-spin**

One of the world's best spin bowlers, he is India's most effective strike weapon. Took 10 for 74 against Pakistan at Delhi in February to become only the second bowler in Test history to take all 10 wickets in an innings. That feat raised his tally to 234 wickets in 51 Tests.

Kumble made his Test debut against England at Old Trafford in 1990 at the age of 19, a few months after playing in his first one-day international against Sri Lanka at Sharjah in the Australasia Cup. His future county team-mate and captain, Allan Lamb, was his first Test wicket.

He claimed his 100th Test scalp in his 21st Test, two fewer than Shane Warne and became the first leg-spinner to take 100 wickets in an English county season since 1971 when he accomplished the feat for Northants in the summer of 1995.

He bowls at a brisk pace, employing a lot of top spin with the ability to move the ball both ways off the pitch.

Twenty of his 105 victims in 1995 were leg-before and 21 were bowled. A large number of batsmen perished from close to the wicket catches and his well concealed googly and flipper, supplemented by quicker deliveries of genuine pace, do most of the damage.

Teetotal, vegetarian, and a graduate in mechanical engineering, Kumble was rested from the national side in 1997, missing the tour to Sri Lanka and the Sahara Cup, but was soon recalled to international service and ranks right up there alongside Warne at the top of the spinning art.

ABEY KURUVILLA
Born 8.8.68 ... **right-hand bat** ... right-arm fast medium

Made his Test debut in the West Indies in 1996-97 and was preferred to Venkatesh Prasad to play in the First Test against Sri Lanka, at Mohali, in November 1997. He took six wickets in the match. Hard-hitting tailender.

VENKAT LAXMAN
Born 1.11.74 ... **right-hand bat**

Made his Test debut against South Africa, at Ahmedabad in 1996-97 and played his first one-day international against Zimbabwe in the Pepsi Triangular series in 1997-98. Played in the Champions Trophy, at Sharjah, in 1998-99 and scored four Test half-centuries in his first 16 innings.

SANJAY MANJREKAR
Born 12.7.65 ... **right-hand bat**

Topped the Test batting averages on his first overseas tour to West Indies in 1988-89 and was described by Imran Khan as the best player of pace bowling in the world after he had scored a double century against Pakistan.

Born in Bombay, his career has been littered with success and failure. He was dropped after the disastrous tour to South Africa in 1992-93, and when Vinod Kambli filled his position in the batting order admirably, it was felt that Manjrekar would slip into the backwaters of domestic Indian cricket.

He has gained some considerable experience, sorted out his technique, but has never quite reached the level of success once forecast and is no longer guaranteed a Test place.

Son of Vijay Manjrekar, one of India's finest batsmen in the 1950s and 1960s, he showed courage and character in shrugging-off a serious a blow over his left eye from Winston Benjamin on his Test debut against the West Indies at Delhi in 1987-88.

He scored his first Test century in Barbados the following winter and when given an opportunity, he has often forged the cornerstone of India's batting.

He averages 37 in close on 50 Tests and after 74 one-day internationals, he was averaging 33 with the bat.

PARAS MHAMBREY
Born 20.6.72 ... **right-arm medium**

Sprang to prominence in 1994-95 when he became India's leading wicket-taker in domestic cricket with 54 victims. He played for India 'A' against the England 'A' tourists and made his Test debut against England at Birmingham in 1996. Played in the one-day Coca-Cola Triangular series for his country in 1997-98.

DEBASHIS MOHANTY
Born 20.7.76 ... **right-arm medium fast**

One of India's most promising pace bowlers, he made his first class debut in 1996-97, taking 22 wickets for Orissa in the Ranji Trophy. Picked for India 'A' for the SAARC tournament in Bangladesh, February 1997 and was a shock choice for India's Asia Cup squad and the Sri Lanka tour. Captured four wickets on his Test debut against Sri Lanka, in Colombo in 1997-98. Played also in the Sahara Cup in Toronto. Has 20 wickets to his name in one-day internationals.

NAYAN MONGIA
Born 19.12.69 ... **right-hand bat** ... wicket-keeper

Successor to his captain and Baroda team-mate, Kiran More, as India's first choice wicket-keeper.

Skilful, neat and tidy behind the stumps, he has fed voraciously off the chances created by India's trio of spinners.

Made his Test debut against Sri Lanka, at Lucknow, in 1993-94 and played his first one-day international in the same series. Toured New Zealand in 1998-99 and by the start of the year was averaging 25.93 with the bat in 36 Tests, with 81 catches and six stumpings.

His record at the one-day game is very impressive with 96 catches and 39 stumpings in 123 internationals by January 19 of this year.

VENKATESH PRASAD
Born 5.8.69 ... **right-arm medium**

Established himself as a world-class pace bowler on India's 1996 tour to England. He exploited conditions conducive to swing and seam admirably, with several victims falling to his dangerous leg-cutter.

A graduate of Dennis Lillee's fast bowling academy in Madras, Prasad first pressed his claim for a Test call-up after taking 50 wickets at only 19 apiece in the 1993-94 domestic season.

He replaced the injured Manoj Prabhakar on the 1993-94 tour to New Zealand, making his one-day international debut for his country at Christchurch.

But he had to wait two further years for his Test debut, against England at Birmingham in 1996, where he took four wickets in England's first innings. He crowned a superb performance in his second Test, at Lord's, by taking seven wickets in the match.

Named International Cricketer of the Year in 1997, he toured New Zealand with India in 1998-99 where he made his 20th Test appearance with 63 wickets to his credit by January 1999.

He had played 104 one-day internationals by mid January of 1999 World Cup year with a tally of 119 victims and will be one of India's chief bowlers in this summer's tournament.

NAVJOT SIDHU
Born 20.10.63 ... **right-hand bat**

Once unkindly labelled the 'Strokeless Wonder' when he made his Test debut for India in 1983-84, Sidhu has transformed his game to become widely acclaimed as 'Six Hit Sidhu'.

An opening batsman, he has led a spectacularly colourful career since breaking into the Indian Test side against the West Indies, at Ahmedabad. Since then he has played more than 51 Tests with an average of 42.13 and had made more than 3,000 Test runs by the time he completed the 1998-99 tour to New Zealand.

He has scored nine Test hundreds and 15 half-centuries and his aggregate in one-day internationals was 4,414 runs at 37.09 after 136 appearances.

He made his one-day international debut against Australia in the 1987 World Cup and appeared for India in both the 1992 and 1996 tournaments.

It was in these one-day matches that he developed into one of the most dangerous exponents of the new-found art of 'pinch-hitting', given free rein at the 1996 World Cup. Instead of settling for 60 runs in the first 15 overs and expecting the tail to slog, openers like Sidhu blazed from the start.

He disgraced himself on India's 1996 tour to England by flying home early after a series of disputes with his captain, Mohammad Azharuddin, but now that harmony has been restored to the Indian dressing-room although he now faces another battle – to hold down a place in the side.

HARBHAJAN SINGH
Born 3.7.80 ... **right-arm off spin**

Made his Test debut against Australia, at Bangalore in 1997-98 and his one-day international debut against New Zealand, at Sharjah, in the Coca-Cola Cup in 1997-98. Dropped from India's squad for Wills International tournament in Bangladesh in 1998 because of a suspect action.

HARVINDER SINGH
Born 23.12.77 ... **right-arm fast medium**

Highly promising youngster after several fine performances for India Under-19 team. Representing India 'A', he took six for 43 against Pakistan 'A' and four for 44 against Bangladesh in SAARC tournament, February 1997. Made his Test debut against Australia, at Chennai in 1997-98 with his first international appearance in the one-dayers coming against Pakistan, at Toronto in the Sahara Cup in, 1997.

ROBIN SINGH
Born 14.9.63 ... **left-hand bat** ... right-arm medium fast

Born in Trinidad in the West Indies, he made his Test debut for India against Zimbabwe, at Harare in 1998-99. One-day specialist, he played his first one-dayer against the West Indies in 1988-89 and by January 19 of this World Cup year he had played 72 limited-overs games, taking 44 wickets and averaging 28.92 with the bat as a lusty hitter. Toured New Zealand with India for the 1998-99 series.

JAVAGAL SRINATH
Born 31.8.69 ... **right-arm fast medium**

The spearhead of India's attack since Kapil Dev's retirement, he is now recognised as one of the world's best pacemen.

Coached at Dennis Lillee's bowling academy in Madras, Srinath has blossomed since producing a modest start to his outstanding Test and one-day international career.

Tall, slim and deceptively quick – batsmen say his quicker delivery is as fast as South African speed machine, Allan Donald – he made his Test debut in Australia in 1991-92, claiming the wickets of Geoff Marsh and Mark Waugh as his first victims.

Courtney Walsh, no slouch with the ball in his hand himself, was so impressed on a West Indies' tour to India that he recommended Srinath to Gloucestershire for the 1995 season. The bowler responded by taking 87 first-class wickets, twice taking 10 in a match.

He returned from a long injury to take 17 wickets in the Test series against Sri Lanka and Australia in 1997-98.

He toured New Zealand in 1998-99 and had taken 124 wickets in 35 Tests by mid January of this year. His one-day record on that date read: 212 wickets at 27.13 apiece in 153 internationals. Played in the 1992 and 1996 World Cups and is likely to be another key man in this summer's competition as India bid for a second World Cup success in England.

❶ TO WATCH **AJAY JADEJA**
Born 1.2.71 ... **right-hand bat** ... right-arm medium

He seems set to establish himself as Sidhu's opening partner after enjoying a successful build-up to the 1999 World Cup on India's tour to New Zealand over the past few months.

Born in Haryana, he is an attractive strokeplayer, who is also blessed with a solid defence. Jadeja has that rare ability to anchor an innings with some obdurate defence or spring from watchful caution to become a dangerous one-day run-getter.

At one stage he was opening the Indian innings in one-day cricket with Sachin Tendulkar, but such is his versatility that when the selectors felt that Manoj Prabhaker would become a more suitable partner for Tendulkar, Jadeja dropped down the batting order.

His value to the team is further highlighted by his outstanding ability in the field, where he can be relied upon to save at least 20 runs per innings, chiefly from his specialist position at backward point. He bowls a useful medium pace, much like Mohinder Amarnath, in one-day internationals.

He made his Test debut against South Africa, at Durban, in 1992-93 and has made steady, if unspectacular progress since then when given an opportunity to play in a powerful batting line-up.

The right-hand bat had played 13 Tests by January 19 1999 but it is at one-day level that he has become of most value to India. He has played a staggering 154 one-dayers since making his debut against Sri Lanka, at Mackay, in the 1992 World Cup and averages 35.88 with the bat, scoring 4019 runs in 139 innings, with four centuries and 23 fifties to his name.

WISDEN WORLD CUP VERDICT
With Dravid and Ganguly coming through to support Tendulkar and Azharuddin, they have an impressive batting line-up. And the bowling, with Prasad likely to support Srinath before ten-wicket Kumble comes on, is pretty good too. India are in with a chance of repeating their surprise 1983 win in England if all goes right — but an injury or two might stretch their resources.

KENYA

GROUP A • England • India • **Kenya** • South Africa • Sri Lanka • Zimbabwe

---

Kenya's rise to become the best of the non-Test playing countries was captured in one colourful freeze-frame moment of their most recent history as an emerging cricket nation.

The date: February 29, 1996. The venue: Pune in central India. The key moment: a catch by Kenya's overweight, bespectacled wicket-keeper Tariq Iqbal to dismiss Brian Lara and start the slide that led to the West Indies' sensational 73-run defeat, the greatest upset in World Cup history.

This match, which represents a golden passage in the romance of World Cup tournaments back to the first one in 1975, marked the defining moment when Kenya finally emerged from the backwaters of contrived international competition to gain the right to mix it with the best cricket playing countries in the world.

No players deserve more recognition in the second half of their careers than their former captain, Maurice Odumbe, and prolific run-scorer Steve Tikolo, who between them have forged the cornerstone of so many fine performances by Kenya in ICC Trophy matches and other competitions in the past decade.

Ironically, Tikolo won the Player of the Match award for Kenya in the 1997 ICC Trophy final against Bangladesh, and Odumbe the Man of the Tournament prize for scoring an aggregate of 493 runs, yet they still had to settle for a runners-up spot in the competition.

Over the past 10 years these two have been as important to Kenya's fortunes as Ambrose and Walsh to the West Indies; Waugh and Waugh to Australia; and Wasim and Waqar to Pakistan.

They arrive in England for the 1999 World Cup as a couple of dangerous one-day specialist match-winners who, given an opening, have the run-making firepower to punish any wayward attack, taking the game by the scruff of the neck.

Their team come carrying the hopes of a grateful nation still talking about that victory over the West Indies three years ago and Kenya's ambition to become a Full Member of the International Cricket Council early in the next millennium.

Back home, development programmes have been set in motion by the Kenya Cricket Association to raise standards at grass roots level as the search for the next Steve Tikolo goes on and several of their leading players are already playing first-class cricket for South African provincial teams.

They will not be phased by entry into World Cup Group A alongside Sri Lanka, India, South Africa, England and Zimbabwe and their confidence is high after the last tournament. They have the players to perform another giantkilling if not progress to the later rounds of the tournament.

They warm-up with matches against Somerset, at Taunton, on Friday, May 7; Gloucestershire, at Bristol, on May 9; and Glamorgan, at Cardiff, on May 11.

Their opening World Cup match is against Zimbabwe, a country they have played regularly in recent years. Kenya have nothing to lose. Zimbabwe, expected to win, will not relish this opener, at Taunton, on May 15.

Three days later they take on England, at Kent's Canterbury ground, in a game Alec Stewart's team should win at a canter. But who would have the courage to place a bet against the chances of a portly wicket-keeper clinging to a catch that turns the match? It's the stuff of World Cup legend!

WORLD CUP HIGHLIGHT

There can be only one — that sensational win over West Indies in 1996. Kenya were bowled out for a very moderate 166 in 49.3 overs but Brian Lara and co were in trouble early on and slumped to 35 for four. They never recovered and were dismissed for 93 in only 35.2 overs. Maurice Odumbe took three for 15 in 10 overs, claiming the vital wickets of top scorers Shivnarine Chanderpaul and Roger Harper.

WORLD CUP RECORD

1975	Did not qualify
1979	Did not qualify
1983	Did not qualify
1987	Did not qualify
1992	Did not qualify
1996	Eliminated at group stage

WORLD CUP ODDS: 50-1

CAPTAIN **ASIF KARIM**
Born 15.12.63 ... **right-hand bat** ... left-armspin

P romoted to skipper after being Kenya's vice-captain in recent seasons, the left-arm orthodox spinner is rated the best slow bowler in the country.

A prolific wicket-taker in the Kenya leagues, he has played in three ICC Trophy tournaments. Represented his country in the 1996 World Cup and took the vital late-order wicket of Courtney Walsh to help set up Kenya's sensational victory over West Indies.

Celebrated figures of three for 31 in ICC Trophy final against Bangladesh and he troubled their best batsmen again, taking five for 33 in Kenya's win in the Triangular Tournament, at Nairobi, October, 1997. Karim has captained Kenya at cricket and at tennis, in the Davis Cup tournament.

RAJAB ALI
Born 19.11.65 ... **right-arm fast medium**

Made his debut against India in the 1996 World Cup and went on to enjoy a brilliant tournament.

Started the collapse which led to West Indies' sensational defeat by Kenya, dismissing Richie Richardson, Brian Lara and Cameron Cuffy to record match-winning figures of three for 17 from 7.2 overs.

He took three for 45 against Australia, claiming the wickets of Mark Waugh, Ricky Ponting and Michael Bevan, and dismissed the Flower brothers and Guy Whittall in the match against Zimbabwe. First choice opening bowler for a number of years, Ali took 13 wickets at 9.85 apiece in the 1997 ICC Trophy.

JOSEPH ANGARA
Born 8.11.71 ... **right-arm medium**

Made his one-day international debut against Zimbabwe, at Nairobi in the 1997-98 President's Cup. Played in the 1997-98 Coca-Cola Triangular series in India. He has returned recently from a six-month coaching spell at the South African Cricket Academy. Once took seven wickets in a league match.

SHAHID BWIBO
Born 15.5.68 ... **right-hand bat** ... right-arm medium

Burly opening bowler and hard hitting batsman. Has yet to represent Kenya but has played for the Kenya Cricket Association against Natal, Border and Northern Transvaal in Nairobi. His best bowling figures include an eight for 28 spell in a national league match.

DIPAK CHUDASAMA
Born 20.5.63 ... **right-hand bat**

Opening batsman who has played for Kenya since 1988. Scored 29 against a full strength India attack, at Cuttack, in the 1996 World Cup. He top scored with 34 for Kenya against Zimbabwe and made 27 against Sri Lanka later in the tournament.

Established world one-day international opening stand of 225 with Kennedy

Otieno, scoring 122 against Bangladesh in a triangular tournament in Nairobi,
October 1997 to beat the previous record of 212 held by Australia's David Boon
and Geoff Marsh against India in 1986-87.

Played in the 1990 and 1994 ICC tournaments and averages 25 in one-day
internationals. He is a medical doctor and is known as 'Doc', surprisingly!

ZAFIR DIN
Born 22.4.77 ... **right-arm leg-spin**

One of Kenya's brightest young prospects. He has yet to represent his country
but came to prominence in 1996 and successfully completed an MCC coaching
course a year later. Born in Nairobi, he plays for the Sir Ali Muslim Club.

SANDEEP GUPTA
Born 7.4.67 ... **right-hand bat**

A leading middle-order batsman for most of the past decade, he is recognised
as one of Kenya's best players of fast bowling. Played in the 1990 and 1994 ICC
Trophy tournaments and toured South Africa with Kenya in 1995. Played
against Sri Lanka, at Nairobi, in the KCA Centenary Tournament in 1996-97.

TARIQ IQBAL
Born 3.4.64... **right-hand bat ...** wicket-keeper

Outstanding wicket-keeper but second choice to Kennedy Otieno recently
with his mediocre batting form one of the reasons why he has lost his place.
He has represented Kenya in three ICC trophy competitions and after missing
part of 1995 season for his club Swamibapa through injury, recovered to play
in their 1996 World Cup shock win against West Indies.

HITESH MODI
Born 13.10.71 ... **left-hand bat ...** right-arm off-spin

Controversial all-rounder who has been called for 'throwing' by umpires in
Kenya league matches. Showed poor form on the tour to South Africa in 1995
but was chosen for the 1996 World Cup squad. Shared a stand of 137 with Steve
Tikolo against Sri Lanka at Kandy in the tournament.

THOMAS ODOYO
Born 12.5.78 ... **right-hand bat ...** right-arm fast medium

The fastest bowler in Kenya, he was rated a teenage sensation when he broke
into the Nairobi Gymkhana league side. Played in recent series' against India A
and on the 1995 tour to South Africa.

MAURICE ODUMBE
Born 15.6.69 ... **right-hand bat ...** right-arm off-spin

Alongside Steve Tikolo, has been the mainstay of his country's batting for the
past decade.

He was given the honour to lead Kenya in the 1996 World Cup, which
represented their breakthrough into senior international cricket. He rose to
the occasion in the opening match against India, at Cuttack, sharing a 96-run
stand with the equally prolific Tikolo.

Chasing Australia's total of 304-7 from 50 overs at Vishakhapatnam, Odumbe led the counter-attack by scoring 50 in 53 balls. His stand of 102 with opening batsman Kennedy Otieno, who made 85, gave Australia a fright before Kenya's challenge faded and they were beaten by 97 runs.

But his finest hour in that tournament and in his career came at Pune when his off-spin accounted for Chanderpaul, Adams and Roger Harper as West Indies perished as they tried to overcome Kenya's total of 166.

He is the younger brother of Kenya's Edward 'Tito' Odumbe.

TITO ODUMBE
Born 19.5.65 ... **right-hand bat** ... right-arm medium fast

Elder brother of Maurice Odumbe. Superb all-rounder with the ability to score quick runs in limited overs matches and adopt a nagging line and length when he is bowling. Played in the 1996 World Cup. Practical joker of the squad.

LAMECK ONYANGO
Born 22.9.73 ... **right-arm fast medium**

Toured Bangladesh and South Africa with Kenya in 1995. Failed to take a wicket on his 1996 World Cup debut against Sri Lanka but scored a useful 23.

KENNEDY OTIENO
Born 11.3.72 ... **right-hand bat** ... wicket-keeper

Kenya's opening batsman and first choice wicket-keeper since scoring a century against Natal in 1993.

He had become an established player by the start of the 1996 World Cup and played superbly against Australia. He put on 102 with Maurice Odumbe and might have scored a century but for cramp. After 50 overs keeping, and another 35 batting, he limped off, collapsing on the boundary. He returned with a runner but Glenn McGrath yorked him for 85.

He played in Kenya's victory over West Indies at Pune later in the 1996 tournament and no player has done more than Otieno to maintain their winning momentum as an emerging cricket nation with full Test ambitions.

He scored a half-century in the 1997 ICC Trophy semi-final against Ireland to secure Kenya's inclusion in this summer's World Cup and cracked a magnificent 144 against Bangladesh in the 1997 Triangular Tournament in Nairobi, the highest score made ever by a Kenyan in a one-day international.

BHIJAL PATEL
Born 14.11.77 ... **left-arm spin**

Son of former Kenya wicket-keeper J.C. Patel, he has become one of the best young spinners in the country. Plays for the Premier Club.

MOHAMMAD SHEIKH
Born 16.6.77 ... **left-arm medium**

Broke into the national side for the Triangular Tournament against Zimbabwe and Bangladesh in 1997. He took a wicket on his debut against Bangladesh.

TONY SUJI
Born 5.2.76 ... **right-hand bat** ... right-arm medium

Toured Bangladesh with Kenya in 1995 and South Africa later that year. Played against Pakistan in the Kenya Cricket Association Centenary tournament in 1996-97. Represented Kenya in the Coca-Cola Triangular series in India in 1997-98.

MARTIN SUJI
Born 2.6.71 ... **right-hand bat ...** right-arm fast medium

Played for Transvaal in 1994 and is one of the few Kenyans with first-class experience. Spearheads the attack with seam and swing and is a useful middle-order batsman. Unlucky to finish on the losing side in the 1994 ICC Trophy final against UAE after taking four for 61. Played in the 1996 World Cup.

DAVID TIKOLO
Born 27.12.64 ... **right-hand bat ...** right-arm medium

Elder brother of Steve, David is a fine all-rounder. Captained Kenya against the United Arab Emirates in the 1994 ICC Trophy final. Played in Kenya's first World Cup 1996 match, against India, and also against Australia and Sri Lanka.

ALPESH VADHER
Born 7.9.74 ... **right-hand bat**

One of the newcomers to the Kenyan national side. Plays for Premier Club. Was involved in the October 1997 President's Cup. Chosen also for the Coca-Cola Triangular series in India in March 1998.

❶ TO WATCH STEVE TIKOLO
Born 25.6.71 ... **right-hand bat ...** right-arm off-spin

Tikolo played a major part in his country's progress to the 1996 World Cup and has been prominent again in producing some wonderful innings to maintain Kenya's progress into the 1999 World Cup in England.

He scored a very impressive 1,959 runs in 18 innings in 1994 with a highest score of 224 from only 108 balls and averaged 49 in the ICC Trophy that year, scoring 67 in the semi-finals against Bermuda and 54 in the final against UAE.

He followed that with 65 in Kenya's opening match against India in the 1996 World Cup and was the game's top scorer with 29 against West Indies. He rounded off a superb tournament for him personally by scoring 96 against a Sri Lanka attack containing Muttiah Muralitharan, at Kandy.

He had a modest run of form with the bat against Zimbabwe and Bangladesh in the October 1997 Triangular Tournament but grabbed four wickets against England 'A' in the first of two one-day matches against the tourists at the beginning of last year. In the second he made 61.

WISDEN WORLD CUP VERDICT
Have rather marked time since their stunning win over West Indies in 1996. Expect the same players to shine (Maurice Odumbe, Steve Tikolo and Kennedy Otieno), and expect at least one upset – perhaps in the first match against Zimbabwe.

SOUTH AFRICA

GROUP A • England • India • Kenya
• **South Africa** • Sri Lanka • Zimbabwe

South Africa brought the curtain up on 21 years of isolation from international cricket when they reappeared from their prolonged exile to play in the 1992 World Cup, hosted jointly by Australia and New Zealand.

They beat Australia comprehensively in the early group matches to leave their cricket supremo Ali Bacher claiming: "This is the greatest moment in South African cricket."

By the time they beat India to book a place in the semi-finals, Dr Bacher was speechless. Sadly, the juggernaut derailed when they failed to make the final after a nerve-tingling, rain-affected battle against England, but falling at the final hurdle meant nothing back home where the management and squad were treated like national heroes on their return to Johannesburg.

A crowd estimated at 100,000 lined the streets to give the team, led by Bloemfontein-born former Australian Test batsman Kepler Wessels, a jubilant welcome.

Cricket was back in business big-time and as ticket sales soared and enthusiasm spread it was possible to feel the euphoria at every level from the street corner to the first-class game.

At the time, caught up in the electrifying atmosphere sweeping the country, you could have mistakenly believed that South Africa, not Pakistan, had won the 1992 World Cup.

The progress clearly made in four years was unveiled for the ICC's family of cricket countries to inspect when South Africa began the 1996 World Cup, hosted by India, Pakistan and Sri Lanka, as if they could lift the trophy without losing a match.

They completed a clean sweep of victories in their group programme, achieving memorable wins against United Arab Emirates, New Zealand, England, Pakistan and Holland, but the new tournament favourites caught the backlash of Kenya's shock victory over the West

Indies when Richie Richardson led his team to triumph in the quarter-finals.

Hansie Cronje's side returned home this time knowing there was still much work to be done before South Africa could be declared world champions.

They prepare for World Cup battle at England 99, seven years on from that historic return to cricket's front-line, better prepared than ever to lift the crown, at Lord's, on Saturday, June 20, 1999.

As Australia's one-day captain Steve Waugh declares so forthrightly in the build-up to the tournament: "The first thing that must be said about the current South African team is that these guys are not easy to beat."

Bob Woolmer, former England and Kent batsman and South Africa's inspirational national team coach, says more cautiously: "For over 20 years South Africa didn't play a Test, so while the current players are very lucky compared to the era that went before them, I think they feel burdened with the responsibility for both the past and the future of South African cricket.'

Deep down Woolmer knows his squad has the ability to win the trophy for the first time. They have played an enormous number of Tests and one-day internationals since their return and the blend of experience and burgeoning talent included in their World Cup squad determines that they begin the tournament as one of the bookmakers' favourites.

They are locked into Group A, which contains World Cup holders Sri Lanka; 1983 winners India; the 1979, 1987 and 1992 losing finalists England; Zimbabwe, competing in their fifth World Cup; and Kenya, sensational winners against West Indies in the early rounds of the last tournament.

Cronje's squad arrive in England determined not to make the same mistakes they did in coming runners-up to Australia in the 1997-98 World Series triangular one-day tournament and losing the subsequent Test series in England when they let a 1-0 advantage become a 2-1 series defeat.

The cut and thrust of one-day cricket is vastly different from the five-day variety but the same principles apply, and in South Africa's case the cruel lesson they have learned in the past 18 months is that, if your opponent is down, keep him there!

This perceived weakness had clearly registered on their psyche by the time they played host to the touring West Indies in 1998-99, when there was no let up until the demolition had been completed.

Woolmer, whose contract with the United Cricket Board of South Africa concludes at the end of the World Cup, said: "West Indies suffered a backlash from England, where we should have won. We learned one very important lesson from that defeat. Now, when we get into a winning position, we're nailing it down."

South Africa's advantage is that several of their top players have knowledge of English conditions, with a coach raised on prime batting pitches at Lord's, Old Trafford and The Oval.

Their strike-force bowlers, Allan Donald and Shaun Pollock, have both played for Warwickshire; Hansie Cronje and Jacques Kallis played one season respectively at Leicestershire and Middlesex; and others have played in the northern leagues.

In terms of entertainment value, South Africa should have few peers at this tournament. The Donald-Pollock new ball attack is world-class; some World Cup spectators will turn up just to see Jonty Rhodes giving an exhibition of fielding at its best; and in Kallis and Lance Klusener they have two of the best one-day specialist all-rounders in the world.

If South Africa have recently been criticised by the ANC for not picking teams that reflect the nation's multi-ethnic reality, their management cannot be accused of not giving the Cape Coloured Paul Adams, Makhaya Ntini and Roger Telemachus every opportunity to shine at the highest level over the past three years.

The trickle of talent from South Africa's deprived areas has begun. Come future World Cups, those humble beginnings of opportunity for the disadvantaged could have turned into a flood.

South Africa have made enormous progress since Kepler Wessels led his men into Johannesburg after the 1992 World Cup. They could be accused of rushing some players through with indecent haste, but after 21 years in isolation, who can blame them?

WORLD CUP HIGHLIGHT

Returning to the international scene in the 1992 World Cup and beating holders Australia by nine wickets in their opening match with skipper Kepler Wessels hitting an unbeaten 81.

WORLD CUP RECORD

1975	Did not enter
1979	Did not enter
1983	Did not enter
1987	Did not enter
1992	Lost to England in semi-finals
1996	Lost to West Indies in quarter-finals

WORLD CUP ODDS: 12-1

CAPTAIN **HANSIE CRONJE**

Born 25.9.69 ... **right-hand bat** ... right-arm medium

Cronje was only 24 when he became South Africa's second youngest Test captain. A naturally gifted leader since childhood, he took over from the injured Kepler Wessels to take charge of the Springboks against Australia, in the Adelaide Test in 1993-94.

Apart from Australia's Mark Taylor, no player in the world is better suited to coping with the cut and thrust demands of international cricket than South Africa's astute captain.

His main attribute, possessed by all great skippers, is the ability to remain icily detached and calm in the heat of battle. No panic, no flawed decisions taken hurriedly, no deterioration in quality of leadership under pressure. The perfect skipper with a record to match.

Cronje's debut as captain in that Adelaide Test ended in a 191 run defeat but following the tour to England later that year, he has been in charge ever since.

Born in Bloemfontein, the leadership skills blossomed from the moment he became captain of Orange Free State at the age of 21. The son of a former OFS player, his credentials for international cricket were sharpened by England's 'rebel' tour to South Africa in 1989-90. He scored a century against Mike Gatting's team for South African Universities and the runs have flowed ever since.

Cronje remains indebted to former OFS captain Joubert Strydom and Kepler Wessels for teaching him the skills of the captaincy business.

"I had three seasons under Joubert when I first played provincial cricket. I also had three years under Kepler at international level. They were the two captains who taught me most," he says.

Cronje had already led South Africa on more occasions than other Springbok leaders when the 1998-99 home series against West Indies began. His record stood at 37 and by the time the 1999 World Cup ends on June 20, he will still be three months short of his 30th birthday, giving himself a strong chance of leading his country in the next World Cup.

Most captains end up getting the sack. In Hansie's case, you sense his future is rock solid, dependant on his decision to give up the job rather than have it taken from him.

Off the edge

- He toured India and the West Indies in 1991-92.
- **One of his best innings was for Orange Free State against Australia in 1993-94 when he scored 251.**
- He had led South Africa in 37 Tests and 92 one-day internationals by the start of the series against West Indies in 1998-99.
- **In that five-match Test series, he steered South Africa to a clean sweep of victories.**
- His father and elder brother played cricket for Orange Free State.
- **He scored five centuries in his first 21 Tests.**
- Hansie played for Leicestershire in the 1995 season in the County Championship.
- **He helped Ireland beat Middlesex in the Benson and Hedges Cup in 1997.**
- A born skipper, he captained Grey Primary School, Bloemfontein and Free State Under-13s.
- **He is a big fan of former England skipper Mike Gatting and studied his captaincy techniques on England's rebel South African tour in 1989-90.**

HYLTON ACKERMAN
Born 14.2.73 ... **right-hand bat**

It was an emotional moment when 'HD', a solid, reliable batsman, was chosen to play in the Second Test against Pakistan at Durban in 1997-98. His father, Hylton also, had been picked to tour Australia in 1971-72 but never gained his cap because of South Africa's political isolation. He crowned the 1997-98 season by scoring 1,373 runs to surpass Barry Richards' 24 year-old record. Member of the 1998-99 squad for West Indies series.

PAUL ADAMS
Born 20.1.77 ... **slow left-arm**

Unorthodox left-arm wrist spinner whose extraordinary, contorted action was described famously as a 'frog in a blender' when he first appeared on the scene in 1995-96.

He introduced himself to England by taking nine for 181 for South Africa 'A' team at Kimberley and had snatched 32 wickets in only five first-class matches when he made his international debut in the Fourth Test at Port Elizabeth against the tourists.

At 18 years and 340 days, he was the youngest Test player South Africa have ever had and only their second non-white cricketer, following Omar Henry.

A Cape Coloured, he went to the same school as England's former batsman Allan Lamb and took eight wickets in his first two Tests but managed only 13 in four Tests in England last summer.

DALE BENKENSTEIN
Born 9.6.74 ... **right-hand bat**

Attacking batsman and flair fielder, he gained recognition when chosen for the 1998 Wills International Cup tournament in Bangladesh. Appointed Natal captain at 22 and led them to the Cup and League double in 1996-97. Hit three league centuries and a fourth against the touring Australians. Captained South Africa 'A' to victory in both the four-day and one-day series' against West Indies 'A' in 1997-98.

NICKY BOJE
Born 20.3.73 ... **left-hand bat ...** left-arm spin

All-rounder with considerable fielding skills. Recognised as a top one-day specialist and future Test prospect. He was fifth in South Africa's domestic first-class averages in 1997-98 with 61.71. Played prominent role in South Africa's Commonwealth Games triumph in Malaysia and did well in the Wills International Cup tournament in Bangladesh in 1998.

MARK BOUCHER
Born 3.12.76 ... **right-hand bat ...** wicket-keeper

Set a world record against England in the Trent Bridge Test in 1998 by taking his 50th catch in only his 10th Test. Took over behind the stumps from long-serving Dave Richardson against Pakistan in 1997-98. The acrobatic 'keeper set a world record ninth wicket stand of 195 with Pat Symcox, against Pakistan in

Johannesburg in his second Test appearance and also equalled the South African record of six dismissals in an innings in successive Tests against Pakistan and Sri Lanka.

DEREK CROOKES
Born 5.3.69 ... **right-hand bat ...** right-arm off spin

Named in the South African squad for the 1998-99 series against the West Indies. Highly promising all-rounder, he averaged 50 in league matches for Natal in 1996-97 and took 25 wickets at 25 apiece after returning from South Africa's tour to India.

DARYLL CULLINAN
Born 4.3.67 ... **right-hand bat**

Shane Warne reckons to have constructed some psychological hold over South Africa's middle-order batsman.

"His temperament is fragile. On the mental side of the game, he is prone to playing the man not the ball," claims the Aussie spin maestro.

But a Test average of 38 before he landed in England with the South African tourists in 1998 indicates the Kimberley-born right-hand bat has had more good days than bad in approaching 50 Tests.

A gifted strokeplayer, he became the youngest South African to score a first-class century at 16, breaking the mighty Graeme Pollock's record for brilliant batting as a teenager.

He has a classical technique and the priceless ability to assess line and length earlier than most. He is relaxed and well-organised against pace, and despite Warne's criticism of his ability to play the turning ball, has neutralised Muttiah Muralitharan.

His maiden Test century against Sri Lanka in Colombo in 1993-94 was made when South Africa were really struggling. He returned from that tour to score 337 not out for Transvaal against Northern Transvaal, a South African record first class score.

And he gave another classic display to compile a rearguard hundred against India in 1996-97 to save a match in Johannesburg.

ALAN DAWSON
Born 27.11.69 ... **right-hand bat ...** right arm medium fast

A serious car accident in his last year at school left him with one leg shorter than the other. But sheer courage drove him to fulfil his ambition to play first class cricket and two encouraging seasons in 1996-97 and 1997-98 for Western Province gained him selection for the South Africa 'A' tour to Sri Lanka. Selected for the Wills International Cup in Bangladesh in 1998.

ALLAN DONALD
Born 20.10.66 ... **right-arm fast**

The fusillade of rib and head crunching deliveries that Allan Donald released on England's Mike Atherton in the Nottingham Test of 1998 became instant x-certificate film footage to rival that of Harold Larwood's 'Bodyline' mauling of Australia's batsmen in 1932-33.

Donald finished with 33 wickets in that series, a remarkable haul for a fast bowler in his 32nd year, and one that carried an ankle injury all tour.

He overtook Hugh Tayfield as South Africa's all-time leading wicket-taker and became the first Springbok to take 200 Test wickets in the series against Sri Lanka, reaching that milestone in exactly the same number of Tests — 42 — as Shane Warne. Only four bowlers have done it quicker.

He joined Warwickshire as a youngster in 1987 after two seasons with Orange Free State, broke into the South African side in 1991-92, and has spearheaded their attack ever since.

He became the first cricketer to receive his government's Sports Award Gold Medal, from President Nelson Mandela.

STEVE ELWORTHY
Born 23.2.65 ... **right-arm fast medium**

Made his Test debut at 33 for South Africa at Trent Bridge in July, 1998. Drafted into the England tour squad when Roger Telemachus dislocated his shoulder, he made his international debut in the triangular one-day tournament involving Pakistan and Sri Lanka three months earlier. Lancashire's overseas player in 1996.

HERSCHELLE GIBBS
Born 23.2.74 ... **right-hand bat**

Opened the batting in South Africa's Test series rout of West Indies in 1998-99. Strokeplaying batsman and superb fielder, he made his first-class debut aged just 16. Enjoyed a highly successful tour to England with South Africa 'A' in 1996 and made his Test debut against India, at Calcutta in November of that year. Tipped for a great future.

MORNANTAU HAYWARD
Born 6.3.77 ... **right-arm fast**

Raw, erratic but genuinely fast and still waiting to fulfil his ambition to become a Test playing regular in the South African side. Developed through the South Africa schools and Under-19s before making his debut for Eastern Province in 1995-96, taking 24 wickets at 16 runs apiece in the one-day matches that season. Captured 15 wickets in three South Africa 'A' 'Tests' against touring West Indies 'A' in 1997-98 and then toured England in the summer.

ANDREW HUDSON
Born 17.3.65 ... **right-hand bat**

Elegant opener, he burst on the international scene when he made a stylish 163 on his Test debut against the West Indies at Bridgetown in 1991-92. Became a regular Test and one-day performer but serious loss of form damaged his progress. Dropped down the order to play all three home Tests against Pakistan in February-March 1998 but modest performances cost him a place on the 1998 tour to England. Shared a World Cup record first wicket stand of 186 with Gary Kirsten against Holland in the 1996 tournament in Pakistan, India and Sri Lanka.

A LOOK AT...

JONTY RHODES

When *Wisden Cricket Monthly* invited readers to vote on their players of the 1998 season, two of them responded to the Fielder of the Season category by writing: 'Guess Who?'

It persuaded editor Tim de Lisle to break all the rules of running a national poll by quite naturally assuming that they meant to say 'Jonty Rhodes', and inked in the name accordingly.

Mr de Lisle will tell you that a poll winner is doing very nicely if he receives 600 votes. Jonty bagged 837, precisely 790 more than second placed Mark Ramprakash.

No fielder has brought more pleasure to Test Match audiences since South Africa's Colin Bland than the man from Natal.

He sprang to fame, quite literally, during the 1992 World Cup in Australia when he launched himself horizontally at the stumps to run out Pakistan's Inzamam-ul-Haq.

He carries that same restless energy that Derek Randall brought to the field for England when he swept in from cover. Jonty patrols the same area, encouraging team-mates and exploding in a blur of energy whenever the ball is in range, which means the segment of field anywhere between gully and mid-off!

He has overcome epilepsy and an erratic start to his international career to become a reliable source of runs in South Africa's middle-order batting. Rhodes reached his zenith in the batting art on the Springbok tour to England in 1998. He electrified Lord's during South Africa's progress towards a 10-wicket victory in the Second Test, scoring 117 — only his second century in 33 Tests — to win the Man of the Match award.

If that innings provided the fulcrum from which South Africa could win the match, his knock of 95 in the earlier Edgbaston Test enabled the tourists to avoid the follow-on.

His rejuvenation as a world-class performer is a lesson to every player. Two years ago his Test career seemed to be over. He began to doubt his ability and lost his appetite for touring. But he buckled down to the task of reviving his career in England and prepares for the World Cup with renewed confidence.

South Africa's captain Hansie Cronje says: "We are a different team without him. We all raise our levels of performance and expectation when he is in the field."

And Jonty says: "I never gave up. I'll never, ever take anything for granted, never stop working. I'm enjoying what I'm doing now more than ever."

That enjoyment shows in his play and such is his talent that he is probably the one player in world cricket that people would actually pay good money to simply watch field.

It is said that Jonty saves on average about 20 runs a game when he patrols the covers and in the one-day game, where every run is a priceless commodity. That is an asset that could take South Africa to triumph this summer.

THE STATS

Full name: Jonathan Neil Rhodes

Born: July 26, 1969 in Pietermaritzburg

Role: Right-hand bat, right-arm medium

Represents: Natal, South Africa

Test debut: For South Africa v India at Durban, First Test, 1992-93.

One-day international debut: For South Africa v Australia at Sydney in the 1992 World Cup.

Finest hour: Rhodes was at his brilliant best earlier this year when he scored a superb 95-ball century against West Indies in the home Fifth Test.

Extras: He took a world record for a fielder of five catches against West Indies in Bombay, 1993-94, three of them sensational.

NOW THAT'S A FACT

● Jonty made his first appearance for South Africa in 1992-93 and at one stage played in 27 consecutive Tests for his country.

● Before scoring 95 and 117 in the Edgbaston and Lord's Tests of 1998, he was averaging 29.61 with the bat in Test Match cricket.

● He was a golf partner of Tico Torres, Bon Jovi's drummer, at Prince's Trust Celebrity golf day at Wentworth in the summer of 1998.

● Rhodes was a top-class hockey player before establishing himself on the Test Match scene and was invited to trials for South Africa's squad for the 1996 Olympics but had to pull out because of a hamstring injury.

● Jonty attended Maritzburg College, Natal University.

● A Christian, he belongs to one of South Africa's many independent church organisations.

● He works hard to promote cricket in the South African townships.

● His hockey prowess made him a hero in Natal after he scored a spectacular goal that earned them the South African provincial title in 1991.

THE THINGS THEY SAY
RHODES ON

❛There was a lot of discipline at home in the leading of our day-to-day lives. We went to church as others did and sometimes had family Bible readings at home.❜ **Jonty on his childhood days**

ON RHODES

❛Somewhere along the way, Rhodes has turned his back upon the notion of fading away.❜ **Former Somerset batsman and now respected cricket writer, Peter Roebuck, after Rhodes' Test century at Lord's in 1998.**

JACQUES KALLIS
Born 16.10.75 ... **right-hand bat ...** right arm medium

One of the world's most talented young batsmen, with the ability to break stands with his useful medium-pace swing bowling as well. He also clings to some magnificent catches in the slip cordon.

Kallis attributes much of his progress to the season he spent at Middlesex in 1997. He opened the batting and bowled when the ball was still new.

"It was a wonderful opportunity to tighten up my technique against some of the best new-ball bowlers around. You would often come face to face with a quality bowler like Waqar Younis, Allan Donald or Devon Malcolm and that can only improve your game," he said.

He averaged 47 with the bat in Championship matches, scoring four centuries and four half-centuries. And 32 wickets in the Championship demonstrated his burgeoning promise as an all-rounder.

He was only 20 when he made his Test debut against England in 1995-96. But he was an altogether different proposition for bowlers in 1998 when he provided one of the highlights of South Africa's England tour.

He scored 132 in the Manchester Test, sharing a 238-run partnership with Gary Kirsten, a second wicket best for the country. Joins Glamorgan in 1999.

GARY KIRSTEN
Born 23.11.67 ... **left-hand bat**

Younger brother of the legendary Peter Kirsten, Gary forges the bedrock for so many lengthy first innings totals established by South Africa.

When Hansie Cronje had finally decided to declare their first innings closed against England in the Third Test at Manchester last summer, Gary had contributed 210 of the runs.

It was his highest Test score and his second double century in successive first-class innings. His knock lasted 10 hours 50 minutes and was the longest in Test Matches by a South African.

He seized his opportunity to become an established Test campaigner as a replacement for the injured Brian McMillan on South Africa's tour to Australia in 1993-94. Within three weeks he had forced his way into the Test side. He scored 67 and 41 in South Africa's famous Test win in Sydney and went on to play 45 successive Tests, equalling the South African record.

He became only the third South African to make two centuries in a single Test when he performed the feat against India in Calcutta in 1996-97 and only the fifth batsman to carry his bat through an innings for his country in making an unbeaten century against Pakistan in Faisalabad in 1997-98.

Superb temperament. Strong through the point area. He is the mainstay of South Africa's one-day batting line-up as sheet anchor.

LANCE KLUSENER
Born 4.9.71 ... **left-hand bat ...** right-arm fast medium

Made a sensational start to Test cricket by taking eight for 64 in the second innings of his debut against India in Calcutta in 1996-97, the best performance by any South African bowler in his maiden Test. Scored a century against India at Newlands in his fourth Test and is now cemented as one of the world's best Test and one-day all-rounders. Missed second half of South Africa's 1998 England tour through injury.

GERHARDUS LIEBENBERG
Born 7.4.72 ... **right-hand bat** ... wicket-keeper

Toured England as reserve wicket-keeper in 1994 but had to wait until 1997-98 to make his Test debut against Sri Lanka. Played in four of the five Tests on South Africa's 1998 England tour but lacked consistency and returned home to work on his technique. Captained Free State to the SuperSport Series title in 1997-98.

SHAUN POLLOCK
Born 16.7.73 ... **right-hand bat** ... right-arm fast medium

Son of Peter Pollock, the former South African fast bowler and now convenor of the national selectors, Shaun has established himself as a frontline bowling all-rounder in the last three years.

He first made his mark in international cricket against the England tourists in 1995-96, taking 16 wickets in the Tests at an average of 23.56 to lead the averages ahead of Allan Donald.

He looked the part with both bat and ball, regularly defying the England bowlers to shore up the tail when they threatened to break through.

Replacing Allan Donald as Warwickshire's overseas player in 1996, he made a sensational start by taking four wickets in four balls on his Benson and Hedges Cup debut against Leicestershire.

Eighteen Test wickets and a batting average of 29 on the tour of England in 1998 confirmed his progress. He captained South Africa's winning team in the Commonwealth Games and is tipped to succeed Cronje as captain.

PAT SYMCOX
Born 14.4.60 ... **right-hand bat** ... right-arm off spin

The oldest player on the international scene. Tall, aggressive spinner and hard-hitting tailender, he became the third number 10 batsman in history to make a Test century when scoring 108 against Pakistan, at Johannesburg in February, 1998. Batting with Mark Boucher, he shared a Test world record ninth wicket stand of 195. Gave up his job as a hospital administrator six years ago to pursue his ambition to become an international cricketer.

ROGER TELEMACHUS
Born 27.3.73 ... **right-arm fast medium**

One of international cricket's unluckiest players. Pulled out of South Africa 'A' tour of England in 1996 with injury, failed a fitness test before South Africa's tour of Australia in 1997-98 and was injured again before playing a match on the 1998 full tour to England. A Cape Coloured, he made his first-class debut for Boland in 1994-95 and became the fifth non-white cricketer to play for South Africa when picked for the 1997-98 triangular one-day tournament with Pakistan and Sri Lanka.

❶ TO WATCH **MAKHAYA NTINI**
Born 6.7.77 ... **right-arm fast medium**

Rarely in cricket history has a player more symbolised the historic change taking place in his country than Makhaya Ntini.

The first black cricketer to represent South Africa, he has emerged as a beacon of hope for millions of his young black countrymen trying to get out of the townships to secure a better future in a land of promise.

He was spotted first in 1993 when South Africa's township development programme, championed by Ali Bacher, moved into his Mdingi village home where the local school had no cricket equipment.

It was the first time Ntini had seen a hard ball and such was his promise that Border added him to their development squad and sent him to Dale College for a proper education.

He played for South Africa at Under-15 and Under-19 level and was fast-tracked onto the Australian Academy in Adelaide and Dennis Lillee's fast-bowling schools in Madras.

Ntini progressed from the Under-19 squad to the senior South African squad for the winter tour to Australia, making his one-day international debut against New Zealand in a triangular World Series match in Perth in January, 1998.

New Zealand captain Stephen Fleming and Adam Parore became his first two victims and, flushed with success, he returned home to play in two Tests against Sri Lanka.

Avarinda de Silva was his first Test scalp on the famous Newlands ground nestling beneath Table Mountain. Ironically, wicket-keeper Mark Boucher, his closest friend and a colleague in junior age group matches for South Africa, claimed the catch.

Ntini dismissed de Silva again on his second Test appearance, at Centurion Park, and the youngster had achieved enough for the selectors to add him to the squad for South Africa's tour to England last summer.

He played in the Old Trafford and Headingley Tests, accounting for Mike Atherton and Robert Croft at Manchester, and Atherton again, Graeme Hick, Ian Salisbury and Darren Gough at Leeds to finish with highly promising figures of 4-72, his best tour performance.

Ntini, one of seven children, has absorbed the glare of media interest with great maturity.

"I don't feel pressure. I see all the other guys around in the townships who are also attempting to achieve what I've done and all I feel I am doing is giving them encouragement to reach the same level, or maybe do better," he says.

WISDEN WORLD CUP VERDICT
Probably the pre-tournament favourites, even though they underachieved in England last year, not reaching the final of the Triangular Tournament. Punishing pace attack, backed up by workmanlike batting and stunning fielding from Jonty Rhodes and his equally acrobatic sidekick Herschelle Gibbs. Expect a final appearance, unless they have an off-day in the semi.

SRI LANKA

GROUP A • England • India • Kenya
• South Africa • **Sri Lanka** • Zimbabwe

In the space of just 29 months, Sri Lanka emerged from the murky backwaters of international cricket to send the doubters and the critics scurrying for cover as they, at last, gained the recognition they had for so long been denied.

The fairytale began on March 17, 1996, on their own Asian continent when their captain Arjuna Ranatunga led them to an astonishing victory by seven wickets against Australia in the World Cup final at Lahore.

It ended at The Oval, London, in August 1998 when an off-spinner named Muttiah Muralitharan bowled them to victory against England by 10 wickets after producing the fifth-best bowling performance in Test history.

Sri Lanka, hitherto considered by some major Test-playing countries as unworthy of a full length series, had beaten mighty England in their own backyard.

They return to England to defend their title at the 1999 World Cup no longer a joke and no longer dismissed as a push-over, incapable of filling grounds and fulfilling the demands of a major series.

They start behind South Africa and Australia in the betting odds for England 99 but with 'Murali's Magic' and one of the most powerful one-day international batting line-ups in the world, they are quite capable of repeating the form and 'Tales of the Unexpected' that carried them to victory at the sixth World Cup.

And Ranatunga can be guaranteed to receive the full attention of television audiences worldwide at the coin-tossing ceremonies before World Cup matches, following the significance of a statement he made before The Oval Test last August.

'It's a bit overcast, we think it might do a bit this morning' has become one of sport's great understatements, a rival for that declaration from the Apollo 13 mission which said: 'Houston, we have a problem!'

Muralitharan's 16 for 220 in the match raised his tally of wickets in Tests to 203 and his profile to that of superstar. He can be guaranteed a warm reception on his return for this World Cup and the start of his new overseas contract with Lancashire at the end of the tournament.

The World Cup planners could not have produced a more appropriate tournament opener than the fixture between England and Sri Lanka, at Lord's, on Friday, May 14. A full-house is guaranteed for this showdown after a short opening ceremony and Ranatunga's players will not be overawed by the occasion.

Their Group A rivals include England, India, South Africa, Zimbabwe and Kenya and Sri Lanka are asked to play arguably the two toughest group matches, against Alec Stewart's team and South Africa in the first five days.

Sri Lanka will field a much better side than they had at the 1996 tournament. Many of their younger players have been exposed to the toughest brand of international Test and one-day cricket since Lahore and some of their older players are showing no signs of wear and tear, as Glenn McGrath and Shane Warne will testify after watching Sanath Jayasuriya rip Australia's attack apart in a one-day international at Sydney on January 13 of this year with an innings of 65 scored from 62 balls.

Behind Jayasuriya come run-makers Kaluwitharana, de Silva, who scored 107 not out in the 1996 World Cup final, Ranatunga and Tillekeratne and if the attack sometimes lacks penetration, you-know-who can be relied upon to produce that flash of genius to turn a lost causes into match-winning celebrations.

No country has managed to win consecutive World Cups since West Indies in 1975 and 1979. Sri Lanka know they have a mountain to climb this summer to follow that but they have done it before.

WORLD CUP HIGHLIGHT
Arjuna Ranatunga lifting the trophy aloft after Sri Lanka had conquered Australia in the 1996 final.

WORLD CUP RECORD

1975	Eliminated at group stage
1979	Eliminated at group stage
1983	Eliminated at group stage
1987	Eliminated at group stage
1992	Eliminated at group stage
1996	Beat Australia in the final

WORLD CUP ODDS: 12-1

CAPTAIN **ARJUNA RANATUNGA**
Born 1.12.63 ... **left-hand bat**

He is overweight, slow in the field, and will be 35 when the 1999 World Cup tournament begins. He gives the appearance of being international cricket's most unlikely performer, and yet you would disregard him at your peril.

This was the man who led Sri Lanka to victory in the 1996 World Cup final in Lahore to firmly establish his country as a major player in the International Cricket Council's family of major cricket-playing nations.

Cricket quiz enthusiasts might like to note that Ranatunga was averaging 120.50 at the end of World Cup 96, thanks chiefly to four not outs. But statistics were a complete irrelevance by the end of the seven-wicket victory he masterminded against Australia in front of 23,826 official spectators and a lot more jammed into the ground in Lahore.

Off the edge

• Ranatunga became the seventh batsman in history to reach 7000 runs in limited-over international cricket, against India in Sharjah, November 1998.

• **He is also the second Sri Lankan to reach that milestone.**

• He scored 238 not out for Sinhalese against Sebastianites in the 1992-93 Sara Trophy, the biggest score by a Sri Lankan on home soil at the time.

• **Arjuna was born in Colombo.**

• He and Asanka Gurusinha batted all day for Sri Lanka against Pakistan in the P.Saravanamuttu Stadium in Colombo in 1985-86.

• **The two put on 240 in that match with Ranatunga undefeated on 135. It was Sri Lanka's biggest partnership at the time.**

Ranatunga made his Test debut against England, at Colombo in 1981-82. When he led Sri Lanka out at The Oval against England last August, he was playing his 82nd Test for his country.

Stocky, affable and a rapid accumulator of runs, his innings of 51 against England in Sri Lanka's first innings raised his aggregate runs in Tests to 4596 at an average of 35.35. He has managed to maintain the same run record at one-day level, scoring 7222 runs at 37.03 in 256 appearances by January 24 of this year.

RUSSEL ARNOLD
Born 25.10.73 ... **left-hand bat**

An opening batsman, he scored 209 off 270 balls against Somerset at the start of Sri Lanka's 1998 England tour. Became Test candidate in 1995-96 when he made 1,475 runs at an average of 70 to break Aravinda de Silva's record for a domestic season. Made his Test debut against Pakistan in 1996-97, sharing stands of 61, 95 and 157 with Sanath Jayasuriya.

MARVAN ATAPATTU
Born 22.11.70 ... **right-hand bat**

A prolific run-getter in domestic cricket who has yet to transfer his obvious talents to the Test stage.

He made his Test debut against India at Chandigarh in 1990-91 after averaging

60 runs per innings against the counties on his first tour to England in 1990.

But runs eluded this clearly gifted batsman at the highest level, and he scored only one run in his first six Test innings and only 108 in his first 14.

The selectors maintained confidence in his sound technique and after 20 Test appearances he was averaging 29.58. He is far more successful at limited-overs cricket, averaging 35.94 after 62 one-day internationals.

MALINGA BANDARA
Born 31.12.79 ... **right-arm leg-spin**

Made his Test debut against New Zealand in Colombo in the First Test of the Kiwi tour in 1997-98. Took 0 for 79 in 21 overs and, still a teenager, is a highly promising product of Sri Lanka's flourishing youth development programme.

NIROSHAN BANDARATILAKE
Born 16.5.75 ... **left-arm spin**

Enjoyed the distinction of taking a wicket with his fifth delivery in Test cricket on his debut against New Zealand in the First Test, at Colombo, in 1997-98. In the Second Test, at Galle, he had match figures of nine for 83 and claimed another five in the Third Test. Finished with 16 wickets in the series.

UPUL CHANDANA
Born 7.5.72 ... **right-arm leg-spin**

Limited-overs specialist, he had made 45 one-day international appearances for Sri Lanka by January 24, 1999 without once making the Test side. In that time he had taken 41 wickets at 32.56.

ARAVINDA DE SILVA
Born 17.10.65 ... **right-hand bat** ... right-arm off-spin

Joined Clive Lloyd and Viv Richards in the record books as the only three batsmen ever to score a century in a World Cup final when his blazing unbeaten 107 led Sri Lanka to triumph over Australia in 1996.

He made his one-day international debut against New Zealand, at Moratuwa, in 1983-84 and played his first Test, against England, at Lord's in 1984. By the time he had played against England, at The Oval, in August 1998, scoring 152 in Sri Lanka's 10-wicket victory, Aravinda had made 74 Test appearances which included seventeen hundreds and 18 half-centuries.

Playing for Kent in 1995, he scored 1781 runs, including seven centuries, and arrived in England for the single Test series last summer having enjoyed the most prolific year in his career. In seven consecutive Tests at home he rattled off scores of 168, 138 not out and 103 not out against Pakistan and 126, 146, 120 and 110 not out against India.

LANKA DE SILVA
Born 29.7.75 ... **right-hand bat**

Another outstanding youngster, he made his Test debut against India, at the Mohali Test in 1997-98 and his one-day international debut against the same opposition in the Asia Cup, at Colombo in the same season.

SAJEEWA DE SILVA
Born 11.1.71 ... **left-arm fast medium**

Made his Test debut against New Zealand, at Hamilton, in 1996-97 and played in the 1996-97 Sameer Four Nations Cup to make his first one-day international appearance. Relies on swing and clever control of line and length to snare batsmen, especially in one-day cricket. Had played 33 one-dayers by April 1998, taking 48 wickets at 24.87.

KUMARA DHARMASENA
Born 24.4.71 ... **right-hand bat ...** right-arm off-spin

Off-breaks and off-cutters bowled with accuracy and at a brisk pace have made him a formidable opponent since he played his first Test against South Africa, at Colombo, in 1993-94. But he became even more impressive at the one-day game, making his debut against Pakistan at Colombo in 1994-95. By October 1998, he had played 94 one-day internationals, claiming 92 wickets at 38.03, and 20 Tests, taking 50 wickets. His best analysis is six for 73 and he played in their 1996 World Cup final triumph.

AVISHKA GUNAWARDENE
Born 26.5.77 ... **left-hand bat**

Made his debut in the third one-day international against Zimbabwe, at Colombo, 1997-98. Played against India in the 1998-99 Champions Trophy.

CHADIKA HATHURUSINGHE
Born 13.9.68 ... **right-hand bat**

Opening batsman who made his Test breakthrough on the 1990-91 overseas tour to New Zealand. Scored 23 and 81 on his debut in the Second Test, at Hamilton, and made 74 in the Auckland Test. On his next Test appearance, at Lord's in 1991, he scored 66. Played his first one-day international in 1991-92 against Pakistan, at Sargodha. Toured England in 1998.

PRADEEP HEWAGE
Born 7.12.78 ... **right-hand bat ...** right-arm medium

Chosen to receive the inaugural Prince of Wales Trophy, awarded to Sri Lanka's Most Promising schoolboy cricketer in 1997-98. Played against the 1997-98 England 'A' touring team and was voted Best Batsman in the 1997 Youth World Cup in South Africa. Educated at Sri Lanka's St Benedict's College.

SANATH JAYASURIYA
Born 30.6.69 ... **left-hand bat**

The `Most Valued Player of the 1996 World Cup' whose assault on England's bowling in the quarter-finals at Faisalabad opened the way for Sri Lanka to exploit the latter stages of the competition and win the ultimate prize.

Opening Sri Lanka's reply to England's 235 for eight, he departed at 113 for one having scored 82 off 44 balls, with three sixes and 13 fours. At one stage he struck Richard Illingworth for four successive boundaries.

He had earlier made scores of 79 against India and 44 against Kenya to confirm his reputation as a savage destroyer of some of the world's best attacks at one-day international level and in the Test arena since his debut at five-day level against New Zealand, at Hamilton in 1990-91.

Became the first Sri Lankan to score a triple century in a Test when he dominated a 576-run stand with Roshan Mahanama to complete an innings of 340 against India in the First Test, at Colombo in August 1997.

That innings had been bettered only by Brian Lara, Garfield Sobers and Len Hutton. He batted 799 minutes, hitting two sixes and 36 fours.

MAHELA JAYAWARDENE
Born 27.5.77 ... **right-hand bat** ... right-arm medium

An all-rounder, he scored 66 on his Test debut against India at Colombo in 1997-98, a match best remembered for Sri Lanka's record total of 952 for six. Followed that with two half centuries in the Colombo Test against New Zealand in May and June of 1998, and in the next Test at Galle scored 167. Played against England at The Oval in 1998. Averaging 44.22 in six Tests by November of that year, he made his one-day international debut against Zimbabwe at Colombo in 1997-98.

PRASANNA JAYAWARDENE
Born 10.9.79 ... **right-hand bat** ... wicket-keeper

Still a schoolboy, was given valuable experience on his first full Sri Lanka tour to England in 1998 as understudy to Romesh Kaluwitharana. Played against the touring England 'A' team in 1997-98.

RUWAN KALPAGE
Born 19.2.70 ... **right-arm off-spin**

Vastly experienced at one-day international level, this Kandy born off-spin bowler had played 82 one-day internationals by January 1998, taking 71 wickets at 39.15. Made his Test debut against India at Colombo in 1993-94 after playing his first one-dayer against Pakistan, at Sargodha, in 1991-92.

ROMESH KALUWITHARANA
Born 24.11.69 ... **right-hand bat** ... wicket-keeper

Became one of the 1996 World Cup's famed 'pinch hitters' in partnership with Sanath Jayasuriya. Shared starts with him of five against Zimbabwe, 53 against India (42 in the first three overs),83 against Kenya and 12 against England.

He made a sensational Test debut against Australia at Colombo in 1992-93, scoring an unbeaten 132. Averaging 32 after 24th Test at The Oval 1998. Game against Australia on January 13, 1999 was his 104th one-dayer.

ROSHAN MAHANAMA
Born 31.5.66 ... **right-hand bat**

Back in favour after a period in the wilderness. Made his Test debut against Pakistan in 1985-86 but had played only 52 times by March 1998, averaging 29. One of the most elegant batsmen in the world, with a superb cover drive off the front foot, he made his highest Test score of 225 against India, at Colombo, in August 1997 in sharing a stand of 576 with Sanath Jayasuriya, a record for any wicket in Test cricket. Ex-opener, he bats down the order these days. Has made over 200 appearances in limited-over internationals.

SURESH PERERA
Born 16.2.78 ... **right-arm medium**

Made his Test debut against England last summer, scoring 43 not out in Sri Lanka's first innings. Born in Colombo, he made his one-day international debut against India at Colombo in 1997-98.

RAVINDRA PUSHPAKUMARA
Born 21.7.75 ... **right-arm fast medium**

One of Sri Lanka's fastest bowlers. Moves the ball both ways in the air and is bowling with more accuracy and economy than on his Test debut against Pakistan, at Kandy, in the 1994-95 Third Test. One-day international debut against India, at Hyderabad in 1993-94. Took 47 wickets in his first 18 Tests by March 1998 and 24 wickets in 29 one-dayers by April that year.

HASHAN TILLEKERATNE
Born 14.7.67 ... **left-hand bat**

Dropped anchor and then exploded to make Sri Lanka's highest score of 73 against Australia, at Sydney, on January 13, 1999, his 169th one-day international since his debut against India, at Sharjah in 1986-87. He averages nearly 30 with the bat in one-dayers, and had scored 2,879 runs at the end of his 53rd Test appearance against England, in Sri Lanka's win at The Oval last summer.

CHAMINDA VAAS
Born 27.1.74 ... **left-arm fast medium**

His decidedly rapid left-arm pace bowling has evoked comparisons with Pakistan's captain Wasim Akram.

Born in Mattumagala near Colombo, his introduction to the Test and one-day international scene in 1994-95 coincided with Sri Lanka's arrival as a major cricket force.

He made his Test debut against Pakistan in the Third Test, at Kandy, in 1994-95, the season after playing his first one-day international at Rajkot against India. He wrote himself a passage in his country's cricketing history when he celebrated match figures of 10 for 90 at the end of Sri Lanka's 241-run Test win against New Zealand, at Napier, in March 1995, the first time a Sri Lankan had taken 10 wickets in a Test.

He played in all the 1996 World Cup tournament matches and by the end of his 26th Test appearance, against South Africa, at Cape Town in 1997-98, he had taken 83 wickets at 29.02. His one-day haul was 119 after taking Adam Gilchrist's wicket against Australia at Sydney, on January 13, 1999, his 97th one-dayer.

MARIO VILLAVARAYAN
Born 22.8.73 ... **right-arm fast medium**

Made his debut in first-class cricket at the age of 23. Caught the selectors' eye in 1995-96 when he playing for domestic champions, Colombo, with his best bowling figures standing at five for 43. Picked for Sri Lanka's tour to England in 1998 but did not play in the triangular one-day tournament or in the Oval Test.

A LOOK AT...
MUTTIAH MURALITHARAN

Sri Lankan captain Arjuna Ranatunga looked at The Oval pitch and declared: "We think it might do a bit."

He promptly elected to field and for the next few days thousands of spectators packed into the ground for the single Test of 1998 between England and Sri Lanka watched a spin-bowling magician destroy the pride of the home side's batting.

The record books show that Muralitharan's match figures of 16 for 220 is the fifth best Test analysis of all time. He took seven for 155 in England's first innings and nine for 65 in the second to pass the 200 Test wicket milestone in the process and bring his tally of victims in 1998 to a phenomenal 68.

So much for the statistics. More important for cricket lovers, a new world star was born. Not since Shane Warne emerged to bamboozle batsmen with his leg-breaks has anyone raised the pulse-rate quite like Muralitharan.

His double-jointed wrist action has become the most photographed delivery in the game. Darrell Hair, the Australian Test umpire, has described his action in a book as 'diabolical' and in Melbourne 1995-96 no-balled Muralitharan seven times for throwing. And Sri Lankan skipper Arjuna Ranatunga took his side off the pitch in protest after umpire Ross Emerson had no-balled Muttiah for the same reason against England in the Triangular series in January 1999.

But he has been cleared of suspicion by the ICC after it was revealed that he has had a physical deformity from birth where he cannot straighten his arm.

The mental torture of being declared a chucker forced him to contemplate early retirement.

"It affected my whole world, my family, friends, and all those who believed in me," says Muralitharan.

He took five wickets to help Sri Lanka to their first Test victory against England in Colombo and has been taking wickets consistently ever since, becoming the first Sri Lankan to take 100 wickets in Tests in New Zealand in 1996-97.

He returned the then best Test figures by a Sri Lankan (12 for 117) against Zimbabwe in 1997-98, took 19 wickets in a series against New Zealand last year, and then destroyed England.

Magnanimous in defeat, England captain Alec Stewart said: "This bloke spins it more than anyone I've ever seen. He's in a league of his own and we could hardly get near him."

Muttiah attributes much of his success to playing street cricket in the historic city of Kandy in childhood.

"Tennis-ball cricket early in a boy's career sharpens his reflexes. You also gain confidence because you are not afraid of suffering physical blows," he says.

And English cricket lovers are now likely to be able to enjoy Muralitharan's magic not only in the World Cup this summer but beyond the tournament as well. He has signed a one-year contract to play for Lancashire after the competition is over although Sri Lanka are said to be reluctant to let him go.

THE STATS

Full name: Muttiah Muralitharan

Born: April 17, 1972 in Kandy

Role: Right-hand bat, right-arm off-spinner

Represents: Tamil Union, Sri Lanka

Test debut: For Sri Lanka against Australia at Colombo, Second Test, 1992-93

One-day international debut: For Sri Lanka against India at Colombo in 1993-94.

Finest hour: His second innings exhibition of brilliance against England at The Oval when he left the England batsmen — and supporters alike — spellbound.

Extras: His skipper, Arjuna Ranatunga, describes Muttiah as "a bowler that comes along once every 100 years."

NOW THAT'S A FACT

● Wasim Akram said he advised Lancashire to sign the Sri Lankan spin wizard after the NatWest Trophy final of 1998.

● Muttiah's family own a confectionary business in Sri Lanka.

● His school bowling attack included Ruwan Kalpage and Piyal Wijetunga, who both played for Sri Lanka.

● He broke a 10-year record in taking 127 wickets for St Anthony's School in one year, back home in Kandy.

● His first international break came in 1991 when he was picked to play against an Australian Cricket Academy XI and the England 'A' tourists.

● His suspect bowling action was repeatedly photographed by a study group from the University of Western Australia.

● Muralitharan averaged a wicket every 59 deliveries in his first 18 Tests.

● Alec Stewart avoided becoming a victim of Muttiah's magic in The Oval Test, 1998. He was dismissed by Suresh Perera in the first innings and was run out in the second.

● He had taken 203 Test wickets by the end of the single Test against England in August 1998.

● He says he is indebted to Dav Whatmore, the half Australian, half Sri Lankan, who coached Sri Lanka before joining Lancashire.

THE THINGS THEY SAY
MURALITHARAN ON

❝I thought it was very cruel❞
On Darrell Hair's decision to no-ball him in Melbourne.

ON MURALITHARAN

❝The way he bowls he will always be a handful❞.
England coach David Lloyd after the Oval Test, 1998.

PRAMODYA WICKREMASINGHE
Born 14.8.71 ... **right-arm fast medium**

The most experienced of Sri Lanka's collection of pace bowlers. He takes the new ball but lack of support in a country largely bereft of decent pace has made the burden of responsibility he carries into international Test and one-day internationals an awesome one.

Born in Matara, his task has been easier of late by the progress made by Chaminda Vaas and Nuwan Zoysa, a new breed of quickies springing from Sri Lanka's development programmes.

He made his international debut in 1990-91 at one-day level, playing for the first time for his country against Bangladesh, at Calcutta, in the Asia Cup. By 1991-92 he was thought good enough for Test baptism, playing for the first time at that level against Pakistan, at Sialkot.

He has been a regular ever since but Sri Lanka's lack of opportunity at Test level meant that when he turned out against England, at The Oval, in August 1998, it was only his 31st cap.

He brought his wicket tally to 60 at an average of 46 apiece in the Oval Test, a modest total for such a hardworking performer. Celebrated his 100th game at one-day level in the match against Australia on January 13. Has over 70 victims.

❶ TO WATCH **NUWAN ZOYSA**
Born 13.5.78 ... **left-arm fast medium**

Shares the new ball with Chaminda Vaas to give Sri Lanka hope of finding an opening attack capable of challenging, if not achieving, the feats of West Indies' Ambrose-Walsh spearhead, South Africa's Donald-Pollock pairing or Australia's McGrath-Gillespie formation.

The new kid on the block from Colombo, he arrived at the Test threshold after some stirring bowling performances for his club side Sinhalese.

He made Chris Cairns his first scalp on an unspectacular Test debut against New Zealand, at Dunedin in March 1997 but snatched six wickets on his second Test appearance at Hamilton a few days later. Figures of three for 47 and three for 53 left a deep impression on New Zealand's batting, despite their win.

Sanath Jayasuriya's match-winning 79 stole the show on Zoysa's one-day debut against New Zealand, at Christchurch in late March 1997, but figures of two for 29 in seven tight overs, followed by two for 47 in the final one-dayer at Wellington spelled immense promise for the future.

He was a member of Sri Lanka's one-day squad for the triangular series in Australia in January 1999 and will only be 21 on May 13 of this year.

WISDEN WORLD CUP VERDICT

Their 1996 pinch-hitting tactics are less likely to come off in England. But their batting techniques are based on classical foundations, so they can't be ruled out. There's a suspicion that the side may be growing old together — only one member of the '96 team (Asanka Gurusinha) is likely to be missing this time, and their over-30s could run out of puff in the latter stages.

ZIMBABWE

GROUP A • England • India • Kenya
• South Africa • Sri Lanka • **Zimbabwe**

Bill Clinton accepted his Democratic party's nomination for the Presidency, John Smith scored a decisive victory to become leader of the Labour Party in the House of Commons and King Juan Carlos opened the Barcelona Olympics.

It was July 1992, best remembered in Zimbabwe as the moment delegates to the International Cricket Council decided to make them Full Members and give them Test Match status.

Seven years later, as they prepare for the 1999 World Cup in England, Zimbabwe stand on the threshold of a glorious future in international cricket.

The Zimbabwe Cricket Union are at last reaping the rewards of well organised cricket development programmes in the high-density suburbs of Harare and Bulawayo by employing the talents at Test level of the first wave of black cricketers to emerge from their coaching initiatives.

Former Australian Test captain Bobby Simpson, invited to inspect progress and offer advice in 1997, returned home with rave reports on Zimbabwe's grass-roots cricket development and his belief that they could, in time, become a major cricket power.

John Traicos, former Zimbabwe spin bowler and chairman of selectors, who is now living in Western Australia, identifies England's 1996-97 tour as another defining moment in Zimbabwe's development as a cricketing nation.

Ball-by-ball coverage relayed by Sky TV cameras gave the sport such a boost for armchair viewers, that Traicos reckons the game of cricket overtook football as the number one sport.

Whatever the theories, Zimbabwean cricket is passing through a golden age from which it can only benefit as their squad prepares to line-up alongside the 11 other countries for the seventh World Cup competition.

Zimbabwe, making their fifth appearance in a World Cup tournament, have never been better prepared to pull off a few shock results than this time, as they line up alongside England, India, Kenya, South Africa and Sri Lanka in Group A.

They play warm-up matches against Worcestershire on May 7; Derbyshire on May 9; and Warwickshire on May 11, during which time they will have alerted their group opponents to the threat they could pose if their more established players and exciting crop of newcomers strike early form on tour.

The tournament proper gives them a comfortable opening World Cup match against Kenya, at Taunton, on Saturday, May 15. They play India, at Leicester, on Wednesday, May 19 and meet World Cup holders Sri Lanka, at Worcester, on Saturday, May 22. England are the next opponents, at Trent Bridge, on Tuesday, May 25, and they meet South Africa in the last group match, at Essex's Chelmsford ground, on Saturday, May 29.

Zimbabwe's programme of matches suggests a gradual spiralling of intensity of competition, beginning with Kenya and ending with South Africa, a format that could assist a predominantly young and inexperienced squad, learning match-by-match.

When Duncan Fletcher led Zimbabwe in their first World Cup, held in England in 1983, the selectors had to choose their squad from a limited field of talent. Andy Pycroft, John Traicos, Kevin Curran, who has just been relieved of the captaincy at Northants, and David Houghton were in that touring party for the finals.

They had made little progress by the time of the 1987 World Cup in India and Pakistan and were in similar disarray in 1992 when they came bottom of the group as Imran Khan led Pakistan to their finest hour in one-day cricket.

This time their chances have been enhanced considerably. They arrive on the strength of victories over India, at Harare in October 1998 — their second-ever Test win — and Pakistan two months later in their first ever winning Test series away from home.

They are no longer pushovers, here for the ride, just happy to be playing Test cricket after years consigned to the international wilderness. They mean to be taken seriously.

Their current Test squad is a combination of proven, experienced stars like Alistair Campbell; the Flower brothers Grant and Andy; the Strang brothers Paul and Bryan; exiles returning home for a slice of the action like Murray Goodwin and Neil Johnson; and an exciting crop of young black players prepared to grasp the opportunities coming their way from the ZCU.

Rising young stars plucked for an international cricket future from the township development programmes include Everton

Matambanadzo, Mpumelelo Mbangwa, Trevor Madondo, Henry Olonga and Mluleki Nkala.

Theirs is a haphazard future in a tough, uncompromising climate at full Test level, but the trickle of talent filtering through the system promises to become a flood with forecasts of success in future World Cups if not the ultimate prize this summer.

They come to England with very little to lose – and plenty to gain. They are now contenders in the world one-day game, if not among the favourites to feature in the latter stages.

Only three countries will qualify from a World Cup group containing England, South Africa, Sri Lanka and India so their chances of making the Super Six are obviously slim but in many ways they have already taken a significant step in the World Cup.

In their previous tournaments, they were considered the lightweights making up the numbers. Now they are more the middleweights, capable of a shock knockout but unlikely to trouble the real heavyweights of the world game, Australia, West Indies, South Africa, Pakistan and the host country.

But their crop of exciting young players will be better cricketers for their involvement this summer and with the experience and talents of the Flower brothers, Paul Strang and captain Alistair Campbell around to nurture that development, Zimbabwe are likely to be capable of competing with those more established cricketing nations on an equal footing when the next World Cup comes around.

WORLD CUP HIGHLIGHT

The minnows of Zimbabwe beat mighty Australia in their first match in the 1983 World Cup in England by 13 runs to record the biggest shock in the tournament's history at the time.

WORLD CUP RECORD

1975	Did not qualify
1979	Did not qualify
1983	Eliminated at group stage
1987	Eliminated at group stage
1992	Eliminated at group stage
1996	Eliminated at group stage

WORLD CUP ODDS: 40-1

CAPTAIN **ALISTAIR CAMPBELL**
Born 23.9.72 ... **left-hand bat**

He was hailed as 'Zimbabwe's David Gower' when he made his debut for Zimbabwe at the age of 20 in the historic inaugural Test Match against India at Harare in 1992-93.

The son of Iain 'Poll' Campbell, headmaster for more than 20 years at Lilfordia, one of Zimbabwe's leading cricketing schools, Alistair grew-up with bat and ball and made history at the school by playing for the first team at the tender age of eight, four years younger than most of his team-mates.

He scored his first century in grade six year, and by the time he moved to Eaglesvale High School, had become a vastly experienced and mature player for one so young.

He announced his arrival by scoring five successive hundreds and went on to graduate for the Fawns, the Zimbabwe Under-15 team.

His electrifying progress led to selection for the full national side while still at school. First, he was picked to play matches against the touring Pakistan 'B' team, including two appearances against them for his full national side, and then became the youngest Zimbabwean to make a first-class century in scoring an unbeaten hundred against touring Glamorgan.

By 1992, Campbell was good enough to play for Zimbabwe in the World Cup, batting in the key position of number three at the age of 19.

When his country were elevated to full Test status, he was an automatic choice to play in that historic Test against India in 1992-93. Still only 20, he scored 45 in the first innings but it took him another season for the timing and fluency to flourish.

The breakthrough happened on Zimbabwe's 1993-94 tour to Pakistan, when he averaged 41 in a three Test series against Wasim Akram and Waqar Younis at their best.

He scored 53 in the First Test at Karachi and in the first innings of the Rawalpindi Test, a swashbuckling 63 from 55 balls, with 11 fours and a six. He defied one of the world's best attacks again in the second innings to make 75 and secure his future in the big time.

He took over as vice-captain for the 1994-95 tour to Australia after David Houghton flew home for personal reasons and then became captain in 1996-97 for the series against England.

Off the edge

- His full name is Alistair Douglas Ross Campbell.
- **Campbell's father insisted that his son bat left-handed despite the fact that, as a child, he did everything else with his right.**
- He scored 11 half-centuries but no 100s in his first 33 Test appearances in international cricket for his country.
- **He is a firm believer that some countries play too much Test cricket.**
- Outside cricket, his other favourite sport is golf.
- **He is also a bit of a gambler – although not on cricket!**
- He reckons that he should still be able to play the game at the top level until he is 40.
- **His first century in the one-day international game came against Sri Lanka.**
- His nickname is Kamba.
- Campbell's World Cup debut was against West Indies on the 29th February, 1992 in Brisbane.

EDDO BRANDES
Born 5.3.63 ... **right-arm fast**

The spearhead of Zimbabwe's attack for more than 10 years. He made his Test debut in Zimbabwe's inaugural Test against India at Harare in 1992-93. Plays for Mashonaland and is a chicken farmer by trade. Man of the Match in the 1992 World Cup win against England, he also picked up a hat-trick against them at Harare in 1996-97.

STUART CARLISLE
Born 10.5.72 ... **right-hand bat**

Made his Test debut against Pakistan in Harare, 1994-95 but had to sit with his pads on for 11 hours while the Flower brothers shared a long partnership — and still didn't bat! Got in on the act on the field though and held three catches in Zimbabwe's victory. A prolific run-getter as a teenager, he represented Zimbabwe Schools on tours to Australia in 1988 and 1991 and England 1989.

MARK DEKKER
Born 5.12.69 ... **left-hand bat** ... left-arm spin or medium

His one-day international debut came against New Zealand in Bulawayo, 1992-93, and he scored half-centuries in his first two appearances in the limited overs games. Made his Test debut against Pakistan at Karachi in December 1993. An opener, he became the first Zimbabwean batsman to carry his bat through a Test innings in scoring 68 not out against Pakistan at Rawalpindi, December 1993.

CRAIG EVANS
Born 29.11.69 ... **right-hand bat** ... right-arm medium

His first-class debut came for Zimbabwe 'B' against Pakistan 'B', in Harare, October 1990. A one-day international debut followed two years later against India, in Harare, but he had to wait a further four years before landing on the Test stage, with his first appearance against Sri Lanka, in Colombo, 1996-97. Plays for Mashonaland and is a specialist one-day player. Evans has admitted to lack of commitment in the past and given his talents, it is fair to say he has under-achieved. Once rated the best amateur golfer in Zimbabwe.

ANDY FLOWER
Born 28.4.68 ... **left-hand bat** ... wicket-keeper

One of the tragedies of Zimbabwe's isolation from cricket's big stage before their breakthrough seven years ago is that Andy Flower has been denied the chance to play on most of the world's major Test Match grounds.

He has averaged over 40 for most of his first 30 Test appearances, yet has never been seen by many cricket followers.

Flower made his first-class debut for the ZCU President's team against Young West Indies in 1986-87 and has been a major influence on Zimbabwean cricket ever since.

He scored 115 not out on his international debut against Sri Lanka in the 1992 World Cup and made his Test debut against India, at Harare, in 1992-93.

The left-hander, brother of Grant, became Zimbabwe's first choice wicket-keeper on David Houghton's retirement after first vying for the job with Wayne James and captained his country in their first ever Test victory, against Pakistan in 1994-95. He has scored more than 2,000 Test runs and almost 3,000 in one-day internationals.

GRANT FLOWER
Born 20.12.70 ... **right-hand bat** ... left-arm spin

One of the most difficult batsmen in the world to remove since making his Test debut against India, at Harare, in 1992-93.

Younger brother of Andy, he was averaging 37.47 with the bat after 32 Test appearances and with his growing experience at international level has come a wider range of strokes after a circumspect start to his career.

A poor tour to Pakistan in 1993-94 was followed by a double century in the First Test against the same opposition back in Zimbabwe the following season. He then averaged 38.66 in Tests against the England tourists in 1996-97 and scored a century in each innings of the First Test against New Zealand, at Harare, in September 1997.

A brilliant fielder in any position, Flower has now scored more than 5,000 first-class runs, a career aggregate second only to former Zimbabwe captain David Houghton, a man who pays Grant the ultimate tribute saying: "I would put him among the top four batsmen in the world."

MURRAY GOODWIN
Born 11.12.72 ... **right-hand bat** ... right arm leg spin

Enjoyed considerable success playing for Western Australia's Sheffield Shield side after emigrating in 1986. He made his WA debut in 1994-95 against England, scoring 91 and 77 but returned home to fulfil his Test ambitions. His Test debut came against Sri Lanka in Kandy, 1997-98 and he scored 42 and 44 in Zimbabwe's win against India in Harare, October 1998, only his country's second win in Test history. Scored an unbeaten 166 from 204 balls in sharing a stand of 277 – record for any wicket for Zimbabwe – with Andy Flower in Bulawayo Test against Pakistan in March 1998.

ADAM HUCKLE
Born 21.9.71 ... **right-arm leg-spin**

His Test debut came against New Zealand in Harare, September 1997. Took two for 32 and three for 84 but marred his international baptism by being fined and received a suspended one-match ban for intimidatory attitude towards an umpire and gesticulating at a batsman. Returned match figures of 11-255 against New Zealand in the Bulawayo Test that series, the first Zimbabwe bowler to take 10 or more wickets in a Test. Sometimes preferred to Paul Strang but often asked to bowl in harness with his leg-spin twin.

NEIL JOHNSON
Born 24.1.70 ... **left-hand bat** ... right-arm medium

Born in Salisbury, he has returned to his birthplace after playing most of his cricket in South Africa.

He celebrated a brilliant maiden century for Zimbabwe in a convincing six-wicket victory over Pakistan in the second one-day international in Sheikhupura in November 1998, saying after the game: "I will cherish this moment for the rest of my life."

A former South Africa 'A' player who has played for Natal, he was granted Zimbabwean citizenship to make his Test debut for Zimbabwe against India, at Harare, in October 1998. His country recorded only their second ever Test win and Johnson celebrated his call-up by dismissing Sachin Tendulkar twice.

He topped Leicestershire's first-class batting averages in 1997 as a late replacement for West Indies Test player Phil Simmons, scoring two hundreds and five half-centuries to average 63.

His best performance with a ball in his hand was in 1993-94 when he took five for 79 for Natal against Boland, at Stellenbosch.

TREVOR MADONDO
Born 22.11.76 ... **right-hand bat ...** occasional wicket-keeper

The first black batsman to be selected for Zimbabwe, he made his Test debut against Pakistan at Bulawayo, March 1998. Considered a role model for young black players, Madondo is a product of Falcon College and Rhodes University, Grahamstown SA. He played for Zimbabwe Schools for two years and was still at school when chosen to make his first class debut, as a wicket-keeper, for Matabeleland against Glamorgan in April 1995. Tipped as the long term wicket-keeping successor to Andy Flower.

MPUMELELO MBANGWA
Born 26.6.76 ... **right-arm fast medium**

Made his one-day international bow for Zimbabwe against Pakistan, at Lahore in November 1996 and his Test debut came at Faisalabad a month earlier. He received his call-up because of injury to Heath Streak and the unavailability of Eddo Brandes and is now rated as one of Zimbabwe's most promising pace bowlers. Coached by Dennis Lillee in Madras and by Clive Rice at Plascon Academy, South Africa, Mbangwa plays for Matabeleland. Under contract to Zimbabwe Cricket Academy Trust.

MLULEKI NKALA
Born 1.4.81 ... **right-hand bat ...** right-arm fast

One of Zimbabwe's most exciting young players, he scored a century in the 1997 Youth World Cup in South Africa. Celebrated his call up for Zimbabwe at 17 by claiming Sachin Tendulkar's wicket with his second ball in the second one-day international at Bulawayo, September 1998.

HENRY OLONGA
Born 3.7.76 ... **right-arm fast medium**

Ten months after making his first-class debut for Matabeleland in March 1994 at 17, he made his Test debut in Zimbabwe's historic first-ever Test win, against Pakistan, becoming the first black cricketer to represent the country in a Test Match. Former Yorkshire and England batsman John Hampshire played a major part in Olonga's early development when he coached in Harare and now he is an established Test regular. He took five for 70 against India, at Harare, in

October 1998 to win the Man of the Match award and was named Zimbabwe's Player of the Series for his performances in their historic first Test series win in Pakistan in December 1998. Henry became a committed Christian in 1992 and names his faith as the most important influence on his life, above cricket.

GAVIN RENNIE
Born 12.1.76 ... **left-hand bat ...** left-arm spin

An opening batsman, Rennie scored a half-century in the second innings on his Test debut against New Zealand at Harare in September 1997 and followed that up with 84, his highest Test score, against India in Harare, October 1998. He swept into the Test frame after scoring a maiden century for Mashonaland 'A' in the Logan Cup in August 1997. Now recognised as opening partner for Grant Flower, after Kevin Arnott's retirement. Younger brother of Test all-rounder John Rennie.

JOHN RENNIE
Born 29.7.70 ... **right-arm medium fast**

Regular Zimbabwe' A' team player but has struggled to make an impact at Test level. Made his Test debut against Pakistan in Karachi in 1993-94. By September 1998 he had made 33 one-day international appearances, after making his debut against South Africa in the Hero Cup in 1993-94. Plays for Matabeleland but has been in the shadow of his younger brother, Gavin, at Test level.

BRYAN STRANG
Born 9.6.72 ... **right-hand bat ...** left-arm medium fast

Younger brother of Paul Strang and son of Zimbabwe umpire Ron Strang, he made his Test debut against Pakistan, at Bulawayo in 1994-95, his first season in first-class cricket. He took nine wickets in two Test appearances against the tourists in that series and has been a regular ever since. Scored his maiden Test half-century off 78 balls against Pakistan in Harare, March 1998. Plays for Mashonaland.

PAUL STRANG
Born 28.7.70 ... **right-hand bat ...** right-arm leg-spin

Despite being overshadowed by the extraordinary feats of Shane Warne earlier in his career, Paul Strang is now firmly established as one of the world's best leg-spinners.

Only 28, he has packed an enormous amount of cricket into his early years in the top flight since captaining Zimbabwe Under-19s in 1989-90.

Born in Bulawayo, the elder brother of Bryan, he made his Test debut against Sri Lanka in 1993-94 and has since represented Kent (1997) and Nottinghamshire (1998) as their overseas player.

He took 57 wickets in his first 20 Tests and 72 in 69 one-day internationals. But he has also made useful contributions with the bat with a Test century to his name and a batting average in the late-twenties in five-day cricket.

HEATH STREAK
Born 16.3.74 ... **right-arm fast**

Appropriately named for a fast bowler, he led the world rankings of Test cricketers, published by Wisden Cricket Monthly, at the start of England's tour to Zimbabwe in 1996-97. At that stage in his remarkable rise to the top he had taken 53 Test wickets at less than 20. By December 1998, he had claimed 106 Test victims at 24.83 apiece in only 26 Test appearances since making his debut against Pakistan, at Karachi in 1993-94. Hampshire's overseas signing in 1995, Heath is the son of Denis Streak, who played for Zimbabwe from 1976-85. An all-action sportsman, he lists his relaxations as shooting, fishing and off-road dirt-biking. A talented all-round sportsman, he represented his country at Under-19 level at rugby.

DIRK VILJOEN
Born 11.3.77 ... **left-hand bat** ... left-arm spin

Zimbabwe's Young Cricketer of the Year in 1996-97, he attended the Adelaide Cricket Academy in 1997. Excelled as a schoolboy, he played for Zimbabwe's Under-19s from 1994-96. An opening batsman, Viljoen scored a double century for the youngsters in 1996 and made the move up to Test level two years later, making his Test debut against Pakistan, at Bulawayo in 1997-98. Also represented Zimbabwe in the Pepsi Triangular Cup one-day tournament at Ahmedabad in 1997-98.

ANDREW WHITTALL
Born 28.3.73 ... **right-hand bat** ... right-arm off spin

Younger brother of Guy Whittall, Andrew is a former Cambridge cricket Blue under John Crawley's captaincy. He scored an unbeaten 91 as Cambridge captain in the 1994 Varsity match and also took 11 wickets that season. Made his Test debut against Sri Lanka at Colombo in 1996-97 and by November 1998 he had played nine Tests and 40 one-day internationals.

GUY WHITTALL
Born 5.9.72 ... **right-hand bat**

Scored a century in Zimbabwe's historic first ever Test win against Pakistan at Harare in February 1995 after making his Test debut against the same country in Karachi 14 months earlier. Also played for Zimbabwe on their 1993 England tour. His first-class debut for Young Zimbabwe came against Pakistan 'B', at Harare, October 1990. Cracked a brilliant, unbeaten 203 for Zimbabwe against New Zealand in the Bulawayo Test in September 1997.

CRAIG WISHART
Born 9.1.74 ... **right-hand bat**

One of his country's most promising young batsmen, Wishart made his first-class debut for Zimbabwe 'B' against touring Kent at Harare in 1992-93. His Test debut came against South Africa at Harare in 1995-96 and two years later he made his career-best Test score of 63 against India, at Harare in October 1998. That followed a quite brilliant 102 against India in the third one-day international, at Harare, September 1998. Plays for Mashonaland.

❶ TO WATCH **EVERTON MATAMBANADZO**

Born 13.4.76... **right-hand bat** ... right-arm fast

Atwin, five minutes younger than his brother Darlington, Everton Matambanadzo represents a symbol of hope for the Zimbabwe Cricket Union's policy to find new players in a country where cricket has been played predominantly by whites.

Matambanadzo, Henry Olonga, Mpumelelo Mbangwa and Trevor Madondo are the first products of this enlightening scheme to bring the game of cricket into every backyard in Zimbabwe, and such has been Everton's rapid progress, the ZCU believe their development programme is second to none in a country where resources are limited.

Everton made his first-class debut for Mashonaland in 1993-94. His bowling was wild and inaccurate in the early days but after established Zimbabwe batsmen Mark Burmester and David Brain had become victims of his lethal yorker, and Andy Flower had also been snared, opportunities for him developed rapidly.

Regular wickets and runs clinched selection for Zimbabwe 'B' against touring English county Worcestershire and he was invited to attend Zimbabwe Cricket Academy nets four days a week for twice-daily coaching in 1996.

They improved his control and stamina and during one of these coaching sessions, new Zimbabwe captain Alistair Campbell informed him that he had been chosen for the full Zimbabwe tour squad to Pakistan.

The youngster anticipated a minor role as net bowler but injury to Heath Streak and the unavailability of Eddo Brandes gave him an unexpected chance to shine. Another injury, this time to Henry Olonga, propelled Everton into a Test debut, aged just 20, in the Second Test in Faisalabad in October 1996.

He removed Pakistan openers Saeed Anwar and Aamir Sohail to claim his first two Test scalps and his Test career was up and running. His final first innings figures of two for 62 and none for 27 in the second proved that the raw material Zimbabwe had blooded needed more experience to flourish in the big time. He also made his one-day international debut on that tour, taking four for 32 at Peshawar.

The return from injury of the more established Zimbabwe bowlers enabled him to learn his trade at a more leisurely and fruitful pace and he was denied an opportunity to play against the England tourists in 1996-97.

A dislocated shoulder, sustained on Zimbabwe's tour to New Zealand in early 1998, blunted his progress and a lack of consistency has become a problem but as his Test team-mate, Guy Whittall, says: "Everton just needs a bit more experience and coaching to become one of our top bowlers."

WISDEN WORLD CUP VERDICT

Campbell's crew could cause an upset or two, especially as they face India and Sri Lanka early on. The batting is strong now: look out for Neil Johnson, who returns to Leicester (where he topped the averages in 1997) for the Indian match. The medium-pacers should contain all right — but there's no obvious enforcer if wickets are needed.

AUSTRALIA

> GROUP B • **Australia** • Bangladesh • New Zealand
> • Pakistan • Scotland • West Indies

Australia approach the 1999 World Cup with a history of success in the six previous tournaments and a wealth of talent on stage and in the wings that is unrivalled by any other cricket playing nation.

No other country has more strength in depth than the Aussies and Sri Lanka, the World Cup holders, will need to be at their best to meet the challenge Steve Waugh's side are likely to pose three years after they met in the World Cup final in Lahore.

Contrary to expectations on that occasion, Sri Lanka controlled their first appearance in a World Cup final to scorch past Australia's total of 241 for seven for the loss of only three wickets, with Aravinda de Silva not out 107 at the climax.

It was no consolation to the defeated Aussies that they had become the first side beaten in six finals by a team batting second.

This time the tournament is played on more familiar territory for the Australians. Many of their squad will have had experience of English conditions, either on the county circuit where they have been recruited on overseas contracts, or in the network of leagues where a young Australian cricketer's education is considered incomplete unless he has sampled English conditions.

The enlightened Australians are different also from most of the other competing countries because of their tried and trusted formula of sending specialist one-day squads to fight World Cup tournaments, with a captain chosen for his expertise in playing the limited overs game rather than any success he might have enjoyed on the Test circuit.

In Steve Waugh, they are fortunate indeed to possess a man for all seasons, one of the world's best Test performers and an exponent par excellence of the one-day game.

Australia have a proud and distinguished history of achievement in previous World Cups. They were runners-up to the West Indies in 1975, the first year the tournament was staged; winners in 1987; and losing finalists in Sri Lanka's finest hour three years ago.

They lost to the West Indies by just 17 runs in the first final played at Lord's in June 1975. From 11am to 8.45pm the teams produced wonderful entertainment.

Put into bat West Indies were in trouble at 50 for three but their captain Clive Lloyd turned the game with a magnificent 102, including two sixes and 12 fours, taking his side to 291 for eight in 60 overs.

Had Ross Edwards clung to a diving catch at mid-wicket when Lloyd had made 26, history could have been rewritten. That fielding lapse and five run-outs in Australia's reply left them holding an inquest on why they had contributed to their own downfall.

There were sound contributions from Ian Chappell, who scored 62, and Alan Turner, who made 40, but the West Indies always had the edge.

Australia's win in the 1987 tournament was another close affair. Watched by a Calcutta crowd of 70,000, just seven runs separated the triumphant Aussies from beaten England.

Australia piled-up 253 for five after man of the match David Boon, who scored 75, and Geoff Marsh had given their side the fifth major opening partnership of the tournament.

England were never properly in the hunt once Graham Gooch and Bill Athey had been parted after their second wicket stand of 65, and with 46 runs needed off the last five overs, and 17 off the final six deliveries from Craig McDermott, the task was beyond tailenders Neil Foster and Gladstone Small.

Australia had to wait nine years before they could make an impact on another World Cup, even though they joint-hosted the 1992 tournament with New Zealand.

On that occasion the tournament was sold with the maximum amount of aggressive hype by Australia television, but the home country's expected easy ride to the knockout stages received a jolt in the first match, when New Zealand beat them by 37 runs.

Kiwi captain Martin Crowe made 100 not out in a total of 248 for six, and then Australia were bowled out for 211, despite a century by David Boon.

Australia's hopes of qualifying for the semi-finals were hit really hard when they lost their second match, comprehensively beaten by South Africa and they never recovered.

Four years later they were back on track, despite a bitterly fought dispute raging behind the scenes before the 1996 World Cup got underway, Australia and West Indies adamantly refused to play their scheduled group games in Colombo, where a bomb had gone off a fortnight before their scheduled match.

The backcloth of dispute was darkened further by Australia's reluctance to participate in the World Cup at all, the backlash of their bribery allegations against Salim Malik have brought death threats from a number of fanatics around Pakistan.

Early matches were forfeited, though Australia and West Indies could make the sacrifice without endangering their progress to the later stages.

Indeed, they met in the semi-finals, Australia winning by a five run margin after Stuart Law and Michael Bevan had dominated their innings of 207 for eight, a target beyond the West Indies despite Shivnarine Chanderpaul's 80.

Australia's subsequent defeat by Sri Lanka in the final was offset by genuine worldwide support for Sri Lanka's breakthrough as a major threat and a lack of rancour in Lahore that March day over the still simmering Salim Malik affair.

The shape of Australia's one-day side has not changed a lot in the three years since that tournament. The Waugh twins, Michael Bevan, Stuart Law, Shane Warne, Glenn McGrath, Damien Fleming and Paul Reiffel, despite recent injury, are still in the frame.

But what must be worrying for the 11 other countries competing in this year's World Cup is that the bulk of the players who represented Australia in the 1996 tournament were still playing well and available for selection for England 99, while a host of new players are coming through the ranks, pressing for inclusion.

Can they win the World Cup for the second time? Current form and enormous playing strength make them a highly fancied contestant by the bookmakers even though gambling is a taboo subject in the Australia dressing-room these days!

WORLD CUP HIGHLIGHT

David Boon's controlled innings of 75 that guided Australia to their first World Cup triumph, against the old enemy in 1987.

WORLD CUP RECORD

1975	Lost to West Indies in final
1979	Eliminated at group stage
1983	Eliminated at group stage
1987	Beat England in final
1992	Eliminated at group stage
1996	Lost to Sri Lanka in the final

WORLD CUP ODDS: 8-1

CAPTAIN **STEVE WAUGH**
Born 2.6.65 ... **right-hand bat** ... right-arm medium

Helmet off, bat raised aloft, the crowd giving a standing ovation...that's the pose the photographers rush to shoot whenever Australia's one-day international captain reaches a century.

It happened again in Melbourne at Christmas, when he gave the England attack another hiding in completing his 17th Test century and went on to run out of batting partners and finish with an unbeaten 122.

There are some shrewd observers who believe that he is a more accomplished batsman than either Sachin Tendulkar or Brian Lara and certainly it is not a high-risk stake to place a wager on this tough, battle-hardened batsman reaching at least a half-century every time he walks to the crease.

He was only 20 when he made his debut against India in 1985-86. He failed to reach a century in his first 26 Tests but in 1989 the floodgates opened to release a stack of runs against England.

He scored 177 not out and 152 not out in the first two Tests at Headingley and Lord's to finish the Ashes series with a batting average of 126.50 and become Player of the Series.

A lean, clean timer of the ball with massive reserves of concentration, he is the hardest batsman in the world to remove from the crease.

He lost his Test place in 1990-91 but returned to play the anchor role in the middle order for so many huge Australian scores over the past decade.

The twin brother of Mark, who took five years longer to make the Australian team, he was raised by a sports loving family in the Sydney suburbs.

He played backyard cricket with his brother and at 15 the twins were playing for New South Wales youth team, scoring hundreds against boys from private school backgrounds.

He soon made the NSW state side and his all-round talents were exposed to the demands of international cricket when he played a crucial part in Australia's World Cup final victory against England in 1987.

Waugh ran out Bill Athey when the England batsman had reached a potential match-winning half-century and then grabbed two crucial wickets to turn the match decisively in Australia's favour.

In reaching his 7,000th Test run against England at Christmas 1998, only Allan Border (11,174), David Boon (7,422) and Greg Chappell (7,110) had scored more runs for Australia.

Off the edge

• He is the older of the Waugh twins by four minutes.

• **Steve was dropped from the Australian side in 1990-91 to make way for a Test debutant – his brother Mark.**

• Asked to describe his talents, he replied: "Someone who makes the most of his ability."

• **He was one of the Wisden Cricketers of the Year in 1989.**

• He has been out nine times in Test cricket while in the 90s – a joint world record.

• **Waugh does a lot of work for charity and is the patron of a hospital wing for children suffering with leprosy in Udayangram.**

• His middle name is Rodger.

• **He was a clear winner of a vote for a World XI skipper in the Wisden Cricket Monthly last year.**

MICHAEL BEVAN
Born 8.5.70 ... **left-hand bat ...** left-arm spin

Born near Canberra, he became the first player to score five successive centuries in Sheffield Shield competition in 1990-91. Hit 82 on his Test debut against Pakistan in Karachi in 1994-95 and snapped up 10 West Indian victims for 113 runs in the match with his chinamen and googlies in 1996-97. Has experience of English wickets after playing for two seasons with Yorkshire in 1995 and 96.

ANDREW BICHEL
Born 27.8.70 ... **right-hand fast medium**

Cruelly denied an opportunity to shine after gaining selection for the 1997 Ashes tour party, injury forcing him to return home early. Worked hard to make the grade with Queensland against fierce competition from Craig McDermott, Carl Rackemann, Dick Tazelaar and Michael Kasprowicz but once he had accomplished the breakthrough, wickets began to tumble. Made his Test debut against the West Indies in 1996-97 after gaining promotion from Australia's one-day side. Toured South Africa.

GREG BLEWETT
Born 29.10.71 ... **right-hand bat ...** right-arm medium

Made a sensational start to his Test career against England in 1994-95, scoring centuries in each of his first two Tests at Adelaide and Perth. Periods of lean form have created a chequered Test career record but he made the 1997 Ashes tour squad and returned to blistering form in 1998-99 to become only the sixth batsman to score more than 1,000 runs in an Australian season before the end of December, 213 of them in an unbeaten innings against England.

MATTHEW ELLIOTT
Born 28.9.71 ... **left-hand bat**

Compared often with Bill Lawry, the Victorian emerged in 1995-96, scoring two double centuries to top the Sheffield Shield averages. Made his Test debut against the West Indies in 1996-97 scoring 78 in the Sydney Test but collided with batting partner Mark Waugh and retired hurt, missing the rest of the series. Made maiden Test century at Lord's in 1997 and came within one run of a double century at Headingley that summer. Wisden Almanack Cricketer of the Year in 1998.

DAMIEN FLEMING
Born 24.4.70 ... **right-arm medium fast**

Celebrated figures of four for 75 against Pakistan on his Test debut at Rawalpindi in October 1994. Then took 10 wickets in three Tests against England in the 1994-95 Ashes series but has not been an automatic choice since. Injured shoulder badly and has struggled to return to full potential for Victoria. Recalled for the Test against England at Brisbane last November, he draped his Aussie blazer over his bed before the game as motivation. In the Second Test at Perth his outswingers claimed five wickets for the first time in a

Test. His selection for the Christmas Test at Melbourne was his 10th appearance for his country in the international five-day game.

ADAM GILCHRIST
Born 14.11.71 ... **left-hand bat** ... wicket-keeper

Topped Young Australia's England tour averages in 1995 with 495 runs at 61.87 and claimed 38 victims. Made his Sheffield Shield breakthrough with New South Wales but moved to Western Australia where he made an immediate impact. In 1995-96 season he averaged 52 in Sheffield Shield matches and broke his own wicket-keeping record in Shield competition with 54 dismissals. Scored 189 not out in the Sheffield Shield Final that season. A better batsman than Ian Healy, he now has the 'keeper's position in the one-dayers.

JASON GILLESPIE
Born 19.4.75 ... **right-arm fast medium**

He has a pony-tail, wears earrings and marks his run-up with a tape-measure a full hour before play begins. He rides a motorbike and has children named Star and Sapphire. Jason Gillespie certainly carries the hallmark of a rebel but there is no more disciplined member of the Australian dressing-room than this extravagantly gifted bowler.

Likeable, quiet, determined, he seized the opportunity granted him when he was drafted into Australia's 1996 World Cup squad as a replacement for the injured Craig McDermott.

He earned the right to achieve that breakthrough on the strength of a remarkable start to his first Sheffield Shield season with South Australia in 1995-96, when he claimed 51 victims.

His promotion to Test status arrived in 1996-97 against the touring West Indies at Sydney. He tore an intercostal muscle in the next Test and missed the rest of the series but made great strides on his first tour to South Africa.

A brilliant spell of pace bowling at Headingley in the Ashes series of 1997 confirmed his development into a world-class performer. He took seven England wickets for 37 runs, the best ever figures achieved on the Yorkshire ground by a touring Australian.

Unlike Glenn McGrath, his close friend, there is no room for histrionics. He simply beats the outside edge of the bat and walks back to his mark to prepare for the next delivery. And in harness with McGrath, the two have a chance to become as famous a double act as Lindwall and Miller and Lillee and Thomson.

MICHAEL KASPROWICZ
Born 10.2.72 ... **right-arm fast medium**

He made his mark as a pace bowler of exceptional promise on joining Essex in 1994. But the burden of responsibility for filling the boots once worn at Chelmsford by Allan Border and Mark Waugh proved too much for an inexperienced 22-year-old and he was released after one season.

He took 60 first-class wickets at an average of 31 runs apiece and on hearing he would not be re-engaged, he promptly dismissed seven Somerset batsmen for 83 runs to give a glimpse of the form that eventually emerged to grant him Test status.

Brisbane-born, he received a classic cricket upbringing, playing for young Queensland teams before making the Australian Under-17 side.

He was just 17 when he made his first-class debut for Queensland and he took nine wickets in his first 'Test' against England for the touring Australian Young Cricketers in 1991.

A year later he was second leading wicket-taker in the Sheffield Shield with 51 scalps at an average of 24.

He went back to England in 1995 as a member of the Young Australia tour party, taking 27 wickets and returned home to maintain the same form by taking 64 wickets, a Queensland record.

Kasprowicz received a call-up for one-day international duty but was disappointed to be omitted from the 1996 World Cup squad. But he did receive the nod at the five-day version and made his Test debut against the West Indies in 1996-97.

Since then he has had a chequered career, with a recall against England in the 1998-99 Ashes series his reward for his determination to succeed at a time when there is so much competition for places.

IAN HEALY
Born 30.4.64 ... **right-hand bat** ... wicket-keeper

The most successful wicket-keeper in Test history. Before the Brisbane Test against England in 1998, he had claimed 362 dismissals, 19 more than his mentor, Australia's Rodney Marsh. A rousing century in the First Test against England in 1998-99 left him needing only 204 runs to overtake Alan Knott's record tally for a gloveman of 4,389. Selected for the 1988-89 tour to Pakistan after playing only three first-class matches and only injury has kept him out since. But has been forced to take a back seat behind the stumps in the one-dayers since Adam Gilchrist's arrival.

BRENDON JULIAN
Born 10.8.70 ... **right-hand bat** ... left-arm fast medium

Talented all-rounder of Polynesian descent, he played for Surrey in 1996, scoring 759 runs, including his first two first class centuries, and took 61 wickets. First came to England on 1993 Ashes tour when he won a Man of the Match award in a Texaco one-day international and then scored his first Test half-century to stave off defeat at Trent Bridge. Opportunities limited by Australia's wealth of talent but he did return to England with the Ashes tour in 1997.

JUSTIN LANGER
Born 21.11.70 ... **left-hand bat**

He is so proud of his Test breakthrough against the West Indies in 1992-93 that he keeps the baggy green cap he was awarded in that series hanging from his bedpost in Perth. As he says: "I collect cricket memorabilia but my greatest possession is that cap."

The circumstances surrounding his first series against the West Indies will remained burned on his memory for as long as he plays Test cricket. The West

Indies pace attack gave him a fearful working over on his introduction to the top flight after he stepped into the breach created by Damien Martyn's injury in fielding practice.

He scored 54 on his Test debut at Adelaide but played only five more Tests over the next three years, until forcing his way back into the side against the West Indies in 1996-97.

Born in Perth, he has become a prolific run-scorer for Western Australia in recent years and made his highest score for them against South Australia in 1996-97, when he made an unbeaten 274.

He joined Middlesex as their overseas player in the 1998 season and made an immediate impact at Lord's. Four Championship centuries and six half-centuries propelled him to the top of the county's averages as he piled up 1,393 runs at an average of 66.33.

STUART LAW
Born 18.10.68 ... **right-hand bat** ... right-arm medium

Made his first-class debut for Queensland at 20 and scored 179 on his second appearance for them. Introduced to the Test arena against Sri Lanka at Perth in 1995-96, scoring an unbeaten 54, and then toured England with Young Australia in 1995. Played all 17 one-day internationals for Australia in 1995-96 including seven appearances in the 1996 World Cup. Joined Essex in 1996 and was Man of the Match in their NatWest final triumph against Warwickshire. Topped Essex's 1998 Championship averages with 982 runs at 40 with two hundreds and three half-centuries and returns there after the World Cup.

SHANE LEE
Born 8.8.73 ... **right-arm medium**

Reliable one-day specialist who made a big impression against England and Sri Lanka in triangular series this year. Took five for 33 against Sri Lanka at Melbourne in February, his best in one-dayers. Plays for NSW.

DARREN LEHMANN
Born 5.2.70 ... **left-hand bat** ... left-arm spin

Made his first class debut for South Australia in 1987-88 and after a three- year period with Victoria returned to his native Sheffield Shield state in 1993-94. Recorded his highest ever score in the 1996-97 season when he hit 255 against Queensland and then joined Yorkshire as their overseas player, distinguishing himself in his first season at Headingley by scoring 1,575 Championship runs at an average of 63.

In 16 Championship innings last summer he scored 969 runs at an average of 60.56 with three centuries and four fifties. He has not always endeared himself to authority. His exit from South Australia for Victoria in 1990-91 caused aggravation and he declined an opportunity to tour the Caribbean with the Australian Academy to get married.

His Test debut was forecast as far back in 1989-90 when he was named in the squad as a 19-year-old. But it took him a further nine years to make the grade, winning his first Test cap against India at Bangalore, where he scored 52 on a .

Part of the successful Ashes squad of 1998-99, Lehmann's recognition as a one-day expert is illustrated by the 33 one-day internationals he had played by

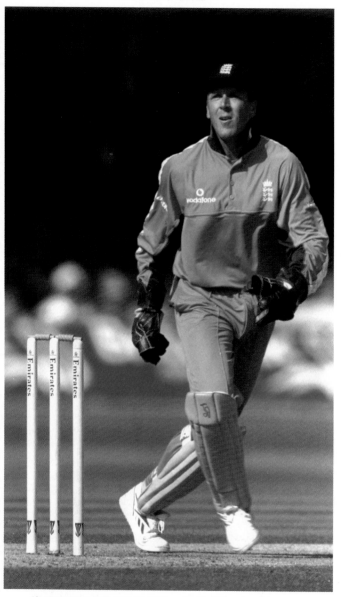

Alec Stewart leads the England challenge for World Cup glory this summer.

Sri Lanka skipper Arjuna Ranatunga lifts the Wills World Cup aloft in 1996.

A fitting venue for the final chapter of the 1999 Cricket World Cup.

SHOUT OF AFRICA...1

South Africa's lethal weapon, Allan Donald, traps Mike Atherton.

Kapil Dev's India in 1983...

Allan Border's Australia in 1987...

Imran Khan's Pakistan in 1992.

Australia's Mark Waugh celebrates another 100, this time against Kenya in 1996.

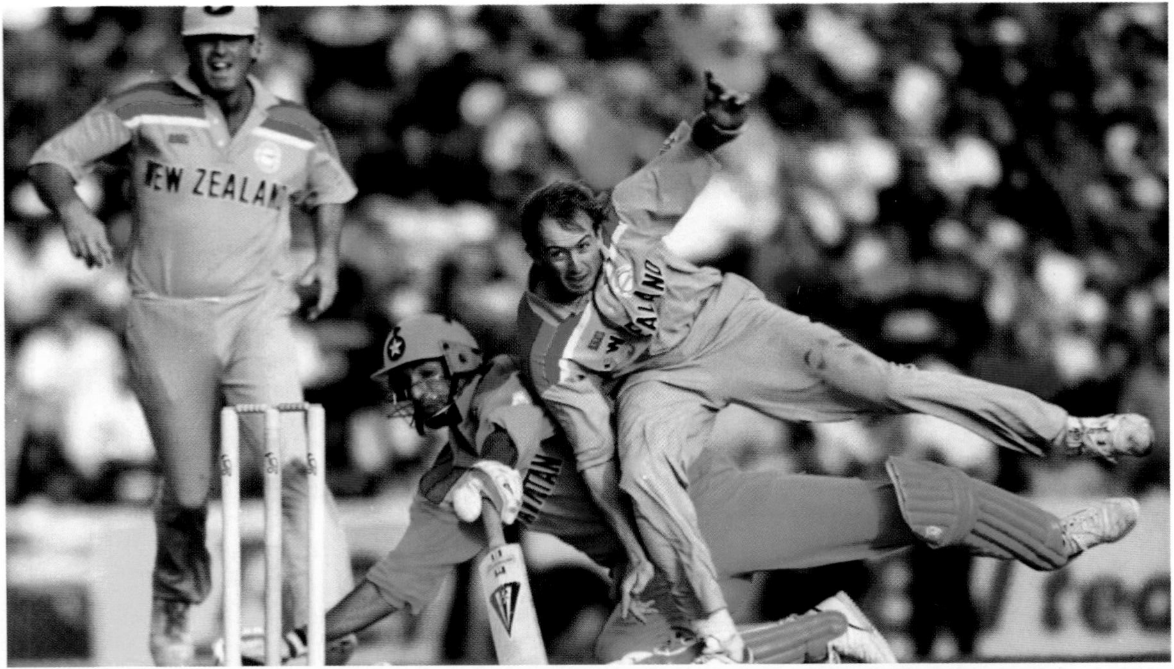

January 26. Has experience of English wickets in his time with Yorkshire and his big ambition is to play in the World Cup.

STUART MACGILL
Born 25.2.71 ... **right-arm leg-spin**

Understudy to Shane Warne, he gave his career a terrific boost by bowling so well against England in the 1998-99 Ashes series. Lacks much of the master's control but once he starts pitching properly, can turn the ball like a top on most surfaces. Bowled a 'jaffa' of a googly to dismiss Nasser Hussain in the First Test at Brisbane and gave England problems again at Adelaide and in the Melbourne Test, taking four for 61 in the first innings and three for 81 in the second. But he saved his best performance for last where he put even Warne in the shade with match figures of 12 for 107 in the deciding Sydney Test.

GLENN McGRATH
Born 9.2.70 ... **right-arm fast**

The enforcer of an Australian team rated unofficial world champions. He is quick and nasty with it.

During the 1998-99 Ashes series, a stump microphone picked up his voice telling England's John Crawley: 'This is going to be your last Test Match.' He might not have achieved that pledge to Crawley but he has clearly become a career threat to Michael Atherton, removing the England opener on many occasions in their frequent battles from the start of the Ashes series in 1997.

He targeted Atherton and England captain Alec Stewart for his special brand of malevolence with a cricket ball in the 1998-99 Ashes Tests.

On hearing that Atherton was troubled again by his problem back condition before one of the Tests, he declared: "I'm looking forward to bowling at Athers. I've heard he's got a dodgy back. He will probably not be getting under them too well, so I might loosen him up with a couple of short ones. I think there's a lot to the old West Indian strategy, where the four fast bowlers would try to target the opposition captain and bring the team down around him."

But like him or loathe him, the New South Wales paceman has become one of the world's top three fast bowlers since taking eight for 38 in the Second Test against England in 1997, the best figures ever by an Australian at Lord's.

He broke the 100-wicket barrier in only his 23rd Test – the same time as Shane Warne – to confirm his right to be considered one of the best.

COLIN MILLER
Born 6.2.64 ... **right-arm fast medium and off-spin**

Born in Tasmania, he broke into the Australian Test side at the age of 34 when chosen to play against Pakistan at Rawalpindi last October. A rare species, he can operate as a pace bowler or slip into the role of off-spinner. Returned from Pakistan to play in the 1998-99 Ashes series, achieving some success in the Adelaide Test by taking three of the first four England wickets to fall in their forlorn bid to score 443 for victory. Described as 'streetwise' by journalist and former Hampshire skipper, Mark Nicholas.

A LOOK AT...
SHANE WARNE

The first delivery Shane Warne bowled in Test cricket in England made him a legend before he had broken sweat. It was bowled to Mike Gatting, an acknowledged master of playing spin, at Old Trafford, on June 4, 1993.

The ball set off on the line of Gatting's pads, dipped and drifted wide of the leg-stump until it was alleged to be at least 18 inches from the nearest stump. By this time Gatting was beginning to lose interest. A mistake! The ball bounced, turned alarmingly and ripped across the England batsman to clip the off-bail.

Gatting stood rooted to the crease for several seconds in disbelief before walking slowly to the pavilion.

Dickie Bird, the umpire at the bowler's end, remarked: "Cor, that was magical. Mike had everything covered, or appeared to. It turned so much, I've never seen anything like it." It was acclaimed as 'the ball of the century'.

So began the Test career of the world's greatest ever leg-spin bowler and as the 1999 World Cup prepares for take-off, batsmen all over the world have yet to unravel the mysteries of Shane's sorcery.

Australia's Test captain Mark Taylor says: "I've never seen anyone dominate Warney. He bowls so few bad balls and he's got so much variety. He has to be considered as one of the greats."

South Africa's captain Hansie Cronje believes he has Warne's measure and Brian Lara, the West Indies skipper, once took 26 off 14 deliveries but the Australian wizard had the last word in that little battle, enticing the great man to edge a catch to Ian Healy.

Once asked how he would play Warne, former Australian captain Allan Border observed: "Use your feet. Get down the pitch and hit him over the in field." Easier said than done.

The golden boy of Aussie cricket, with blond hair highlights and gold trinkets jangling under a burning sun, has averaged nearly five wickets a Test.

An operation on his spinning finger kept him away from the international scene for six months and shoulder surgery cost him his Test place at the start of Australia's Ashes series last winter. When he did return he was put in the shade by the match-winning exploits of Stuart MacGill.

Warne had already bagged 315 wickets by the end of January 1999 and could go on to become the greatest Test wicket-taker of all time. But perhaps his greatest legacy will be the fact that he triggered a renaissance in the art of wrist-spin bowling.

Youngsters all over the world are now trying to copy the great man's style, the run-up, the delivery, the elation at another wicket – the sheer wizardry that is Shane Warne.

Along with Sri Lanka's Muttiah Muralitharan, Indian master Anil Kumble and Mushtaq Ahmed of Pakistan, the Australian has put spin bowling very firmly back on the Test scene and that can only be good for cricket after an avalanche of quick and medium pace bowlers had threatened to dominate this great game.

THE STATS

Full name: Shane Keith Warne

Born: September 13, 1969 in Melbourne

Role: Right-hand bat, right-arm leg-spin

Represents: Victoria, Australia

Test debut: For Australia v India in Sydney, Third Test, 1991-92.

One-day international debut: For Australia v New Zealand in Wellington, 1992-93.

Finest hour: The so called 'ball of the century' that beat Gatting at Old Trafford in June, 1993.

Extras: In the 1993 calendar year, Warne took a staggering 72 wickets.

NOW THAT'S A FACT

● Shane was a great fan of Aussie Rules football as a kid and dreamed of making a career in the sport.

● Warne departed the Australian Cricket Academy because of ill-disciplined behaviour in 1990.

● He played his first Test against India in January 1992 after appearing in just four Sheffield Shield matches for Victoria.

● He took 1-228 against India and some said the selectors' gamble had totally backfired.

● Shane gave up beer to raise the standard of his fitness for Test cricket.

● He yielded 107 runs from 22 wicketless overs in the first innings of the opening Test against Sri Lanka in Colombo in 1992.

● Warne averages nearly five wickets per Test Match.

● By the end of 1996, he had dismissed Graham Gooch, Michael Atherton, Alec Stewart and Graham Thorpe six times each in 11 Tests.

● Against England in 1994-95, he captured 27 wickets, including a hat-trick in Melbourne.

● He was fined A$8,000 by the Australian Cricket Board in 1995 for taking cash from an illegal Indian bookmaker, the incident kept secret by ACB until 1998.

THE THINGS THEY SAY
WARNE ON

❝I must emphasise that I have never been involved in any match-fixing or bribery in any cricket matches at any stage in my career.❞ **Statement issued when the betting scandal broke in December 1998.**

ON WARNE

❝If only we could pick a computer to bat against him instead of rank him.❞ **Simon Hughes, former Middlesex pace bowler.**

TOM MOODY
Born 2.10.65 ... **right-hand bat** ... right-arm medium

His Test debut came in 1989-90 but has really made his mark playing as a one-day international specialist for Australia. Signed a one-year contract for Warwickshire after scoring a century against them for the touring Australians in 1989. He hit centuries in his first three first-class matches for Warwicks, and seven in first eight matches. He took advantage of declaration bowling to score fastest ever first-class century against Glamorgan in 26 minutes. Has played for Worcestershire since 1991 and was a member of Australia's 1996 World Cup squad. Experienced World Series action in 1997-98.

MATTHEW NICHOLSON
Born 2.10.74 ... **right-arm fast**

Made his Test debut against England at Melbourne last December after playing only eight first-class matches. Lean, strong and 6ft 6ins tall, he was coached by Dennis Lillee at the Adelaide Academy before breaking into the Western Australian state side. He runs in straight and delivers with a chest-on action. His dismissal of Mark Ramprakash in England's second innings at Melbourne with a delivery that nipped between bat and pad illustrates the danger he could pose batsmen in the years ahead.

RICKY PONTING
Born 19.12.74 ... **right-hand bat**

A product of the Australian Academy, he is destined to become the curse of bowling attacks worldwide over the next decade.

A prodigious run-getter from Launceston, Tasmania, he fell to a controversial lbw decision when he had scored 96 on his Test debut against Sri Lanka at Perth in 1995. But that was a short-lived setback for a young batsman whose pedigree for Test cricket assures him a successful career.

His struck his first international century in a World Series match against Sri Lanka and made another against the West Indies in the last World Cup in India.

He scored 88 against the West Indies in Brisbane in 1996-97 but loss of form cost him his Test place and he was omitted from the tour to South Africa.

Ponting regained form to make the squad chosen for the 1997 Ashes series, scoring 127 in the Fourth Test at Headingley, and he returned home with a Test average of 48 that summer.

Known affectionately at `Punter' because of his fondness for gambling, he has been fighting to overcome a drink problem recently.

PAUL REIFFEL
Born 19.4.66 ... **right-arm fast medium**

Jason Gillespie's advance has reduced his Test chances but there is no more dangerous bowler in the English conditions that this World Cup will produce. Took eight wickets on his Ashes debut at Headingley in 1993, claimed another six victims at Birmingham and finished the series on top of the Australian bowling averages with 19 wickets at 20.84 apiece. Took 11 Test wickets against England on 1997 Ashes tour and showed he was more than capable with the bat but has had strictly limited opportunity to shine since.

MICHAEL SLATER
Born 21.2.70 ... **right-hand batsman**

He made a dramatic start to his Test career at Old Trafford in the 1993 Ashes series when he shared the first day's honours with Mark Taylor, both from the New South Wales town of Wagga Wagga.

An opening stand of 128 established a stranglehold on the Test that Australia never relinquished and a glittering Test career was forecast.

Unfortunately, erratic form and severe losses of concentration have blunted his progress since that promising beginning and there is still a question mark against this dashing opening batsman six years later.

He played well in his first two Ashes series but for a time he lost his place to Matthew Elliott and Matthew Hayden as Australia's rich seam of batting talent gave the selectors so many options.

That maiden Test 50 at Manchester was followed by a century in the Second Test at Lord's, when he delighted the crowd by giving a jig of delight and tearing off his helmet to kiss the Australia badge.

He scored 416 runs in that series and plundered the England attack again in Australia in 1994-95, scoring 623 runs with three more centuries.

He had a modest season with the bat by his standards at Derbyshire in 1998 but regained his Test place against England in the 1998-99 Ashes series and scored a magnificent 123 out of Australia's total of 184 to help his country to victory in the Fifth Test.

MARK WAUGH
Born 2.6.65... **right-hand bat** ... right-arm medium

The younger of the Waugh twins, he took five years longer than his brother Steve to break into Test cricket. Once he did, replacing Steve against England at Adelaide in 1990-91, he announced his arrival with a majestic 138 and has remained an automatic choice ever since.

His style of play lends itself to bad patches and two blips in his outstanding Test career have cast doubts over whether he can be termed one of the 'greats'. He made two 'pairs' in Sri Lanka in a three-match Test series and had a particularly bad time in the Ashes series in England in 1997.

Before the 1998-99 Ashes series began, he had scored 15 Test centuries, four of them in eight Tests in 1997-98. He is the only Australian to score 3,000 runs in a calendar year and with Steve has beaten the record of 43 Test matches together as brothers established by Ian and Greg Chappell.

Waugh has three passions: food, gambling and cricket. He owns racehorses, plays golf, is an avid follower of all televised sport and loves sleeping.

Last December he and Shane Warne admitted to having received payment from an Indian bookmaker for providing information about pitch and weather conditions in Sri Lanka four years earlier. The ACB fined him A$10,000.

But a run of prolific form at the 1999 World Cup to follow his record breaking achievement of hitting three centuries in the 1996 tournament will take him into his country's hall of fame and make him a national hero again.

❶ TO WATCH **ANDREW SYMONDS**
Born 9.6.75 ... **right-hand bat**

One of the most controversial players of his generation. Born in England, Australian-bred, he decided not to take the easy option of declaring himself English at once and has set out to prove himself Down Under.

A product of the Australian Cricket Academy in 1993-94, he joined Gloucestershire in 1995 and did so well in the west country that he was chosen for the England 'A' winter tour of 1995-96.

But he shook the administration at Lord's by declining the offer, claiming he wanted to remain eligible to play for Australia.

Few players have caused more of a stir in their formative years than Symonds. After two seasons at Bristol, in which he produced some magnificent innings, he had gathered as many critics as he had made friends and it was no surprise that he returned to Queensland, leaving English cricket followers and administrators feeling their hospitality had been abused.

Born in Birmingham, he was brought-up in Queensland, where his forceful run-getting soon made an impact. He played for Queensland Colts in 1993-94 and the full state side the following season. A highlight of that debut year was a century against the touring England side in 1994-95.

He hit a world record 16 sixes in his innings of 254 not out for Gloucestershire against Glamorgan in 1995 and still managed to ruffle a few feathers of those attending the match at Abergavenny.

Wisden editor Matthew Engel wrote afterwards: "I was lucky enough to be at Abergavenny to see the 16th six of Andrew Symonds' innings sail over the outfield, a hawthorn bush and a patch of bindweed and on to a nearby tennis court, giving him a world record.

"Interviewed later, he said he was entirely unconcerned by the record; what mattered was playing the best he could for his team etc etc. This is supposed to be the sort of thing one says in these circumstances.

"What was worrying was that he sounded sincere...Did it really mean nothing to Symonds? If so, it is dispiriting that such gifts could have been given to someone with so little appreciation of what they mean to the rest of us."

Nevertheless, Symonds was voted the Professional Cricketers' Association's Young Player of the Year in 1995 and had a second season at Gloucestershire in 1996.

He became ineligible for the county a year later after selection for the Australia 'A' squad against West Indies. But if still unpopular with some people in England, he clearly has a bright future in his adopted Australia.

WISDEN WORLD CUP VERDICT
No Taylor, no Healy ... but two of the world's best bowlers (Warne and McGrath), the best one-day batsman of the moment (Bevan) and his young pretender (Gilchrist), not to mention a Waugh or two. They can't be written off: expect a repeat of the '98 Commonwealth Games final, when South Africa upset the Aussies.

BANGLADESH

GROUP B • Australia • **Bangladesh** • New Zealand
• Pakistan • Scotland • West Indies

The Bangladesh squad sweep into England for the 1999 World Cup tournament as champions of the non-Test playing nations.

Their arrival signals the dawn of a new era of cricket opportunity for a country riddled with poverty and deprivation.

A stroll in the scorching sun round the perimeter stonework of the National Cricket Stadium in Dhaka is to see desperately sad scenes of sickness, starvation and helplessness which mirrors the misery of a large proportion of Dhaka's 100 million population.

But the gates leading to the interior of that famous old cricket stadium now carry the hopes and dreams of a grateful nation for a better future following Bangladesh's remarkable journey to England 99.

Respected Bangladesh journalist Utpal Shuvro caught the mood of the nation when he wrote eloquently in the 1998 Wisden Almanack: 'Not since independence from Pakistan in 1971 had the country celebrated with such togetherness. When the team won their semi-final against Scotland and thus made sure of their World Cup place, processions started all over the country and young people began sprinkling coloured water. Ecstasy was not without its share of undesirable excess – three fatalities were reported.'

Hundreds of thousands of people thronged the airport to receive and salute their returning heroes from that ICC Trophy win in Kuala Lumpur.

Each player was given a new car and mobile phone, and Gordon Greenidge, the West Indian batsman whose inspired coaching turned Bangladesh from emergent cricket nation into potential World Cup giantkillers at the 1999 tournament, was made a Bangladeshi citizen as a special honour from a grateful government.

The crippled, the diseased and the penniless will continue to ring the perimeter fencing of Dhaka's National Stadium in their desperate misery but yet again the game of cricket, Bangladesh's national sport, is seen as some beacon of hope in a country almost drowned by floods in 1998 and reliant on overseas aid.

The dream of graduation from isolated cricket backwater to a country nearly ready to play and compete with illustrious neighbours India, Pakistan and Sri Lanka and other high-powered members of the ICC's Test playing fraternity, has been there for many years.

Bangladesh have been competing in the ICC Trophy since it began in 1979. From those humble beginnings to their 1997 trophy-winning exploits, Bangladesh's record stood at 33 one-day internationals played, with 17 victories, 14 defeats, and two no-results. Twice, in 1982 and 1990, they reached the ICC Trophy semi-finals but, unfortunately, on both occasions, they ran into Zimbabwe, then the dominant force among the ICC Associate members.

MCC teams have flown the flag in Dhaka, the Test-playing nations of Asia are regular visitors and the West Indies U-19 touring team was beaten in all three matches by their Bangladesh counterparts four years ago.

The big breakthrough was anticipated at the 1996 World Cup after it was announced that three Associates would take part in the tournament. But all the hype and optimism was ill-founded as Nairobi 1994 became a graveyard for Bangladesh's immediate future. They lost to the United Arab Emirates, Holland and Kenya, and they, not Bangladesh, went through to the World Cup.

Their bold and successful bid to host the Wills International Cup in Dhaka last October and November attracted teams from Australia, England, India, New Zealand, Pakistan, South Africa, Sri Lanka, West Indies and Zimbabwe. It was a huge success and, arguably, did as much for the future of Bangladesh cricket in terms of public relations as the achievements of their rapidly improving national side.

Bangladesh's bid for ICC Full Member status could be completed by the year 2000, according to Saber Hossain Chowdhury, President of the Bangladesh Cricket Board, but despite the Wills tournament triumph, his country did not have the happiest of times in the 1997-98 season.

They struggled in Kenya and New Zealand and in their own Silver Jubilee Independence limited-overs tournament. India and Pakistan beat them in the first three days of the competition in January 1998 but Zimbabwe's entry into the Test Match family has clearly helped expand Bangladesh's horizons.

England international cricketers Neil Fairbrother, of Lancashire, and Worcestershire's Richard Illingworth have been recruited to bring experience of the first-class game to their domestic competitions, and internationals giants Wasim Akram of Pakistan, and Sri Lanka pair

Arjuna Ranatunga and Sanath Jayasuriya are treated like gods when they arrive on special visits arranged by the cricket board.

The potential for development was clear to ICC chief executive David Richards as long ago as 1993 when he was surprised to see 15,000 spectators watching a league match at the Dhaka stadium between two clubs of modest aspirations and ability.

Now the country are set to make their bow in the big time. They face an intriguing opening World Cup match against New Zealand, on Monday, May 17.

On paper, Bangladesh stand no chance against the Kiwis but any betting man would be happy to risk a wager on the possibility of the new boys causing a shock result on the tournament's third day, especially if all their supporters staffing the south-east region's Indian restaurants pour into Chelmsford that day to cheer their visiting heroes.

They start favourites to beat Scotland in Edinburgh on Monday, May 24 and even though their group includes fixtures against the powers of international cricket, Australia, West Indies and Pakistan, England 99 could represent the defining moment when Bangladesh shrug off their eternal struggle for recognition to become a cricket power in their own right with a bright future in the new millennium.

Any success in this summer's tournament will certainly give the people of Bangladesh something to smile about at last.

WORLD CUP HIGHLIGHT

Beating Scotland in the semi-finals of the ICC Trophy by 72 runs to clinch a place in the final and with it World Cup qualification. They then beat Kenya with a leg-bye off the last ball to win the final on a higher comparative score after rain had reduced their target to 166 in 25 overs.

WORLD CUP RECORD

1975	Did not qualify
1979	Did not qualify
1983	Did not qualify
1987	Did not qualify
1992	Did not qualify
1996	Did not qualify

WORLD CUP ODDS: 100-1

CAPTAIN **AKRAM KHAN**
Born 1.2.67... **right-hand bat...** right-arm medium

The Bangladesh captain and their most experienced player. He made his debut for his country in an Asian Cup one-day international against Pakistan in 1988-89 at Chittagong, the place of his birth.

By May 1998 he had played in 21 one-day internationals, averaging 22.65, with 59 his highest score.

He represented Bangladesh in the Coca-Cola Triangular Series in 1997-98 but victory over Kenya in the 1997 ICC Trophy final in Kuala Lumpur has been the highlight of his career.

Not only did he lead his team to a famous victory by two wickets to qualify for the 1999 World Cup but he also shared a match-winning stand of 53 in nine overs with Aminul Islam to ensure Bangladesh would reach their target.

Has experienced British conditions after touring Scotland with Bangladesh last year but the World Cup will provide the biggest challenge of his career.

AMINUL ISLAM
Born 2.2.68 ... **right-hand bat...** right-arm offspin

Nicknamed 'Bulbul', he has become a cricketing legend in Bangladesh's rise to prominence as a cricketing nation.

Made his international debut against India, at Chittagong in the 1988-89 Asia Cup and had made 21 appearances in one-day internationals by May 1998 with a batting average of 31.

Born in Dhaka, he played a crucial part in Bangladesh's qualification for the 1999 World Cup in England by sharing a match-winning stand with Akram Khan of 53 in nine overs for the fourth wicket against Kenya in the ICC Trophy final in Kuala Lumpur.

He top scored in the innings with 37. His biggest international knock is 70 and he has two half-centuries to his name as he approaches this summer's extravaganza.

Made a brilliant start to the 1998 Bangladesh Silver Jubilee Independence tournament by scoring an undefeated 69 against India in the opening match of January 1998.

Another who has sampled British conditions on the tour of Scotland with Bangladesh last year and will be looking to make an impression on the biggest stage he will have played on.

ATHAR ALI KHAN
Born 10.2.62 ... **right-hand bat...** right-arm medium

Born in Dhaka, he made his debut for Bangladesh against India in the 1988-89 Asia Cup tournament. Had played 19 times for Bangladesh by May 1998, averaging 29.55 with three half-centuries under his belt. Played his part in the 1997 ICC Trophy final victory over Kenya in Kuala Lumpur and will relish the chance of taking on the cream of the international cricket world in England this summer.

ENAMUL HOQUE
Born 27.2.66 ... **left-hand bat** ... left-arm spin

Made his debut for Bangladesh against New Zealand in the 1989-90 Australasia Cup. Had made 12 appearances in one-dayers by May 1998 with just 71 runs to his credit, averaging just 7.88, with his five wickets costing 73 apiece. Played in the 1997-98 Coca-Cola Triangular series. Born in Comilla and nicknamed 'Moni', he played in Bangladesh's 1997 ICC Trophy final winning team in Kuala Lumpur. Tasted British conditions last summer when he toured Scotland with his countrymen.

HABIBUL BASHAR
Born 17.8.72... **right-hand bat**

Made his debut for Bangladesh against Sri Lanka, at Sharjah in the 1994-95 Asia Cup. Took part in the 1997-98 Silver Jubilee Independence Cup and had made eight international appearances by May 1998, with a highest score of 70.

HASIBUL HOSSAIN
Born 3.6.77... **right-arm fast medium**

Made his debut for Bangladesh against Sri Lanka at Sharjah in the 1994-95 Asia Cup and by the turn of this year had played in 15 one-day internationals, taking 13 wickets.

Hasibul's quick thinking was chiefly responsible for Bangladesh beating Kenya to win the 1997 ICC Trophy final and thus qualifying for the World Cup in England with the trophy in their hands.

The final ball of a gripping match bowled by Kenya's Martin Suji struck Hossain on the pad and he scampered the winning run with Khaled Masud. Earlier, he had shared the new ball with Saiful Islam.

He also played in the 1997-98 Coca-Cola Triangular series and toured Scotland with Bangladesh last year.

JAHANGIR ALAM
Born 19.4.68 ... **right-hand bat** ... left arm medium

Made his debut for Bangladesh against Australia at Sharjah in the 1989-90 Australasia Cup. Infrequent call-ups after that but made a comeback to play against Zimbabwe at Nairobi in the 1997-98 AK President's Cup.

JAVED OMAR
Born 25.11.76 ... **right-hand bat**

Made his debut for Bangladesh against India at Sharjah in the 1994-95 Asia Cup. Played against Pakistan at Dhaka in the 1997-98 Silver Jubilee Independence Cup.

KHALED MAHMUD
Born 26.7.71 ... **right-hand bat** ... right-arm medium

Made his debut for Bangladesh against India at Dhaka in the 1997-98 Silver Jubilee Independence Cup and also played in the Coca-Cola Triangular series in the same period.

His highest score in his first six one-day internationals was 47. Played a significant part in his country's finest hour by removing the dangerous century-maker, Steve Tikolo, in a two for 31 bowling stint against Kenya to help set up Bangladesh's victory in the 1997 ICC Trophy final. Scored a superb 47 against India in the opening match of the Bangladesh Silver Jubilee Independence Cup tournament, at Dhaka in January, 1998.

MAFIZUR RAHMAN
Born 10.11.78 ... **right-hand bat** ... right-arm medium

Made his debut for Bangladesh against Sri Lanka at Colombo in the 1997-98 Asia Cup. Also played in the AK President's Cup in Nairobi the same season.

MEHRAB HOSSAIN
Born 22.8.78 ... **right-hand bat** ... right-arm medium

A youngster who had his first experience of international cricket for Bangladesh against India at Mohali in the 1997-98 Coca-Cola Triangular series.

MINHAJUL ABEDIN
Born 25.9.65 ... **right-hand bat** ... right-arm off-spin and medium

One of Bangladesh's longest serving players, he made his debut against Pakistan at Colombo in the 1985-86 Asia Cup and was still a leading player when appearing in the 1997-98 Coca-Cola Triangular series.

Has made 23 appearances for his country and played a vital part in Bangladesh's victory over Kenya in the 1997 ICC Trophy final, at the Tenga Sports Stadium, Kuala Lumpur.

He shared a partnership of 50 in seven overs with Mohammad Rafique to steer his team towards a win and qualification for the 1999 World Cup.

MOHAMMAD HASANUZZAMAN
Born 15.1.75 ... **right-hand bat** ... right-arm medium

Highly promising all-rounder, expected to feature prominently in the next few seasons but was unsure of selection for the Bangladesh World Cup squad.

MOHAMMAD RAFIQUE
Born 15.5.70 ... **left-hand bat** ... left-arm spin

Valuable member of the Bangladesh bowling attack and useful batsman. He made his debut against India at Sharjah in the 1994-95 Asia Cup and also played in the 1997-98 Coca-Cola Triangular series.

Has taken over 15 wickets for his country in only 12 matches and has a highest knock of 77.

Enjoyed his finest hour in the 1997 ICC Trophy final when he shared a very useful partnership of 50 in seven overs with Minhajul Abedin to help Bangladesh to victory over Kenya. Earlier, he had taken three for 40, including Maurice Odumbe's vital wicket, to reduce Kenya to 241 for seven. He bowled superbly also in the semi-final against Scotland, taking four quick wickets for 25 to steer Bangladesh to victory by 72 runs.

Top scored with 29 against Pakistan in Bangladesh's second match in the Silver Jubilee Independence Cup tournament, at Dhaka in January, 1998.

NAIMUR RAHMAN
Born 19.9.74 ... **right-hand bat ...** right-arm off-spin

An opening batsman, he made his debut against Pakistan at Sharjah in the 1994-95 Asia Cup. Played in the 1997-98 Coca-Cola Triangular series but was still waiting for his maiden half-century after his first eight appearances, which included a duck in Bangladesh's victory over Kenya in the ICC Trophy final. A member of their tour party to Scotland last year.

SAIFUL ISLAM
Born 1.4.69 ... **right-hand bat ...** right-arm medium fast

Made his debut for Bangladesh against Sri Lanka at Calcutta in the 1990-91 Asia Cup. Played in the 1997-98 President's Cup in Nairobi and opened the bowling in the 1997 ICC Trophy final victory over Kenya, taking two for 39 in nine overs.

SANUAR HOSSAIN
Born 5.8.73 ... **right-arm off-spin**

Made his debut for Bangladesh against India at Dhaka in the 1997-98 Silver Jubilee Independence Cup and was also a member of the side that played in the Coca-Cola Triangular series the same year.

SHAFIUDDIN AHMED
Born 1.6.73 ... **right-hand bat ...** right-arm fast medium

Made his debut for Bangladesh against Zimbabwe at Nairobi in the 1997-98 President's Cup. Played in the Silver Jubilee Independence Cup at Dhaka the same year. Claimed the prized wickets of Saurav Ganguly and Mohammad Azharuddin in his 10 overs against India in the opening match, at Dhaka, January, 1998. His best bowling figures were three for 42 after his first five appearances.

SHAHRIAR HOSSAIN
Born 1.6.76 ... **right-hand bat**

Made his debut for Bangladesh against Kenya at Nairobi in the 1997-98 President's Cup. Played in the 1997-98 Silver Jubilee Independence Cup in Dhaka but still lacks real international experience.

SHEIKH SALAHUDDIN
Born 10.2.69 ... **right-hand bat ...** right-arm off-spin

His first international appearance for Bangladesh came against Pakistan at Colombo in the 1997-98 Asia Cup. Played in the 1997-98 President's Cup in Nairobi and gained experience of British conditions in preparation for the 1999 World Cup when he toured Scotland with Bangladesh in 1998.

ZAKIR HASAN
Born 1.12.72 ... **right-hand bat ...** right-arm fast medium

Was part of the Bangladesh side that played India at Colombo in the 1997-98 Asia Cup, his debut for his country. Played in the 1997-98 Silver Jubilee Independence Cup in Dhaka but has little international experience, especially against the calibre of opposition Bangladesh will face this summer.

❶ TO WATCH **KHALED MASUD**
Born 8.2.76 ... **right-hand bat** ... wicket-keeper

First choice wicket-keeper, he made his debut for Bangladesh against India at Sharjah in the 1994-95 Asia Cup.

Played in the 1997-98 Coca-Cola Triangular series and has 16 international one-dayers to his name coming into this year.

Was one of the star performers for Bangladesh in their triumphant march into the 1999 World Cup on the strength of their 1997 ICC Trophy win in Kuala Lumpur.

Masud was top scorer with 70 in Bangladesh's semi-final victory over Scotland and was rock solid again in shoring up the innings with an unbeaten 15 to help complete victory over Kenya in the final. An ICC judging panel named him wicket-keeper of that tournament, a point he emphasised with a smart stumping to remove Kenya's captain Maurice Odumbe in the final.

He performed admirably throughout the tournament and will be looking to show he can handle the pressure of scoring runs and keeping soundly in the pressure-cooker environment of the World Cup this summer.

WISDEN WORLD CUP VERDICT
They have struggled since winning the ICC Trophy, and may find it hard on English (and Scottish and Irish) pitches. A 100 per cent record — of defeats — looms.

BANGLADESH v KENYA
ICC Trophy Final at Tenaga Sports Ground (Kilat Kelab), April 12, 13. Bangladesh won by a higher comparative score in a reduced-overs match. Toss: Bangladesh.

KENYA

Asif Karim b Saiful Islam	0
S.K.Gupta c and b Khaled Mahmud	16
†K.Otieno lbw b Saiful Islam	2
S.Tikolo c Saiful Islam b Khaled Mahmud	147
*M.Odumbe st Khaled Masud b Moh'd Rafique	43
T.Odoyo b Mohammad Rafique	1
Hitesh Modi not out	12
A.Suji st Khaled Masud b Moh'd Rafique	1
B 1, l-b 9, w 9	19
TOTAL (7 wkts, 50 overs)	**241**

BOWLING: Saiful Islam 9-0-39-2; Hasibul Hassan 6-0-15-0; Ather Ali Khan 5-0-22-0; Khaled Mammud 7-1-31-2; Enamul Haque 10-0-41-0; Naimur Rahman 4-0-21-0; Mohammad Rafique 6-1-40-3; Akram Khan 3-0-22-0.

BANGLADESH

Naimur Rahman b M.Suji	0
Mohammad Rafique c Odumbe b A.Suji	26
Minhazul Abedin c Patel b Odoyo	26
Aminul Islam b Asif Karim	37
*Akram Khan c Odoyo b Odumbe	22
Enamul Haque c Gupta b Asif Karim	5
Saiful Islam c Odumbe b Asif Karim	14
†Khaled Masud not out	15
Khaled Mahmud st Otieno b Odumbe	5
Hasibul Hassan not out	4
B 3, l-b 4, w 5	12
TOTAL (8 wkts, 25 overs)	**166**

BOWLING: M.Suji 4-0-28-1; S.Tikolo 4-0-29-0; Odoyo 5-0-27-1; A.Suji 5-0-26-1; Asif Karim 4-0-31-3; Odumbe 3-0-18-2.

FALL OF WICKETS
1/0 2/15 3/58 4/196 5/212 6/230 7/241

FALL OF WICKETS
1/0 2/50 3/63 4/116 5/118 6/123 7/139 8/151

NEW ZEALAND

GROUP B • Australia • Bangladesh • **New Zealand**
• Pakistan • Scotland • West Indies

New Zealand arrive to compete in the World Cup better prepared to do damage to the more fancied countries than at any time since the first tournament was held in 1975.

New Zealand Cricket Inc have transformed the Test side, sorted out their cricket management and administration, developed coaching schemes, dug up and revitalised 'tired' pitches, and created a more open, honest approach to cricket after many years of acrimony behind the scenes.

The most inspired decisions have been to ensure Australian team coach Steve Rixon receives the backing his energy, enthusiasm, coaching and leadership skills deserve, and to appoint Stephen Fleming as captain in succession to the under-achieving Lee Germon.

In 1996-97 they won three Tests, lost three and drew one, the first time since 1989-90 that wins were not exceeded by defeats. And since then progress has gathered momentum, culminating in the Kiwi's 1998-99 Test home series win against India in the build-up to England 99.

There is a refreshing zeal about New Zealand's cricket at present with a host of young Test prospects available and several old hands recapturing lost form.

Chris Cairns, who should have emulated the cricketing feats of Kiwi legends Sir Richard Hadlee and Martin Crowe, has returned to his best form as one of the world's leading all-rounders, highlighted by his recent innings of 126 and six-wicket haul against India in the Third Test at Hamilton.

Bryan Young announced he was far from being a spent force with an undefeated 267 against Sri Lanka in March 1997, the highest score of his career, and was still considered good enough to play in the 1998-99 one-day series against India, at Napier.

Meanwhile, Daniel Vettori, a left-handed batsman and left-arm spinner, prepares for his first World Cup as the bright new kid of Kiwi cricket. He became New Zealand's youngest ever Test cricketer when he made his debut against England in February 1997 and under Rixon's shrewd management seems destined for a brilliant future.

The blend of youth and experience makes New Zealand one of the unknown quantities of this World Cup with Rixon and Fleming having set about creating a team spirit that has been missing from the New Zealand camp since Hadlee's heyday.

Rixon believes the turning point was the 2-0 Test series win against Sri Lanka in March 1997. Young made his double century in the First Test and Vettori enjoyed match figures of nine for 130 in the next Test.

He recalls: "I remember when they won the First Test the champagne corks were popped and there were all sorts of celebrations but there was a change of attitude after the next Test win at Hamilton.

"I asked: 'What's the difference?' They replied: 'We expected to win' and that's what I wanted to hear. They have been so lacking in self-esteem in the past but now they're on a roll."

Fleming puts the transition down to the loss of an inferiority complex. "In the past the New Zealand attitude had always been to get into a position where you couldn't lose the game before you attempted victory. Now, we're prepared to risk losing to win," he says.

The new captain still has much to prove. He was averaging 36.72 in Tests at the turn of 1999 with only two centuries. He is no Martin Crowe but he thrives on responsibility, and now that a Kiwi captain can expect full support from administrators and management without needing to watch his back, Fleming has the ambition to seize his chances in this World Cup and keep the his country's bandwagon rolling in overdrive.

WORLD CUP HIGHLIGHT

New Zealand topped the nine-team group infront of their home fans in the 1992 World Cup but bowed out in the semi-finals to Pakistan. Kiwi skipper Martin Crowe did give the home support something to cheer however with a quite majestic 91 in that match to confirm his status as the tournament's most consistent batsman.

WORLD CUP RECORD

1975	Lost to West Indies in the semi-finals
1979	Lost to England in the semi-finals
1983	Eliminated at the group stage
1987	Eliminated at the group stage
1992	Lost to Pakistan in the semi-finals
1996	Lost to Australia in the quarter-finals

WORLD CUP ODDS: 33-1

CAPTAIN **STEPHEN FLEMING**
Born 1.4.73 ... **left-hand bat**

He shares the same April Fool's birthdate as David Gower and bats in the same stylish, fluent way as the former England batsman. Very strong off his legs, he has a penchant for hooking anything short of a length.

The Kiwi skipper was hailed as the most exciting New Zealand batsman to emerge since Martin Crowe when he made his Test debut against India, at Hamilton, in 1993-94.

He struck a glorious 92 on his first appearance and followed that with another 90 off 107 balls in the one-day international at Napier. But those 90s became an albatross in his development as he struggled to convert them into maiden hundreds at Test and one-day level. The breakthrough finally came in a one-day series against West Indies in 1995-96 and in the home Test series against England in 1997-98.

The elegant left-hander reached his maiden Test century after hitting 10 fifties in 22 Tests, at Auckland in January 1997. He defied England's attack for six hours, striking 18 fours and a six in an innings of 129.

By the Third Test in that series he had replaced the injured Lee Germon as captain to become New Zealand's youngest Test skipper. It became a baptism of fire as England scored the 13th highest fourth-innings total to win a Test with a score of 307-6.

Fleming has since taken over permanently from Canterbury's batsman-keeper to lead New Zealand at the 1999 World Cup.

He came fifth in New Zealand's domestic batting averages with 58.14 at the end of the 1997-98 season and his appointment as New Zealand's captain draws a final curtain across the most controversial chapter of his distinguished career.

Aged 21, he returned home in disgrace from New Zealand's tour to South Africa after he, Matthew Hart and Dion Nash had been jointly accused of smoking cannabis during a game against Boland, at Paarl in December 1994.

Off the edge

- Fleming is New Zealand's highest run-maker in youth 'Tests'.
- His innings of 90 against India in his first one-day international was the highest score by a New Zealander on his limited-overs debut.
- When Lee Germon was injured before the Third Test against England at Christchurch in February 1997, Fleming became New Zealand's youngest Test captain at 23 years 319 days.
- Lee Germon's sacking after the 1996-97 series and Fleming's subsequent appointment as skipper caused a public outcry in New Zealand. Petitions were signed but Fleming kept the job.
- One of Fleming's best one-day displays was against India at Dunedin last December. He hit 73 off only 64 balls.
- He captained New Zealand at the 1998 Wills International Cup tournament in Bangladesh.
- When New Zealand beat Sri Lanka in back-to-back Tests at Dunedin and Hamilton in March 1997 under his captaincy, it was only the third time in Test history that the Kiwis had accomplished that successful double feat.
- He was averaging 30.47 with the bat after 65 one-day international appearances.
- He scored two centuries and 18 fifties in 69 Test innings.

GEOFF ALLOTT
Born 24.12.71 ... **left-arm fast medium**

Made his Test debut against Zimbabwe, at Hamilton in 1995-96 and removed Nick Knight, Alec Stewart, John Crawley and Andy Caddick in a four for 74 performance in the Christchurch Test, February 1997. Took two for 49 on his one-day international debut against England at Napier later that month.

NATHAN ASTLE
Born 15.9.71 ... **right-hand bat** ... right-arm medium

A pugnacious batsman with a cynical disregard for the finer points of the MCC coaching book.

Astle is a bludgeoner of runs with a good eye and an unorthodox technique. His aggressive style often leads to periods of infuriating inconsistency but by the end of October 1998 he had played well enough to make 22 Test appearances and play in 75 one-day internationals.

Born in Christchurch, he began his career as a bowler who could bat. But by the time he made his one-day international debut against West Indies, at Auckland in 1994-95 and played his first Test against Zimbabwe, at Hamilton in 1995-96, he had reversed that assessment.

His best performances with bat and ball include a knock of 191 for Canterbury against Wellington, at Christchurch in 1994-95 and a six for 22 spell against Otago in 1996-97.

He was named Man of the Match against England in the 1996 World Cup after scoring 101 from 132 balls at Ahmedabad and batting with Matthew Horne, he established a New Zealand record fourth wicket stand of 243 in the Second Test against Zimbabwe, at Auckland in February 1998. Astle making 114.

Has experience of English wickets after playing county cricket for Nottinghamshire in 1997, averaging 40 in first-class matches, backed-up by a useful haul of 22 wickets.

He is a safe fielder in the slip-gully cordon, can also perform heroics in the deep and is likely to be one of New Zealand's key men this summer.

MARK BAILEY
Born 26.11.70 ... **right-hand bat** ... right-arm medium

Newcomer with huge promise. Came eighth in New Zealand's domestic averages in 1997-98 with 786 runs at 52.40. Made his debut at one-day international level against Zimbabwe, at Dhaka, in the Wills International Cup in October 1998. Plays for Northern Districts.

MATTHEW BELL
Born 25.2.77 ... **right-hand bat**

Made his debut in the Second Test against India, at Wellington in 1998-99 and his one-day international debut last October against Zimbabwe in the Wills International Cup in Bangladesh. Plays for Northern Districts.

CHRIS CAIRNS
Born 13.6.70 ... **right-hand bat** ... right-armfast medium

One of the world's leading all-rounders for the past decade but criticised often for under-achievement.

A matchwinner, more with the bat than with the ball since he declared himself a batsman who bowls. He hits hard and straight, is technically very correct and is certainly capable of tearing an attack apart but tends to bat too low in the New Zealand order at one-day level.

Cairns made his Test debut aged 19 against Australia, at Perth in 1989-90 and his one-day international debut against England, at Wellington, in 1990-91.

He had played in 35 Tests by the start of January 1999, averaging 27.69 with the bat with his 109 wickets costing 32.73 runs apiece. His record in the one-day international game at the time read an average of 27.15 with the bat after 100 one-day appearances, with his 92 wickets costing 32.94 runs each.

The all-rounder played a starring role in the drawn Test against India, at Hamilton, in January 1999, with an aggressive 126 and a six wicket haul.

Another Kiwi who has played county cricket for Nottinghamshire but his flamboyant attitude has sometimes had its critics.

Suffered heartbreak four years ago when his sister was killed in a train accident.

HEATH DAVIS
Born 30.11.71 ... **right-arm fast**

Has cut his tearaway pace to develop rhythm and control. Made his one-day international debut against Sri Lanka in the 1993-94 Australasia Cup in Sharjah and won his first Test cap against England, at Trent Bridge in 1994. Suffered knee and heel problems in the 1996-97 Test series in Sri Lanka.

SIMON DOULL
Born 6.8.69 ... **right-arm medium**

Rated New Zealand's second best bowler behind the great Sir Richard Hadlee since making his Test debut in the early 1990s.

Doull has the ability to swing the ball alarmingly both ways and Sri Lanka's powerful batting line-up struggled badly against him in the two-Test series in March 1997, when the movement he generates through the air and off the pitch defeated their resistance.

He took five for 58 and three for 82 at Dunedin and four more wickets in the next Test at Hamilton. A month earlier he had taken five for 75 in England's first innings at the Wellington Test.

Doull's Test debut came against Zimbabwe, at Bulawayo in 1992-93 and he celebrated his one-day call-up in the same town on that trip. He had claimed 95 victims in 26 Test appearances by this January and had scalped 34 batsmen in 38 one-dayers.

CHRIS HARRIS
Born 20.11.69 ... **left-hand bat** ... right-arm medium

Limited overs specialist all-rounder. Hard-hitting batsman, bowls a dangerous leg-cutter and is lithe and athletic fielding at point or at square leg.

Scored 130 against Australia in the 1996 World Cup quarter-finals. Has played in 120 one-day internationals but only 14 at Test level.

MATTHEW HORNE
Born 5.2.70 ... **right-hand bat**

Made his Test debut against England, at Christchurch in 1996-97 and played his first one-day international on the same ground that season against Sri Lanka. Had played 13 Tests, averaging 36.97, and 29 one-dayers by January 29 of this year. Made 157, his highest Test score, against Zimbabwe, at Auckland, in February 1998 and gave his side some solid starts against India in 1998-99.

GAVIN LARSEN
Born 27.9.62 ... **right-hand bat** ... right-arm medium

New Zealand's vice-captain on the 1994 England tour. An economical bowler, he made his one-day international debut against India, at Dunedin, in 1989-90. Celebrated his Test debut against England at Trent Bridge in 1994 and had taken 103 wickets in 106 one-dayers by January 19, 1999. Had made eight Test appearances, taking 24 wickets at the same stage.

CRAIG McMILLAN
Born 13.9.76 ... **right-hand bat** ... right-arm medium

The rising all-round star of New Zealand cricket. Played a significant part in New Zealand's 1998-99 Test series win against India. Made his one-day international debut against Sri Lanka, at Hyderabad, in the 1996-97 Independence Cup and gained his first Test cap against Australia, at Brisbane, in 1997-98. After 10 Tests he was averaging 49, with two hundreds and six half-centuries. Has played in 36 one-dayers for the Kiwis.

DION NASH
Born 20.11.71 ... **right-hand bat** ... right arm medium

Rose to international stardom at the age of 22 on New Zealand's tour to England in 1994. He took 17 wickets in three Tests, highlighted by match figures of 11-169 in the Lord's Test, the best by a Kiwi bowler against England.

Nash made his debut for Northern Districts in 1990-91 and became a shock selection for the 1992 tour of Zimbabwe and Sri Lanka with just three first-class games behind him. He made his Test debut at Harare and his one-day international debut at Bulawayo on that tour.

Joined Middlesex in 1996 but played only one Championship match before he broke down with back trouble and was released.

Scored 107 for Northern Districts against Central Districts in December 1997, the maiden first-class century of his career, and returned to Test cricket against Zimbabwe in early 1998, taking seven wickets in the two-Test series. Had taken 57 wickets in 18 Tests and 44 in 51 one-dayers by January 19, 1999.

SHAYNE O'CONNOR
Born 15.11.73 ... **left-arm medium**

One of New Zealand's brightest prospects since making his one-day international debut against Sri Lanka, at Hyderabad, in the 1996-97 Independence Cup tournament.

A new-ball bowler, he made his Test breakthrough on the Kiwi's tour to Zimbabwe in 1997-98. He was awarded his first cap in the First Test, at Harare, in September 1997 but finished with an undistinguished bowling analysis of one for 104 in the first innings. In the second, he dismissed Zimbabwe's top three batsmen to take three for 73 in 26 overs.

He spearheaded New Zealand's attack with Chris Cairns and Gavin Larsen in all three one-day internationals and clearly has a bright future in both one-day and five-day disciplines if he continues to progress.

BLAIR POCOCK
Born 18.6.71 ... **right-hand bat**

A steady, unspectacular opening batsman, he made his Test debut againstAustralia, at Perth in 1993-94. Played one Test against England on the 1994 tour but faded from the scene with shoulder trouble. Was recalled for the 1996-97 home series against England, averaging 30 in three Tests.

MARK PRIEST
Born 12.8.61 ... **left-arm spin**

Made his Test debut against England, at Nottingham, in 1990 and played in the one-day international series against India, at Colombo in 1997-98, eight seasons after his debut against Australia in the 1989-90 Australasia Cup.

CRAIG SPEARMAN
Born 4.7.72 ... **right-hand bat**

Made the first of his eight Test appearances against the Pakistan attack of Waqar Younis and Wasim Akram, at Christchurch in 1995-96. Scored 112 against Zimbabwe in his third Test. Has played 31 one-day internationals since debut against Pakistan, at Dunedin in 1995-96.

ALEX TAIT
Born 13.6.72 ... **right-hand bat** ... right-arm medium

An all-rounder, he made his one-day international debut against Zimbabwe, at Dhaka, in the Wills International Cup in October 1998.

ROGER TWOSE
Born 17.4.68 ... **left-hand bat**

Never made the full England squad so departed Warwickshire at the end of the 1995 season to fulfil an ambition of playing Test cricket for New Zealand.

He achieved that objective shortly after arrival when he was called-up for the Second Test against India, at Madras in 1995-96. He also made his one-day international breakthrough on that trip, celebrating his debut against India at Jamshedpur.

Returned from a miserable tour to the West Indies in 1995-96, announcing his retirement from international cricket for 'business reasons'. He was appointed Wellington's captain in 1996-97 but returned from the international wilderness to score 87 against India in the Test draw at Hamilton, in January 1999.

A LOOK AT...

ADAM PARORE

He became the first Maori to play Test cricket at the age of 19 when he was plucked from the sidelines and thrust into the limelight in the Birmingham Test of 1990.

Parore, the tour rookie, had travelled to England with the New Zealand squad as reserve understudy to established wicket-keeper Ian Smith. But when Smith was injured shortly before the game, the Auckland-born stumper grabbed his big chance to play in the Test, significant chiefly not for his arrival but the high profile departure of Sir Richard Hadlee, making his final appearance in a Test Match.

Adam's arrival on the Test scene was dramatic by any standards. He was a member of the New Zealand Under-19 side that toured England in 1989, scoring 96 when the tourists won the first 'Test' at Scarborough and a vital 90 at Old Trafford to prevent England from drawing the series in the final meeting.

So, his opportunities to play first-class cricket had been rare when he captured the final place in the tour squad for England the following summer.

He made an immediate impact on the cricket scene when he equalled the Auckland record of five catches in an innings on his first-class debut in 1988-89 and held six more behind the stumps in only his second Test against England in Auckland in 1992.

By September 1997 he had played only 46 Test Matches, due in part to injuries and lack of opportunity for a Kiwi squad often in disarray and not always given the international exposure it needs. A total of 1,979 runs at an average of 27.48, with one century and 12 half-centuries, told only half the story.

Hadlee has often described Parore as 'technically the best batsman in the side, who can occupy the crease, judge the line well, and can score runs freely' but the right-hander, who has succeeded ex-skipper Lee Germon as wicket-keeper, has lacked consistency at the highest level of international cricket.

Wisden Cricketers' Almanack said he was the only New Zealand player to advance his claims as a genuine top order Test batsman on the disappointing Kiwi tour to South Africa in 1994-95.

He fell out with new team coach Glenn Turner, sometimes engaging in open warfare with the dogmatic former Test opener as he attempted to instill discipline into New Zealand's under-achieving squad.

But since those gloomy days New Zealand have improved, extended their international and domestic cricket commitments, and Parore has emerged as an important squad member.

He represented New Zealand at the Wills International Cup tournament in Bangladesh last autumn and now looks forward to this summer's World Cup with anticipation with his combination of keeping skills and batting power making him a key man in New Zealand's plans.

THE STATS

Full name: Adam Craig Parore

Born: January 23, 1971 in Auckland

Role: Right-hand bat, wicket-keeper

Represents: Auckland, New Zealand

Test debut: For New Zealand against England at Edgbaston, Third Test, 1990.

One-day international debut: For New Zealand against Zimbabwe at Bulawayo, 1992-93.

Finest hour: Taking six catches in his second Test against England in 1992.

Extras: Glenn Turner used Parore as a batsman so that he could accommodate skipper Lee Germon in the wicket-keeper role when the new coach took over.

NOW THAT'S A FACT

● Parore scored 131 runs in six innings on his first England tour in 1990.

● He also held 14 catches and made one stumping on that trip.

● He top scored for his country in the first innings of their Test match against the West Indies in Bridgetown in 1995-96 with 59 before being caught by Phil Simmons of a first ball delivery by Jimmy Adams that took a wicked bounce.

● He had two stumpings among his first 61 dismissals in Test Matches.

● Parore, who is noted for his speed between the wickets, was run out in both innings of the Second Test against Sri Lanka at Hamilton in March 1997.

● He and Stephen Fleming added 118 in the second one-day international at Sialkot in December 1996 but Pakistan won by 46 runs.

● Parore scored 59 in New Zealand's 156-run victory over a West Indies Board XI in 1995-96. It was the Kiwis' first first-class win in three tours to the Caribbean.

THE THINGS THEY SAY
PARORE ON

❝I have learned so much about wicket-keeping from Ian Smith, my mentor.❞ On the help he received in his formative years from the former New Zealand 'keeper.

❝What a thrill to play my first Test with Richard Hadlee.❞ On his first Test appearance for his country as Sir Richard was bowing out.

ON PARORE

❝Parore, aged 19, made his Test debut at Edgbaston and although showing that some fine tuning of his glovework was needed, he revealed that he was a technically sound batsman of whom much more should be heard.❞ David Leggat's review of New Zealand's England tour of 1990 in Wisden Cricketers' Almanack.

PAUL WISEMAN
Born 4.5.70 ... **right-arm off-spin**

Made his Test debut against Sri Lanka, at Colombo in 1997-98 and played in the recent 1998-99 series against the touring Indians. He made his first appearance in a one-day international against India at Sharjah in the Coca-Cola Cup in 1997-98.

BRYAN YOUNG
Born 3.11.64 ... **right-hand bat**

An opening batsman, his undefeated 267 against Sri Lanka, at Dunedin, in March 1997 was the highest score of his career and second only to Martin Crowe's 299 as a New Zealand Test record. He made his Test debut against Australia, at Brisbane in 1993-94 and played the first of 70 one-day internationals against Australia in the 1990-91 World Series, keeping wicket in the match.

❶ TO WATCH **DANIEL VETTORI**

Born 27.1.79 ... **left-hand bat** ... left-arm spin

He celebrated his 20th birthday at the beginning of World Cup year and looks set to play a starring role for New Zealand over the next decade.

A shaggy haired, bespectacled, orthodox slow left-arm spinner, Vettori became New Zealand's youngest ever Test cricketer when he made his debut in the Second Test against England, at Wellington on February 6, 1997 at the age of 18 years and 10 days, 187 days younger than Doug Freeman in 1932-33.

He earned that call-up partly due to the economy of his bowling on his first-class debut for Northern Districts against Mike Atherton's side a fortnight earlier. He had reeled off 20 overs for 30 runs in England's first innings.

In the Wellington Test, England thrashed New Zealand by an innings to overshadow Vettori's promising performance but the wickets of Hussain and Caddick were compensation for his marathon 34.3 overs, costing only 98 runs.

At the end of that Test series, Vettori was topping the batting (59.00) and bowling (seven wickets at 29.71) averages after two appearances.

The left-hander celebrated the best figures (five for 22) of his career for Northern Districts against Otago in a Shell Trophy match in March 1998 and showed his outstanding promise as an all-rounder in the 1998-99 Test series against India, scoring 57 in the Second Test, at Wellington.

By January 19 of this year, and still only 19, he had taken 54 wickets in 16 Tests and made 31 one-day international appearances with 25 scalps.

WISDEN WORLD CUP VERDICT
They've been called unexciting, but Chris Cairns could change all that. Apart from him, the bowling isn't so much military-medium as slow-medium: Watch out for Craig McMillan — a fast-scoring batsman (and another slow-medium bowler!) who could make his mark. Semi-finalists?

PAKISTAN

GROUP B • Australia • Bangladesh • New Zealand • **Pakistan** • Scotland • West Indies

Cricket quiz fanatics the world over will be having a field day when questions are posed about the 1999 World Cup tournament in England this summer.

If Pakistan manage to win the World Cup for the second time in seven attempts, a favourite question could easily become: 'Who was the Birmingham League player who led his country to victory in a World Cup final?'

Incredibly, Pakistan, one of the favourites to reach the latter stages of World Cup 99 and possibly go on to clinch the trophy for the second time in seven years, will be led into battle by Wasim Akram, a few weeks before he is expected to play his first match for Smethwick in the Birmingham League.

Not even the World Cup's glorious romantic past history has thrown up quite such a bizarre situation as that which confronts the 32-year-old former Lancashire all-rounder who, one moment will be captaining Pakistan in World Cup action before capacity gates, and the next trying to find Smethwick off the M6, who struggle to attract 100 spectators on match days.

But as Wasim led Pakistan on a short tour to India in January 1999, all his attention was riveted on planning a World Cup campaign that will give his country a chance of emulating the feats of Imran Khan's side in 1992.

Reinstated as captain in January after Aamir Sohail had been relieved of the job, Wasim has been given the unenviable task of trying to restore Pakistan to the standards they have achieved in past World Cups, after failing to progress beyond the quarter-finals in 1996.

They reached the semi-final stages of three successive World Cups, in 1979, 1983 and 1987, before winning the trophy for the first and only time in 1992.

Imran Khan, the captain, in his 40th year and nursing an injured right shoulder, declared victory over England in the Melbourne final his finest hour, a claim supported by the pictures of him holding the £7,500 Waterford crystal trophy after ICC chairman Sir Colin Cowdrey had made the presentation at the MCG.

Sitting in a corner of the Pakistan dressing-room that March day was Wasim Akram, who also received an award for Man of the Match.

He pledged to one day lead Pakistan to a similar World Cup triumph, something which eluded him three years ago but will clearly be occupying his mind again as he prepares for his final appearance in a World Cup tournament.

Pakistan will field a squad capable of beating any of the 11 other countries.

They prepare for the tournament with match-winning batsmen of the calibre of Saeed Anwar, Salim Malik, Inzamam-ul-Haq and the new boy Yousuf Youhana at their disposal.

Their bowling is even more impressive with Wasim Akram and Waqar Younis forming a warhead capable of destroying any batting line-up, and if assault and battery fails, they can exploit the subtle varieties of spin and sorcery provided by Mushtaq Ahmed and Saqlain Mushtaq, both superbly efficient at bowling on English pitches after the success they have enjoyed with Somerset and Surrey.

But as so often happens, Pakistan have become their worst enemy in the build up to the big event. They have changed their captains repeatedly since Imran Khan retired and their legal wrangling with Australian stars Mark Waugh and Shane Warne, which involves Salim Malik, continues to offer a murky sideshow to all the success they produce on the field.

It cannot be easy for skipper Wasim to bring peace and tranquillity to the dressing-room when his predecessors Aamir Sohail, Ramiz Raja and Saeed Anwar have all recently been stripped of the honour, and Salim is trying to do his best to forget allegations made by Waugh and Warne that he tried to bribe them in 1994.

But there is nothing new about the smell of cordite wafting through a Pakistan dressing-room, and their World Cup clash with Australia, at Headingley, on Sunday, May 23 has the makings of an absorbing contest played between sworn enemies, before a capacity Yorkshire gate.

Pakistan play their warm-up matches before the tournament proper against Derbyshire, on May 8, Durham, on May 10, and Lancashire, on May 12.

Their opening game in the tournament is against the West Indies, at Bristol, on May 16; followed by Scotland, at Chester-le-Street on May 20; Australia on May 23; New Zealand at Derby on May 28; and Bangladesh, at Northampton, on May 31.

They will not want a repeat of their performances in the early stages of their triumphant 1992 campaign. They won only one of their first five matches! Fortunately, they won all five thereafter.

Pakistan's strength is their knowledge of English conditions, with a batting line-up well-versed in how to combat movement through the air or off the seam; and a bowling attack which has played almost as much cricket in England as it has back home in Asia.

When Pakistan lost to India, at Bangalore, in the quarter-final of the 1996 World Cup, one distraught supporter is said to have taken a loaded gun to his television set and then to himself, while captain Wasim Akram, who was injured and not playing, was burned in effigy.

Pakistan's players were given a torrid time for months after that game, indeed some supporters have not forgiven them, such is the rivalry between the two countries and the 'shame' at losing to their fiercest rival.

Fortunately, Wasim has survived all the slings and arrows that curse Pakistan cricket to return to England for one last campaign in the sunset of a glorious career.

He will have his work cut out to try to bring harmony to their dressing-room and bring the individual talents of so many quality players into a collective unit. Imran managed it seven years ago and the result was World Cup triumph. Can Wasim follow in his footsteps and end his World Cup career as skipper of the world champions — before heading off to Smethwick?

WORLD CUP HIGHLIGHT

Their 1992 success over England in the final with Imran Khan leading his side to their first World Cup triumph by 22 runs. They were awful in the opening group games and only just qualified for the semi-finals but peaked in the last two games of the tournament.

WORLD CUP RECORD

1975	Eliminated at group stage
1979	Lost to West Indies in the semi-finals
1983	Lost to West Indies in the semi-finals
1987	Lost to Australia in the semi-finals
1992	Beat England in the final
1996	Lost to India in the quarter-finals

WORLD CUP ODDS: 12-1

CAPTAIN **WASIM AKRAM**
Born 3.6.66 ... **left-hand bat** ... left-arm fast

English spectators need little convincing that Wasim is one of the world's greatest all-rounders. He has been a crowd-pleaser for a full decade since first wearing the Lancashire sweater in 1988.

Ironically, Wasim struck his maiden Test century against Australia in 1989-90, sharing a stand of 191 with Imran Khan, who four years before the left-armer had made his bow with Lancashire had predicted a great future for him.

If his batting has sometimes failed to live up to its rich early promise, he is arguably the most dangerous all-rounder in the world.

Coming in at number eight, he scored a career best 257 not out for Pakistan against Zimbabwe in 1996-97, the highest score by a batsman from that position in history.

He was appointed captain of Pakistan in 1992-93 but was replaced by Salim Malik on the tour to New Zealand in 1993-94. But by the time Pakistan toured England in 1996, Wasim was back in control, a job he has subsequently lost again – and then regained at the turn of this year.

Wasim was born in Lahore on June 3, 1966 and at 12 was opening the bowling and batting for the school team. At 15 he was captain, his life and ambitions consumed by cricket. He played street games in old Lahore and was soon sent off to a summer camp organised by the Pakistan cricket board for the city's top youngsters.

Brilliant Pakistan batsman Javed Miandad, seeking practice, faced Wasim in the nets and was so impressed with the pace and big inswing that the youngster generated that he named the teenager in a squad for a match against the touring New Zealanders at Rawalpindi. He took seven for 50 in the first innings, and two more in the second. In his second Test at Dunedin, he had a match analysis of 10-128. He was only 18!

Today, he is on schedule to make more than 100 Test appearances and approaches the 1999 World Cup as a proven match winner.

Off the edge

- England's Alan Mullally became his 300th Test victim at The Oval in 1996.
- **Wasim scored 531 runs in 18 Championship innings for Lancashire in 1998, his final season at Old Trafford.**
- He claimed 48 Championship wickets at 21.35 during that period.
- **He once took 5-10 against Leicestershire in a Benson and Hedges Cup-tie in 1993.**
- Lancashire were so impressed with his performances on Pakistan's 1987 tour to England that they signed him in 1988.
- **He launched his Lancashire career with an unbeaten century against Somerset in May 1988.**
- Wasim took 21 wickets in four Tests against England in 1992. In the other tour matches that summer he was even more devastating and finished with 82 first-class wickets at 16 runs apiece.
- **Born in Lahore, his father was mostly concerned with his son's happiness than any sporting success.**
- He attended the fee-paying Cathedral School in Lahore where all the lessons were conducted in English.
- **"I have never faced a bowler like Akram, he is unbelievable, and yet we wore him down like a crying baby wears out its tired mother." Justin Langer talking about Wasim on Australia's 1998 tour to Pakistan.**

AAMIR SOHAIL
Born 14.9.66 ... **left-hand bat** ... left-arm spin

Sohail was stripped of the captaincy of Pakistan after losing the home Test series to Australia and going 1-0 down in the series against Zimbabwe in 1998-99. He then pulled out of the team before a ball had been bowled in the Lahore Test against Zimbabwe last December complaining of sickness.

But his withdrawal was seen by some observers as a protest relating to his grievances against team selection and the wicket preparation.

Wasim Akram was reinstated as captain for the Tests against India after Moin Khan had done the job for the rest of the series against Zimbabwe, leaving Aamir to dwell on a bleak chapter in an otherwise glittering career.

He has filled the role of attacking opening batsman that Pakistan have needed since the days of Mohsin Khan and Majid Khan.

He made his Test debut against England, at Edgbaston, in 1992 and went on to crown a magnificent start to his international career by scoring 205 in the Old Trafford Test, his third appearance. By the end of the series he had scored more than 400 runs at an average of 51.62.

By the time of his 45th appearance in the First Test against Zimbabwe in November 1998, he was averaging 36.53. He had played 149 one-day internationals at that stage with an average of 32 and had taken 82 wickets.

AKHTAR SARFRAZ
Born 20.2.76 ... **left-hand bat**

Made his one-day international debut against West Indies, at Sharjah, in the 1997-98 Champions Trophy. Member of the Pakistan squad at the Wills International Cup in Dhaka in October 1998.

AQIB JAVED
Born 5.8.72 ... **right-arm fast medium**

His bowling career has been overshadowed by the exploits of Wasim Akram and Waqar Younis but Aqib's contribution to Pakistan, especially at one-day level, has been underrated.

He made his Test debut as a teenager against New Zealand at Wellington in 1988-89 and his one-day international debut against West Indies, at Adelaide, in the 1988-89 World Series.

He was an outstanding success in the 1992 World Cup, taking 11 wickets, including two against England in the final.

His appearance against Zimbabwe in the First Test at Peshawar last November was his 22nd for his country, with 54 wickets. He had taken 182 wickets in 163 one-dayers at that stage. Played for Hampshire in 1991 season.

ARSHAD KHAN
Born 22.3.71 ... **right-arm off-spin**

Born in Peshawar, he made his Test debut against the West Indies in the First Test in 1997-98 on his home ground. Given his one-day international baptism against Zimbabwe in the 1992-93 Wills Trophy in Sharjah. Had played two Tests and 12 one-dayers by November 10, 1998.

ASIF MAHMOOD
Born 18.12.75 ... **right-hand bat**

Played his first two one-day internationals against Australia, at Peshawar and Lahore in November 1998. Born in Rawalpindi, he plays for Rawalpindi Division Cricket Association.

AZAM KHAN
Born 1.3.69 ... **right-hand bat**

Born in Karachi, made his Test debut against Zimbabwe, at Sheikhupura, in 1996-97, his only Test appearance to date. Had played five one-day internationals by the time he appeared against Australia, at Karachi in 1998-99. Averaging 23.20 with one half-century.

AZHAR MAHMOOD
Born 28.2.75 ... **right-hand bat** ... right-arm fast medium

The great hope in Pakistan is that he can progress to become the next 'Imran Khan'. A genuine all-rounder, he is a hard-hitting orthodox batsman and can raise his pace for Test appearances. Azhar made his one-day international debut against India, at Toronto in the 1996-97 Sahara Cup and played his first Test against South Africa, at Rawalpindi in 1997-98. Averaged 40 with the bat in Tests after 21 innings with 25 wickets at 37.64. Had taken 34 wickets in 49 one-day internationals after playing the third of the one-dayers against Zimbabwe on November 24, 1998.

IJAZ AHMED
Born 20.9.68 ... **right-hand bat**

He was 18 when he played his first Test against India, at Madras, in 1986-87. Reliable middle-order batsman who played his 50th Test against Zimbabwe, at Lahore in December 1998. At that stage he was averaging 39.98, with 10 hundreds and 11 half-centuries in 74 innings. Played his 215th one-day international against Zimbabwe, at Rawalpindi on November 24, averaging 32, with nine hundreds and 30 half-centuries.

INZAMAM-UL-HAQ
Born 3.3.70 ... **right-hand bat**

One of Pakistan's greatest batsmen, he has the technique to grind out a Test innings against some of the world's best attacks or cut loose with such savagery in a one-day international to change the course of a match in a few overs of blistering aggression.

Born in Multan, an ancient cultural town in the lower Punjab, he has become Pakistan's most consistent batsman in all forms of cricket since making his first tour to England in 1992 and winning his first Test cap, at Edgbaston.

He earned selection for that tour on the strength of his impressive form in the 1992 World Cup, highlighted by an innings of 60 from 37 balls against New Zealand in the semi-finals to earn him the Man of the Match award, and 42 (35 balls) in Pakistan's triumph over England in the final in Melbourne.

Inzamam was averaging 42.70 from 51 Test appearances after playing the First Test against Zimbabwe, at Peshawar in November 1998. Three days earlier he had made his 171st appearance in a limited-overs international, also against Zimbabwe, at Rawalpindi, with an average of 38.35 and a run aggregate of 5,369 with five hundreds and 37 half-centuries.

MOHAMMAD AKRAM
Born 10.9.74 ... **right-arm fast**

Made his Test debut against Sri Lanka, at Faisalabad, in 1995-96 only a few days after his 21st birthday. Toured Australia but had no luck in the first two Tests where catches were spilled off his bowling. Made his one-day international debut against Sri Lanka, at Gujranwala in 1995-96. Has played only six Tests but made his 13th one-day international appearance against Zimbabwe, at Sheikupura in November 1998. Northants' overseas player in 1997.

MOHAMMAD HUSSAIN
Born 8.10.76 ... **left-hand bat** ... left-arm spin

Made his Test debut against Zimbabwe, at Faisalabad in 1996-97 and played his first one-dayer against New Zealand, at Mohali, in the 1996-97 Independence Cup. Played his second Test against Australia, at Rawalpindi, in 1998-99.

MOHAMMAD NAVEED ASHRAF
Born 4.9.74 ... **right-hand bat**

Received a shock call up when his captain Aamir Sohail and Inzamam-ul-Haq pulled out of the Pakistan team before the Second Test against Zimbabwe at Lahore in December 1998. Opened with Saeed Anwar and scored 32 in his first (and only) innings. Chosen for 1999 tour to India.

MOHAMMAD WASIM
Born 8.8.77 ... **right-hand bat**

Shot to fame scoring an undefeated 109 on his Test debut against New Zealand, at Lahore, in November 1996. A middle-order batsman, he made his one-day international debut against New Zealand, at Karachi in 1996-97. Had played 11 Tests and 21 one-dayers by October 1998.

MOHAMMAD ZAHID
Born 2.8.76 ... **right-arm fast**

From the same region as Waqar Younis, he launched his Test career in sensational style, aged 20, by claiming match figures of 11 for 130 in the Second Test against New Zealand, at Rawalpindi in November-December 1996. Made his one-day international debut, at Karachi, in same series. Recovering from a back operation after injury on tour to Sri Lanka.

MOIN KHAN
Born 23.9.71 ... **right-hand bat** ... wicket-keeper

Pakistan's first choice wicket-keeper and vice-captain on recent 1999 tour to India. He made his Test debut against West Indies, at Faisalabad, in 1990-91 and was picked for his 42nd against Zimbabwe, at Lahore, in December 1998. At that stage he was averaging 30 with the bat, having scored three centuries and nine 50s, taking 74 catches and 11 stumpings. He played his 118th one-day international against Zimbabwe, at Rawalpindi, on November 24, 1998.

A LOOK AT...
WAQAR YOUNIS

Few bowlers have emerged to make a more sensational impact on the international cricket scene than Waqar's arrival at the end of the 1980s.

Born in Burewala in the Vehari region of the Punjab, he was a day short of his 18th birthday when he was asked to make his Test debut against India, at Karachi in 1989-90. He took 55 wickets in his first 11 Tests, capturing five wickets in an innings five times.

In that time he provoked Martin Crowe, New Zealand's captain, into saying that he had never faced pace and swing bowling of such quality. He also forced the great Kiwi batsman to wear a helmet grille for the first time.

An astonishing number of Waqar's wickets have been clean bowled or have come from leg-before decisions. His lethal dosage depends on blinding pace and late swing, in which he either shatters the stumps, batters pads, or bruises toes.

He joined Surrey in 1990 on Imran Khan's recommendation and terrorised the county circuit. In the 1991 English season, he took 113 wickets in 582 overs at a mere 14.65 apiece.

In 1992 he was named one of Wisden's Five Cricketers of the Year and, with the left-arm pace of Wasim Akram, formed one of world cricket's most lethal spearheads.

When chosen to tour India at the start of 1999, he had taken 275 wickets in 55 Tests at an average of 21.57. He had claimed five wickets in an innings on 21 occasions and 10 wickets in a Test five times.

His Test-playing history is laced with one-day international appearances also. He made his 172nd appearance for Pakistan in one-dayers when he played against Zimbabwe, at Rawalpindi, in the third one-day international last November.

A staggering 283 wickets at 23 apiece illustrates the problems he is certain to pose if form and fitness enable him to play in the 1999 World Cup competition this summer.

He joined Glamorgan on a two-year contract in 1997 and took a hat-trick against Lancashire a few weeks after making his debut, the first Glamorgan player to do so since Ossie Wheatley achieved the feat in 1968.

He recorded his best bowling performance for the Welsh club in his first season, taking eight for 17 against Sussex, at Swansea as Glamorgan swept to the county Championship.

Beyond doubt, Waqar Younis is an outstanding bowler. When Imran Khan recommended him to Surrey, the Pakistan captain had only seen him bowl on television. Since then he has refined Waqar's run and action, taught him the fundamentals of swing, and persuaded the 'Burewala Express' to make life as uncomfortable as possible for the world's best batsmen.

And should Pakistan make a major impact in this summer's tournament, Waqar is sure to feature heavily in those displays as he sets out to prove that his injury problems are behind him and he is still to be considered as one of the most destructive bowlers in the game.

THE STATS

Full name: Waqar Younis

Born: November 16, 1971 in Vehari

Role: Right-arm fast, right-hand bat

Represents: Glamorgan, Pakistan

Test debut: For Pakistan against India in Karachi, First Test, 1989-90.

One-day international debut: For Pakistan against West Indies in Sharjah in 1989-90.

Finest hour: Helping Pakistan to Test series victory in England in 1992.

Extras: Injury forced him out of Pakistan's 1992 World Cup triumph.

NOW THAT'S A FACT

● The right-arm quickie played in the 1996 World Cup tournament, helping Pakistan reach the quarter-finals.

● In 1990-91 he took 10 for 106 against New Zealand at Lahore and followed it up with 12 for 130 in the next Test at Faisalabad.

● He was at his brilliant best against Sri Lanka in 1994-95 when he took 11 for 119 in the Third Test.

● Waqar helped Glamorgan to the county Championship in 1997, their first success in 28 years.

● Matthew Maynard, the Welsh club's skipper, described Waqar as "probably the best signing Glamorgan have ever made."

● He headed the bowling averages in 1997 with 68 wickets at 22.80 each.

● His contract at Glamorgan was said to be the biggest pay deal ever offered to a county player in England.

● Imran Khan spotted Waqar's potential while he was watching a local match on TV in a hospital.

THE THINGS THEY SAY
WAQAR ON

❝We tried our best but England are a very strong side at home.❞ **Answering allegations that members of the Pakistan team took a bribe during their tour of England in 1992.**

ON WAQAR

❝The one thing that makes Waqar stand out above many other bowlers is the numbers of wickets he takes through hitting the stumps.❞ **David Gower talking about Waqar's accuracy with the ball.**

MUSHTAQ AHMED
Born 28.6.70 ... **right-arm leg-spin**

A member of the Holy Trinity of leg-spin wizards alongside Warne and Kumble, Mushtaq reached the zenith of his wrist-spinning powers between November 1995 and August 1996 when he claimed 45 wickets in six Tests.

A regular on the English county circuit since joining Somerset in 1993, he is one of the most enthusiastic cricketers in the world, despite a workload that is heavier than most Test Match bowlers.

He says: "I like the English four-day Championship because it gives spin bowlers a good chance to bowl long spells. And one-day cricket is exciting to watch and play in. A good cricketer can play all types of cricket."

His impressive record in Test and one-day internationals for Pakistan testifies to the accuracy of that remark. He had made 41 appearances when he played in the First Test against Zimbabwe, at Peshawar, in November 1998 and his record at one-day level stood at 130 appearances after the limited-overs contest against South Africa, at Capetown in the 1997-98 Standard Bank Series.

He had taken 165 Test wickets at 29 apiece and 144 one-day wickets at 33 by the end of November 1998.

England were the victims of two of his finest bowling performances in the 1996 series when Mushtaq spun them to defeat on the final afternoons at Lord's and The Oval. He regarded his six for 78 performance at The Oval as his best ever.

NADEEM KHAN
Born 10.12.69 ... **left-arm spin**

Such are the mysteries of Pakistan cricket that Nadeem hardly appeared on the international front after making his debut against the West Indies in the Third Test, at Antigua, in May 1993, with Desmond Haynes and Brian Lara becoming his first two Test victims. Received a shock recall from the wilderness for the squad named to tour India at the start of 1999.

SAEED ANWAR
Born 6.9.68 ... **left-hand bat**

One of the world's best opening batsmen and another Pakistan player with the ability to tighten his game for the demands of Test cricket or relax to turn on the flamboyance needed for World Cup duty.

A Test regular since the start of the decade, he reached the peak of his batting powers on Pakistan's 1996 tour to England. He marked his opening first-class match of the tour with a double century against Glamorgan and scored two more hundreds in his next three first-class games.

He maintained his form to score 74 and 88 in the First Test at Lord's and reserved his best innings that summer for a paceless Test pitch at The Oval where he scored 176, his highest Test score.

He ended that trip with 1,224 runs at 68.00 to top Pakistan's first-class averages and was named one of Wisden's Five Cricketers of the Year in 1997.

Born in Karachi, Pakistan were nearly denied his cricketing services. In 1973 his father, an engineer, moved to a job in Teheran, and Saeed stayed there until 1977 playing football, the only sport available.

He made his Test breakthrough against West Indies, at Faisalabad in 1990-91 after playing his first one-day international against the Windies, at Perth, in the 1988-89 World Series.

When named in the Pakistan squad to tour India in early 1999, he had played 36 Tests, averaging 45.64, with seven hundreds and 17 half-centuries. In 161 one-day internationals, he was averaging 40, with 15 hundreds.

SALIM ELAHI
Born 21.11.76 ... **right-hand bat**

Made his 18th appearance in a one-day international against Australia, at Karachi, in November 1998. He averages 29.94 and has scored one century and three 50s. Made his Test debut against Australia, at Brisbane, in 1995-96.

SALIM MALIK
Born 16.4.63 ... **right-hand bat**

Salim seems to have become embroiled as much in cricket politics as he has in influencing the results of matches with his brilliant strokeplay since arriving on the Test scene in the early 1980s.

In the build up to the 1999 World Cup, he admitted that accusations by Shane Warne and Mark Waugh that he had tried to bribe them in 1994 had 'upset him and spoilt his cricket'.

But Salim, named in Pakistan's squad for the India tour at the start of 1999 after making a shock comeback for his 100th Test appearance in the Second Test against Zimbabwe, at Lahore, in December 1998, is best known as the 'Crown Prince' of Pakistan's batting for the best part of two decades.

He played his first Test against Sri Lanka, at Karachi in 1981-82 and made his one-day bow the same year against West Indies, at Sydney, in the World Series Cup.

His storybook courage against the West Indies at Faisalabad in 1986 has gone down in Pakistan Test folklore. A rearing delivery from Courtney Walsh fractured his wrist. He retired, but returned in the second innings, batting at number eleven. He faced the first ball batting left-handed but returned to right-handed to put on 32 vital runs.

Malik played county cricket for Essex and was one of Wisden's Five Cricketers of the Year in 1988.

He had scored 5,641 Test runs at 44.76 when he set off for India recently and averaged 33 at one-day level after 276 internationals.

SAQLAIN MUSHTAQ
Born 27.11.76 ... **right-arm off-spin**

The only good thing to come out of Pakistan's disastrous home series against Sri Lanka in 1995-96 was the discovery of an 18-year-old off-spin bowler.

He took a wicket with his seventh ball in Test cricket on his debut in the First Test, at Peshawar, and by the time he was named in their 1999 squad to tour India, he had taken 65 wickets in 17 Tests and 176 wickets in 88 one-dayers.

Born in Lahore and currently a valued member of the Surrey staff after joining them in 1997, Saqlain is rated the second best off-spinner in the world behind Muttiah Muralitharan, some even say he's the best.

He took 32 first-class wickets at 19 apiece and 63 last summer at 17.76 in his first two seasons at The Oval. He bowls with an easy, rhythmic action and possesses a lethal 'floater' which drifts away from the right-hander.

SHAHID AFRIDI
Born 1.3.80 ... **right-hand bat ...** right-arm leg-spin

A last-minute replacement for Pakistan in the 1996-97 Kenya Centenary Tournament, the hard-hitting top-order batsman played a sensational first innings in a one-day match, against Sri Lanka, at Nairobi, by smashing a century off 37 balls. He made his Test debut against Australia, at Karachi, last October and appeared in the series against India this year. A one-day specialist, he has over 70 international one-dayers to his name.

SHOAIB AKHTAR
Born 13.8.75 ... **right-arm fast medium**

Has the capability to become one of Pakistan's quickest pacemen. Made his Test debut against West Indies, at Rawalpindi in 1997-98 and played his first one-day international against Zimbabwe in the same season. Picked to tour India at the start of 1999 after eight Tests and five one-dayers.

❶ TO WATCH **YOUSUF YOUHANA**
Born 27.8.74 ... **right-hand bat**

Yousuf came out of the dense fog shrouding Lahore for the Second Test between Pakistan and Zimbabwe last December to score a brilliant maiden Test century.

Making his seventh appearance in five-day cricket for Pakistan, he scored an unbeaten 120 out of 325 for nine declared, showing tremendous temperament and a wide range of strokes to dominate the Zimbabwe attack.

The fog was still threatening when he reached his century in 277 minutes from 186 balls. He hoisted Adam Huckle for a six to celebrate his arrival at the three-figure milestone and his unbroken 50-run partnership in 48 minutes with Waqar Younis left Pakistan in control when the declaration came.

Yousuf was given his big chance of Test cricket in South Africa when chosen to play in the Second Test at Durban in 1997-98 and he made his one-day international debut against Zimbabwe at Harare. When he played against Zimbabwe again, at Rawalpindi, in November 1998 he had played 13 times, averaging 53 with 479 runs from 11 innings. His Test record is no less impressive. He averages 40.72 with 448 runs in 12 innings.

WISDEN WORLD CUP VERDICT
It's handy to have one-day cricket's leading wicket-taker as your skipper, in familiar conditions. Some of the batsmen haven't played much in England, though, and may get found out by the moving ball. Super Six qualifiers.

SCOTLAND

Scotland entered a golden passage in their long history of fighting for recognition when they qualified for World Cup 1999, their first appearance in the tournament.

They clinched it by achieving victory over old rivals Ireland in the 1997 ICC Trophy third place play-off in Kuala Lumpur. The two countries had been regular cricket adversaries over the years but never had they met in a more important match than the one which decided who would progress to the World Cup finals.

Ireland could complain that rain pursued them to the last. It caused the match to be reduced to 45 overs and under the Duckworth-Lewis method, they faced a revised target of 192. It proved too much for them and they were bowled out for 141 in 39 overs.

George Salmond, Scotland's long-serving captain, recognises that victory as the 'proudest moment' of his long and distinguished cricket career.

But if that crucial match result was special, the prospect of an opening Group B encounter with Australia has mouth-watering possibilities.

They are locked in a group that offers the toughest series of matches Scotland have faced in their history. Australia, World Cup 87 winners; West Indies, World Cup 75 and 79 winners; Pakistan, World Cup 92 winners; New Zealand and Bangladesh provide their opposition for what promises to become an absorbing introduction to the greatest cricket tournament on earth for Scotland's largely inexperienced squad.

Their progress to the finals is a triumph for Scottish Cricket Union general manager Alex Ritchie, national coach Jim Love, and a squad prepared to battle against heavy odds whenever they complete in ICC Trophy tournaments, against visiting Test-playing touring teams, or in Benson and Hedges Cup or NatWest Trophy matches.

Scotland, granted £2.2 million Lottery money recently to build a cricket academy, can no longer be dismissed as cannon-fodder for cricket's big guns.

Former Yorkshire batsman Love has injected a professionalism into all aspects of practice and match performance that has helped steer Scotland on to the World Cup stage.

George Salmond explains: "In the old days, our batsmen would blame the pitch if they got out. Jim preaches honesty, urging us not to seek excuses for failure but to address the problems.

"When he first came to Scotland he struggled to come to terms with the fact that cricket was not always the main thing in players' lives, that we all had jobs outside cricket.

"But he's turned it round and given a sharp edge to our game. Now, we make all opposition work hard for victory and cricket is almost as important as work, hence the time out from our business interests some of us are taking to play in the tournament.

"Our opening World Cup match against Australia is as big as it gets. Our intention is to go out and enjoy games in the tournament. If we perform above ourselves, and opponents underachieve, who knows, we might pull off a giantkilling."

Scotland will have home advantage for two of their group matches, against Bangladesh on May 24 and New Zealand in their final first round match seven days later.

Raeburn Place will host those two games and support should be strong for George Salmond's side. If they are to produce an upset it is likely to be in one of those two encounters rather than against the all-powerful combination of Pakistan, West Indies and Australia.

WORLD CUP HIGHLIGHT

Beating Ireland in that crucial third-place play-off in Malaysia to reach the World Cup finals for the first time in their history.

WORLD CUP RECORD

1975	Did not qualify
1979	Did not qualify
1983	Did not qualify
1987	Did not qualify
1992	Did not qualify
1996	Did not qualify

WORLD CUP ODDS: 100-1

CAPTAIN **GEORGE SALMOND**
Born 1.12.69 ... **right-hand bat**

The easiest decision for the Scottish Cricket Union in planning their World Cup campaign was to name George Salmond as skipper.

His inspirational captaincy has done more than anything to steer Scotland through the most successful chapter in its history and he can be expected to exploit all the experience he has gained in doing the job since 1995.

He will be making his 105th appearance when he leads Scotland in their first group match against World Cup favourites Australia, at Worcester, on May 16.

But when challenged to say whether that red-letter date in his diary will represent the proudest moment of his year, he offers a cautious response.

"I'd say one of them," he replies. Salmond's reluctance to talk only cricket this year is governed by his decision to marry his fiancée Angela Bogie. Their date at the altar has been fixed for April and honeymoon plans have had to be put on ice until after the World Cup.

> # Off the edge
>
> • Salmond averaged 36 with the bat in Scotland's successful participation in the 1997 ICC Trophy.
>
> • **George and his Scotland team were stranded in Malaysia for a while after their triumph in the ICC Trophy. They had been booked on an early flight back during the competition by their pessimistic authorities but their extended success in the tournament meant the party had to re-book a later flight, which proved very difficult until the president of the Malaysian Cricket Association smoothed their way!**
>
> • His marriage to Angela Bogie will take place on April Fools Day – but the honeymoon will be put on hold until July.
>
> • **A primary school teacher at George Watson's College, Edinburgh, the Scotland skipper has been given time out by his employer for the World Cup campaign.**

"Put it this way," he explains. "Playing against Australia will be the proudest moment of my cricket life! It will be my crowning glory in some wonderful times playing for Scotland over the past decade. But don't tell Angela!"

An exciting strokeplayer and brilliant fielder, Salmond is one of the most successful ever products of Scotland's youth system. He captained them at Under-16, Under-19 and B-team levels before gaining full international honours.

Most of his batting success has been accomplished at Ireland's expense in annual fixture lists frustratingly curtailed against top first-class opposition. He scored a century in the first innings and 95 in the second against the Irish in 1992 and made his highest-ever score of 181 against them in 1996.

But World Cup 99 will present the biggest challenge of his cricket career and it is one that he is looking forward to taking on.

"To play against the likes of Australia, Pakistan and West Indies will be a real test of our ability but we are ready for the task," he says.

"We have a tremendous team sprit in the squad and a shock result is not out of the question."

MICHAEL ALLINGHAM
Born 6.1.65 ... **right-hand bat** ... right-arm medium

Plays for Heriot's Former Pupils. Debut for Scotland in 1991, scoring 50 against The England Amateur XI. Played almost 50 matches for Scotland with a top score of 64 not out against Transvaal Under-23 in Johannesburg. Scrum-half for Scotland 'B' before knee injury curtailed his rugby career.

JOHN BLAIN
Born 4.1.79 ... **right-arm fast medium**

He became Scotland's youngest-ever player when given his debut against Ireland three years ago at 17. Since then he has made regular appearances for Scotland in the Benson and Hedges Cup competition.

Born in Edinburgh, Blain celebrated the offer of a playing contract at Northants by making his first-team debut for them in 1997. He took five for 24 on his Sunday League debut against Derbyshire that season but chances to shine on the county circuit have been limited since then.

He was a member of the Scotland Under-19 side at the International Youth Tournament in Holland in 1994-95 and represented Scotland in the European Championships in Denmark in 1996, going on to captain his country's Under-19 team in the 1997 Youth World Cup.

He left for New Zealand at the end of the 1998 season to play club cricket and prepare for the World Cup.

A promising footballer as a teenager, he signed schoolboy forms for Hibernian and Falkirk, making youth and reserve team appearances before committing his future to cricket. But he still plays soccer, and also enjoys golf and listening to music.

JAMES BRINKLEY
Born 13.3.74 ... **right-arm fast medium**

Scotland's main strike bowler with a wealth of experience of first-class cricket gained at Worcestershire and in Zimbabwe and Australia.

Brinkley has never quite produced the match-winning form he threatened when some outstanding performances for Matabeleland in Zimbabwe's domestic competitions five years ago alerted Worcestershire to his growing potential.

Born in Helensburgh, Scotland, he produced career-best bowling figures of six for 35 against Mashonaland Country Districts in Harare in 1994-95 and took hat-tricks in Worcestershire 2nd XI Championship and Bain Clarkson Trophy matches against Surrey and Somerset.

Given a rare first-team chance in the Championship he took six for 98 against Surrey at The Oval in 1994 on his UK debut.

He played Benson and Hedges Cup and Sunday League matches but never quite made the grade at New Road.

After five seasons at Worcestershire, he signed for Essex on a match-by-match contract in 1998 and made his first appearances for Scotland in their Benson and Hedges Cup squad.

GREG BUTCHART

Born 17.6.78 ... **right-hand bat** ... right-arm medium

Member of Scotland's Under-19 World Cup squad of 1997. Uncapped at full international level, he plays for Heriots FP Club. Comes from same Arbroath district that produced Scotland's captain, George Salmond.

ASIM BUTT

Born 2.5.68 ... **left-arm fast medium**

Born in Lahore, Asim made his Scotland debut on his 30th birthday last summer. It was the culmination of protracted negotiations to gain qualification to play for his adopted country.

A member of the Heriot's Former Pupils club, he shares the new ball in attack with James Brinkley.

He produced the performance of his life last summer in the Benson and Hedges Cup-tie against Yorkshire at Linlithgow by clinching the gold award. He trapped Anthony McGrath leg before for nought and then dismissed Darren Lehmann and Craig White in three deliveries.

"He has that extra edge of speed lacking in so many pacemen in Scotland," says Asim's national team captain, George Salmond, who will look to Butt and Brinkley for early success with the ball in their group matches.

DAVID COWAN

Born 30.3.64 ... **left-hand bat** ... right-arm medium

Leading member of triumphant Village Cup winning Freuchie team at Lord's in 1985. Plagued by injuries but what he lacks in pace, he compensates for with guile. Late swing with metronomic accuracy.

STEPHEN CRAWLEY

Born 16.9.62 ... **right-hand bat** ... right-arm medium

Regular Minor Counties player for Cheshire from 1982 until 1993, when he moved to Scotland. Aggressive 'pinch hitting' opener, medium pace bowler and sharp close catcher. Was on Lancashire's staff between 1982-84 although he moved to Scotland in 1993 and is now qualified by residence. Sales director of an Edinburgh brewery.

ALEC DAVIES

Born 18.4.62 ... **right-hand bat** ... wicket-keeper

Born in Rawalpindi. Made his Scotland debut in 1993 and has gone on to make 59 appearances for his country. Played for Surrey second team against touring Sri Lankans a decade ago, where he rivalled Alec Stewart for the 'keeping berth. Stylish bat, joined West Lothian from Grange last season. By trade, a sports development officer for West Lothian Council.

NICK DYER

Born 10.6.69 ... **right-arm medium**

Made his first-class debut against Ireland in 1997 and played out the last 15 deliveries with his partner to save the match with nine wickets down. Renowned for his nagging accuracy in the limited-over game. Plays Sussex

League cricket and is a primary school teacher in Hampshire by trade with time booked off this summer, no doubt!

SCOTT GOURLAY
Born 8.1.71 ... **right-hand bat** ... right-arm medium

Consistent all-rounder and certainly a useful late-order bat. He made his debut in the 1995 Triple Crown Tournament but reserved his best bowling figures for the ICC Trophy in 1997, taking three for 26 against Kenya. Has represented his country on more than 20 occasions.

DOUGLAS LOCKHART
Born 19.1.76 ... **right-hand bat** ... wicket-keeper

Highly promising opening batsman and likely to take over wicket-keeping duties from Alec Davies when he retires. Captained Scotland's Under-19 team in 1995 International Youth Tournament, winning Player of Tournament award. Impressed again when he scored 119 not out against the Earl of Arundel's team in 1996.

BRYN LOCKIE
Born 5.6.68 ... **right-hand bat**

Opening bat who made his Scotland debut in 1995. Scored a classy 74 against MCC at Lord's a year later and also shared in a match-winning partnership against Ireland of 198 in 1996. Began the 1998 season with three half centuries, two in the Benson and Hedges Cup. Plays for the Carlton Club, Edinburgh. A contemporary of Warwickshire's Dougie Brown at the Arns in Alloa with Clackmannan County, Lockie has taken a year off his job as assistant PE head at Daniel Stewart's Melville College, Edinburgh to prepare for the World Cup, spending the winter playing for Perth, WA.

CRAIG MACKELLAR
Born 30.5.79 ... **left-arm medium**

A reliable medium pace bowler who plays club cricket for the Royal High Stewart's Melville Club. Not expected to feature prominently in Scotland's World Cup campaign, though.

GREGOR MAIDEN
Born 22.7.79 ... **right-hand bat** ... right-arm off-spin

Member of the Scotland squad for the 1997 Youth World Cup in South Africa. A sound lower-order batsman, he is likely to understudy medium pacer and off-spin rival Nick Dyer. A brilliant outfielder with safe hands and powerful throwing arm, he made his Scotland debut against MCC at Lord's in 1998. Plays for West of Scotland Club, Glasgow and is a student at Loughborough University.

DREW PARSONS
Born 26.2.75 ... **left-hand bat** ... left arm medium

Made his Scotland debut in 1997 against Durham in the Costcutter Cup. Aggressive batsman, who bowls occasionally. Graduated from Scotland Under-16, Under-19 and 'B' levels. Plays for the Prestwick Club and recently spent a second winter playing in Australia. Has taken a year out of his studies to stake his claim for a World Cup place for this summer's tournament.

BRUCE PATTERSON
Born 29.1.65 ... **right-hand bat**

The date Sunday, May 16, 1999 is already marked in red ink in this man's diary. Barring accident, he will make his 99th appearance for Scotland on that day against Australia in their opening group match of this summer's World Cup.

Patterson has been a prolific run-scorer since crowning his debut for Scotland in 1988 with a century against Ireland. But arguably his best innings was the 70 he scored against Allan Border's touring Australians in 1989. He had to negotiate Merv Hughes at his best in playing against a powerful line-up which included Steve Waugh.

Born in Ayr, he has shared the burden of Scotland's run-getting with his opening partner, Iain Philip, for the past decade. He plays for his hometown club now after spells as a professional cricketer with Edinburgh Academicals and Clydesdale before returning to his roots in 1995.

The disappointment of exclusion from Scotland's squad for the ICC Trophy tournament in Malaysia in 1997 was offset by a century against Denmark on his return to the side and is now geared up for the challenge of World Cup cricket.

Patterson holds a sports coaching diploma and works as an estate agent in Glasgow — but not on May 16!

IAIN PHILIP
Born 9.6.58 ... **right-hand bat**

Known as the 'Legend', he has scored a record aggregate of 4,730 runs for Scotland since making his debut in 1986.

He will be making his record 130th appearance for his country if he is chosen to open the batting against Australia in the opening group match of the World Cup at Worcester on May 16.

And he can expect some jocular 'sledging' from the Aussies, for Philip spends six months a year playing cricket in Perth, Western Australia where he spent his formative years.

Born in Stenhousemuir, he moved to Australia at the age of 11 so he would have been delighted in more ways than one with the century he scored last summer against an Australian 'A' attack which included Jason Gillespie and Brendan Julien.

Philip took his place in the history books in 1991 with an innings of 234 against MCC, the highest ever individual score by a Scotland player and he is now his country's most capped player.

He has also scored more centuries (11) for his country than any other batsman and has even kept wicket in a number of one-day matches for Scotland in various competitons.

Temperamentally sound, an elegant timer of the ball, with a sublime cover drive, he is a member of Stenhousemuir Cricket Club.

KEITH SHERIDAN
Born 26.3.71 ... **left arm spin**

Made his Scotland debut against the MCC aged 18 in 1989 and is the product of coaching schemes run by former national coach Omar Henry.

Has played more than 50 matches for Scotland with a best bowling performance of 5-48 against Transvaal University on Scotland's South Africa tour of 1992.

Hit the headlines when he scalped Mark and Steve Waugh in a five for 65 performance against the touring Australians in 1997 and also took four for 34 in the ICC Trophy third place play-off win against Ireland that year.

MICHAEL SMITH
Born 30.3.66 ... **right-hand bat** ... right-arm medium

Under-achieving, gifted top order batsman who struggles to convert 30s into half-centuries. Scored 79 against Ireland on his Scotland debut back in 1987 but fell out of favour with the Scotland selectors from 1990 to 94. Returned to the international scene and hit an unbeaten century against MCC at Lord's in 1994. Plays for Aberdeenshire Club. Born in Edinburgh, he is the son of a doctor.

IAN STANGER
Born 5.10.71 ... **right-hand bat** ... right-arm medium

A superb all-rounder with match-winning qualities, he made his debut for Scotland in 1992. Has gone on to make 57 appearances and would have made many more had he not been handicapped by a string of injuries.

He was Scotland's Young Cricketer of the Year in 1992 and 1993 and joined Leicestershire the following year but was released at the end of the 1994 season.

Stanger has played for Scotland 'B' and captained his country at Under-16 and Under-19 levels and also led Scottish Universities when he was studying at Dundee University.

He has spent two winters away, playing cricket in Perth, Western Australia in 1988-89 and for Stellenbosch, South Africa in 1994-95, where he also acted as assistant coach to Omar Henry, head of cricket at Stellenbosch University.

He was one of his side's most successful batsmen against the touring Australia 'A' team last summer and will be looking for a repeat performance against the Aussies when they meet in World Cup action on May 16.

PETER STEINDL
Born 14.6.70 ... **right-arm medium**

Victim of Scottish hospitality. From Bundaberg, Queensland, he joined Cupar Club as professional in 1991 and has stayed ever since. Married a Scottish girl and has two daughters. Made 23 appearances for Scotland without playing regularly at club level and despite being troubled by a back injury, bowled well for Scotland last season. He was a professional at Edinburgh Academicals before joining Grange Club as an amateur but has now left them and is currently in between clubs.

ANDREW TENNANT
Born 17.2.66 ... **left-arm spin**

Made his Scotland debut in 1994 and has also played for the 'B' team. Gave his best performance in the 1996 Benson and Hedges Cup match against Yorkshire at Headingley where he came up against frontline Australian Michael Bevan and recorded match figures of 10-1-29-2. Imparts more spin than Keith Sheridan but lacks his control.

KEVIN THOMSON
Born 24.12.71 ... **right-arm fast medium**

Made his Scotland debut in 1992 and offers strong opening bowling support to the Brinkley-Butt spearhead. He is a product of the Scotland Under-15, Under-16, Under-19 and 'B' teams. Nearing 50 caps but blighted by injury problems. He was offered trials by Durham and now plays for Aberdeenshire Club but struggles to get time off work as a plumber.

FRASER WATTS
Born 5.6.79 ... **right-hand bat**

Opening batsman. Made his Scotland debut last summer against Bangladesh. Tipped to take over from Bruce Patterson when he retires but is not expected to figure in Scotland's World Cup first team. Superb outfielder, the Loughborough University student is tipped as one for the future and is sure to get his chance soon.

GREIG WILLIAMSON
Born 20.12.68 ... **right-hand bat ...** right-arm medium

Made his Scotland debut in 1989 but was then omitted from the international scene until 1993. Re-established himself and has been a regular ever since.

His best performance was against the touring West Indies in 1995, taking three for 68 and then scoring 57 against a side containing Courtney Walsh, Winston Benjamin and Rajindra Dhanraj.

One of Scotland's Players of the Year in 1996, he is more of a middle-order bat than a bowler.

Given the christian names John Greig after the legendary Glasgow Rangers and Scotland football captain, Williamson plays his league cricket for the Clydesdale Club.

CRAIG WRIGHT
Born 28.4.74 ... **right-hand bat ...** right-arm medium

Given his Scotland chance in 1997 against Ireland and is another product of his country's flourishing youth system. Took five wickets against Worcestershire in the NatWest Trophy in 1998. Plays for West of Scotland Club and is a Development Officer with the Scottish Cricket Union. Born in Paisley, he is a seam bowling all-rounder and is another tipped to have a great future in the game.

❶ TO WATCH **GAVIN HAMILTON**

Born 16.9.74 ... **right-hand bat** ... right-arm fast medium

The conversation between David Graveney, Chairman of the England selectors, and the young Yorkshire all-rounder was short and sweet.

It happened during the Fifth Test between England and South Africa at Headingley and went something like this: "Excuse me, but given the opportunity, would you like to be considered for England?" asked Graveney. "Certainly, sir, I'd love to give it a go" replied the player. "Then I suggest you keep your options open," suggested Graveney.

Those 'options' have caused a major headache for the Scottish Cricket Union in planning their World Cup campaign. For Broxburn-born Gavin Hamilton, whose international opportunities hitherto have been confined to matches for Scotland, has suddenly been given the chance to play for England.

At the turn of the year, the Yorkshire all-rounder was the subject of much debate between officials of ECB, SCU and ICC, with his registration to play for England, Hamilton's preferred choice, or Scotland, much in doubt as the World Cup 1999 approached.

Fortunately, there is understanding and compassion rather than any tug-of-war on all sides as this outstanding player with dual qualification was permitted to play for Scotland with no risk to an England future.

He, naturally, wants to play Test cricket, whilst retaining gratitude and fond memories of his time with Scotland in his formative years. Understandably, national coach Jim Love retains slim hopes of picking him for Scotland. His selection for England's squad for the Super Max 8s tournament in Perth last October, which was cancelled at the last minute, caused further confusion over his future at international level. Then it was thrown into total chaos when Hamilton was the shock name in England's 30-man World Cup squad.

Hamilton, whose father was a long-serving player for West Lothian and his brother a regular for Scotland and Aberdeenshire, says: "Once I had listened to David Graveney, I knew my future lay with England and not Scotland."

His form with bat and ball for Yorkshire last summer propelled him into international contention. He produced the second-best all-round performance in Yorkshire's history, after George Hirst, in grabbing 10 wickets and scoring 149 in the match against Glamorgan, and finished with match figures of 11 for 72, which included a career-best seven for 50 against Surrey.

Of the cancelled England trip to Perth under Mike Gatting's management, he said: "The England trip would have been the icing on the cake at the end of a season in which everything began to click for me. There has never been any contest between England and Scotland but who knows what the future holds."

WISDEN WORLD CUP VERDICT

There's a joke that Scottish dictionaries don't include the words 'Second phase of the World Cup'. The phrase won't be needed this time, either, and the Scots will be out to avoid heavy defeats when they take on the four Test teams in their group. They'll be confident of a home victory against Bangladesh in Edinburgh, though.

WEST INDIES

GROUP B • Australia • Bangladesh • New Zealand • Pakistan • Scotland • **West Indies**

No country competing in the 1999 World Cup has achieved better results in the tournament than the West Indies.

They won the first tournament, held in England in 1975, and when Lord's hosted the 1979 World Cup final, Clive Lloyd raised the Prudential Assurance trophy high on the balcony to signal another famous triumph.

Incredibly, West Indies battled to the World Cup final in 1983 to make it a hat-trick of appearances at Lord's, but this time the trophy went to India, the underdogs, in a 43-run victory.

Many of the West Indies stars in those days counted England as their second home. A large proportion of the squad held overseas contracts with the English counties and England as a venue for the first three tournaments was as familiar as playing kids cricket in their own backyard.

The removal of the World Cup from England between the 1983 tournament and its return in 1999 has coincided with West Indies' failure to mount the same impact on the competition that they had in the early years.

When the World Cup was played in India and Pakistan in 1987, England destroyed their hopes of reaching the later stages with two victories over them on a triumphant march to the final.

The fifth World Cup in 1992 confirmed the West Indies loss of momentum as the calypso kings of limited-overs cricket when defeat by South Africa left them with an uphill task of making progress from the preliminary group matches — a task they failed.

If the 1992 tournament gave the West Indies Cricket Board cause for concern, the 1996 tournament proved their side was in disarray and that the Caribbean was no longer the cricketing stronghold it had been for three decades.

Paradoxically, they managed to reach the semi-finals, where they were slain by Australia but not before they had been made victims of the most famous giantkilling act in World Cup history. They were routed by Kenya!

Fielding a side containing only one professional player, Kenya bowled out the West Indies for 93 in response to their score of 166.

Roused by an unbeaten 93 from their beleaguered captain Richie Richardson, they beat Australia four days later to reach the last eight and then defeated favourites South Africa to make the semi-finals on the strength of a brilliant match-winning century by Brian Lara.

Australia beat them in the semis to leave the West Indies a battered cricket force and the selectors needing to launch a team rebuilding programme with some urgency.

Three years later they now arrive in England to contest their seventh World Cup in the midst of the overhaul the Caribbean cricket authorities duly ordered.

Since the 1996 tournament their form has fluctuated between the impressive and promising to the worrying and downright disappointing.

Lara has yet to stamp his full authority as captain; the West Indies board are short of funds; and the game at domestic level in the Caribbean lacks the sponsorship it needs to thrive.

Overseas contract offers from English counties are less plentiful than they were when Clive Lloyd and Viv Richards were Test captains and the lure of the American dollar is persuading some youngsters from the islands to seek sporting fame and fortune in the USA, rather than take the traditional gravy train to cricketing glory that Sir Garfield Sobers and countless others have ridden for the past 40 years.

But it will be a brave man who dismisses this part-revitalised team's chances of clinching a third World Cup title when they line up in Group B alongside Australia, Pakistan, New Zealand, Bangladesh and Scotland.

They have the toughest of opening matches against 1992 World Cup winners Pakistan at Bristol on Sunday, May 16 and then they face the prospect of a colourful fixture against World Cup newcomers Bangladesh in Dublin on Friday, May 21 where they once suffered catastrophic defeat by the Irish.

West Indies approach the 1999 tournament in slightly better fettle than they did the last one. Lara has been ensconced as captain after losing the job briefly last autumn when both he, and Carl Hooper, the vice-captain, were involved in a dispute over terms and conditions before the West Indies' tourists departure for South Africa.

The acrimonious showdown was sorted out in an hotel near Heathrow airport, and when the reinstated Lara finally led his men to Johannesburg, he stepped off the aircraft to announce: "We are sorry if we caused offence and we apologise to the people of South Africa for the delay. These things happen in sport!"

But they had a nightmare time on the tour and were soundly thrashed in the Test series by Hansie Cronje's team as further questions were asked of the West Indies talent — and application.

But the composition of recent West Indies squads make them irresistible value for money. Lara remains the most dangerous slayer of all types of bowling in Test and one-day cricket. Carl Hooper has at last emerged from the cocoon of mediocre scores that shrouded his early Test career to become a full blown matchwinner although he went back into his shell on the recent tour to South Africa.

Shivnarine Chanderpaul's six hours and 20 minutes stay of occupation to score 182 against South Africa 'A' just before Christmas illustrates his capacity to play the anchor-role to Lara's blitzes.

There are ominous signs also that as Curtly Ambrose and Courtney Walsh, surprisingly sacked by Gloucestershire in December, begin to fade from the scene of so many wicket-shattering triumphs, their famous footholds will be filled by another battery of fastmen, which includes Franklyn Rose, Nixon McLean and Mervyn Dillon.

Dinanath Ramnarine and Hooper, who provide a spin option if the pace fails, complement an attack that begins to look like it could carry the same damaging menace of former West Indies strike-forces.

Inevitably, Lara holds most of the keys to West Indies' hopes of maintaining progress as a world cricket power. He has yet to bring the same authority Frank Worrell, Garfield Sobers, Clive Lloyd and Viv Richards brought to the job and he was hurt by the criticism over the debacle in South Africa but the signs of maturity are beginning to show. Now he faces the awesome responsibility of leading a proud cricketing country along a comeback trail that could yet lead to glory.

WORLD CUP HIGHLIGHT
Becoming the first holders of the World Cup after skipper Clive Lloyd's majestic ton had helped them to a 17-run win over Australia at Lord's.

WORLD CUP RECORD

1975	Beat Australia in the final
1979	Beat England in the final
1983	Lost to India in the final
1987	Eliminated at group stage
1992	Eliminated at group stage
1996	Lost to Australia in the semi-finals

WORLD CUP ODDS: 10-1

CAPTAIN **BRIAN LARA**
Born 2.5.69 ... **left-hand bat**

O ne of the truly great West Indies batsmen to emerge since the last War and certainly the most exciting player in the world to watch when he is on top form at the crease.

The 'Lara versus Tendulkar' debate on who has the right to be called the 'King of Cricketers' will rage through the 1999 World Cup and beyond. Clearly both are blessed with genius, and if the Indian has that extra measure of consistency, then the West Indies captain can claim greater box office appeal.

The unparalleled glut of batting records that fell to him between April and June 1994 amazed the cricket world — and made an impact further afield.

He made a world record shattering Test score of 375 against England in Antigua, a world record first-class score of 501 not out for Warwickshire against Durham, and completed a unique sequence of seven hundreds in eight innings.

At the height of this avalanche of runs he passed the 1,000 mark in an English season in only seven innings to equal Don Bradman's record.

Born in Cantaro, a village in Trinidad's Santa Cruz Valley, he shaped his future career in cricket by using a broom stick to hammer a 'ball', fashioned from chunks of lime or marble, against a garage door.

At three, his father gave him a cutdown bat and at six he was receiving professional coaching.

He emerged as a 'tour de force' in the 1992 World Cup, scoring 333 runs in the eight matches, and confirmed his threat to all-comers playing the longer game by scoring 277 against Australia in the Sydney Test the following year.

Former West Indies star Rohan Kanhai observed: "That was one of the greatest innings I've ever seen."

And after his world best 375, he dedicated his innings to his late father's memory, saying: "I had some bad influences in my time and, if my parents weren't there to straighten me out, things might have gone haywire. I thank them for that."

He replaced Courtney Walsh as West Indies captain for the series against England in 1997-98 and was appointed Warwickshire's captain in 1998, in his second spell there.

Off the edge

• More than half the 333 runs he made in eight World Cup matches in 1992 were scored in boundaries.

• **Lara took five Tests to score his first century.**

• He was voted Trinidad and Tobago's Sportsman of the Year in 1993.

• **The left-hander reclaimed his old Red Stripe Cup record in 1994 with 715 runs in five matches.**

• Of the 219 runs scored against Jamaica when he was at the wicket for Trinidad in 1994, all but 39 came from his bat.

• **His father was superintendent at a government agricultural station.**

• He bats left-handed but plays golf right-handed and can often be found at the Belfry.

• **When scoring his 4,000th run in Tests, he was averaging 54 per innings with 10 centuries and 20 fifties.**

• He is a close friend of Manchester United's Trinidad-born striker, Dwight Yorke.

• **During his world record 501 not out against Durham, he hit 174 runs before lunch on one day.**

JIMMY ADAMS
Born 9.1.68 ... **left-hand bat ...** left-arm spin

One of the most underrated members of the West Indies squad. In recent years, when the top-order batting has wobbled under pressure, the Jamaican left-hander has often steadied the innings and given his side an outlet from which they have turned disaster into triumph.

Born in Port Maria, Jamaica, his Test potential as an all-rounder surfaced on a tour to England in 1985 with West Indies Young Cricketers. He played three `Tests' that summer and went on to tour Australia with Young West Indies in 1988.

A member of the West Indies 'B' touring squad to Zimbabwe in 1986 and 1989, he proved that all the grooming and groundwork had not been wasted years when he made an impressive start to his Test career against South Africa in 1991-92.

He scored an unbeaten 79 and took four crucial wickets to reward the selectors' faith in their belief that they had uncovered a player of rare substance.

Since then reliability has become his trademark. He averaged 62 against England in the Caribbean in 1993-94 and scored unbeaten centuries against India in Nagpur and Chandigarh in 1994-95. He completed that three Test tour with 520 runs, averaging 173, and went on to score 151 against New Zealand.

Adams played one season for Nottinghamshire in 1994 and toured England in 1995 with unspectacular results. He still struggles on occasions, making no impression on the West Indies home series against England in 1997-98 but the ability is there.

He flew home from the 1998-99 tour to South Africa after cutting a tendon in his hand with a bread-knife on the outward flight. He didn't play a game on the tour, which given their poor form was probably a blessing in disguise for him.

CURTLY AMBROSE
Born 21.9.63 ... **right-arm fast**

Mike Atherton's assessment of Australia's fast bowler Glenn McGrath at the end of the 1997 Ashes tour to England was short and succinct. "He's just like Curtly, gives you nothing!" said the England opener.

Those seven words were as much a tribute to the great West Indian fast bowler as they were to the Aussie newcomer.

Few pacemen in cricket history have mastered the art of bowling the 'dot ball' better than the giant Antiguan, often delivered at speeds ranging between 80-90 mph.

Rated the most feared fast bowler on the world circuit for a full decade, it is hard to believe that the 6ft 7ins giant was more interested in basketball than cricket as a teenager.

He made his mark in the West Indies regional competition in 1987-88, his first full season, by taking a record 35 wickets costing only 15.51 runs apiece.

The West Indies selectors worked swiftly to harness his talents, thrusting him into Test cricket in April, 1988 against Pakistan at Bourda.

He toured England for the first time in 1988 but it was at Bridgetown in 1989-90 that the cricketing world first recognised his potential. He took a career best eight for 45 against England, producing the lethal yorkers and bouncers that were to become his trademark over the next decade.

He celebrated his contract with Northants in 1989 by taking a wicket with his first delivery in the Championship and the wickets have tumbled ever since.

And Ambrose has his name firmly etched in history now as one of only an elite quartet of West Indies bowlers to have taken more than 300 Test wickets.

KEITH ARTHURTON
Born 21.2.65 ... **left-hand bat ...** slow left arm

Only the third Test cricketer to come from the island of Nevis. A dashing, left-handed strokemaker who has learned to be more patient and selective after seeking the counsel of Sir Garfield Sobers and Geoffrey Boycott. Became established as quality middle-order batsman on the 1992-93 tour to Australia but has lost his way a bit since the England tour of 1995.

KENNY BENJAMIN
Born 8.4.67 ... **right-arm fast medium**

Plagued by injuries since Test debut against South Africa in 1991-92. Joined Worcestershire in 1993 but suffered recurring hamstring problems and was given an early release after taking 37 wickets in his 11 matches. Claimed 22 England victims in 1993-94 and clinched series saving victory in India with five for 65 in 1994-95.

IAN BISHOP
Born 24.10.67 ... **right-arm fast**

A stress fracture of the back has repeatedly threatened his career. Had established himself in front rank of world's best bowlers when he first broke down in 1990-91 but after an absence of 20 months he returned successfully to play against Australia in 1992-93. His back flared up again after two home Tests against Pakistan in 1992-93 but he was leading Test wicket-taker with 27 on 1995 England tour. Played fewer than 40 Tests in a decade.

COURTNEY BROWNE
Born 7.12.70 ... **right-hand bat ...** wicket-keeper

Made his debut for Barbados in 1990-91 and two years later set a record for the most dismissals in a domestic season with 23 catches and four stumpings. Made his first Test appearance against Australia in 1994-95 to crown a remarkable season. Led Barbados to Red Stripe Cup in his first season as captain in 1994-95 but has now fallen behind Ridley Jacobs as the first-choice wicket-keeper for West Indies.

SHERWIN CAMPBELL
Born 1.11.70 ... **right-hand bat**

Only 20 when he made his first-class debut for Barbados. Took four years to establish himself, finishing fourth behind Brian Lara, Stuart Williams and Jimmy Adams in the West Indian first-class averages with more than 500 runs, including three centuries, at an average of 54.70. Former captain of West Indies Youth, he made his Test debut in New Zealand, scoring 51 and 88 in his first two Tests. Sporadic appearances since.

SHIVNARINE CHANDERPAUL
Born 18.8.74 ... **left-hand bat ...** right-arm leg-spin

Solid, reliable, higher-order batsman who is likely to play a key role in the West Indies' side for the next 10 years.

He became the first teenager to play Test cricket for the West Indies for more than 20 years when he made his debut against England at Georgetown in 1994.

Some critics suspected his inclusion was designed to attract the Indian community in his native Guyana but the youngster more than justified his call-up by scoring the first of four half-centuries he produced in his first four Tests.

He is best remembered in that series for playing second fiddle to part of Brian Lara's world record breaking Test innings of 375. He shared a stand of 219 with Lara in that Antigua Test, displaying all the maturity of a proven Test batsman with an innings of 75 not out.

Chanderpaul finished third in the Test batting in that series, averaging 57.60 behind Brian Lara and Jimmy Adams, and his future was cemented.

Two Test appearances on the tour to England in 1995 enhanced his growing reputation and by the time England went to the Caribbean in 1997-98, he was an established performer with a bright future.

A century – his second in Tests – against England at Guyana in February 1998 won him the Man of the Match award and by the time he scored 182 against South Africa 'A 'in Pietermaritzburg in December 1998 he had become the lynchpin of a sometimes fragile West Indies batting line-up.

Has occasionally been pushed up the order by his captain to open the batting in the one-day game.

RAJINDRA DHANRAJ
Born 6.2.69 ... **right-arm leg-spin**

Became the first leg-spin and googly bowler to play for the West Indies for nearly 18 years when he made his debut against India in Bombay in 1994-95. Took eight for 51 against Barbados a year earlier and was given another chance to shine on the international scene against New Zealand and then again on the West Indies' tour to England in 1995. But Dinanath Ramnarine's emergence as a top flight leg-spinner has reduced the Trinidadian's Test chances and he has fallen behind his rival in the pecking order.

MERVYN DILLON
Born 5.6.74 ... **right-arm fast**

One of the West Indies' brightest prospects as they search to replace Curtly Ambrose and Courtney Walsh. Former Hampshire and West Indies great, Malcolm Marshall, rates the Trinidadian highly. Cuts ball into batsmen off the seam but is working to move it the other way. Sometimes short on stamina and often injury troubled. He made his Test debut against India in 1996-97 and took four wickets for 148 runs in that series. Toured South Africa in 1998-99.

A LOOK AT...
CARL HOOPER

Hooper has been described as the great enigma of West Indies cricket. He was hailed as a future Test captain when he emerged from the Guyana youth side in the mid-1980s. But that bold forecast has never really materialised.

And he was rated so highly by former West Indies captains Clive Lloyd and Viv Richards that if Brian Lara was destined to become the Windies greatest batsman of the modern era, 'Hoops' was reckoned good enough to run him close. Again, that early optimism was ill-founded.

He scored only four centuries in his first 86 innings, averaging barely 30, but since then he has produced the brilliant strokeplay that he kept hidden for so long, shedding much of that reputation for underachievement.

Once asked to explain the erratic start to a Test career that began when Pakistan toured West Indies in 1987-88, he said: "In the past it's been difficult to exclude all the conflicting advice, and it's possible I've taken too much. I refuse to put more pressure on myself now, and our heavy workload has definitely undermined my technique on occasions as well."

There were times when only his steady off-spin bowling, which had clearly developed potency when England toured the Caribbean in 1997-98, and brilliant catching at slip, have kept him in the West Indies side.

But by the time England had completed their tour last winter the Guyanese-born Hooper had done much to establish himself in the West Indies team.

He joined Kent as their overseas recruit in 1992, and apart from non-availability for two seasons, consistently remained their heaviest run-getter until his departure at the end of the 1998 season.

A gently spoken, reserved man, he did take aboard one piece of advice in his time at Kent. The then coach Daryl Foster advised him to use a longer bat, to stand straighter with feet closer together.

"He's a good coach and shrewd judge," said Carl afterwards, as the runs began to flow again from his restless bat.

He was re-instated as the West Indies vice-captain for the tour of South Africa last winter after leading a protest with Brian Lara over the financial terms of the tourists playing contracts and looks set to play an important role in this summer's main event.

A hero in his time with Kent, Carl holds a special place in the history books of the club as one of only two men who have successfully cleared the lime tree at the Canterbury ground with bat in hand.

But while that challenge has been accepted and completed, the task of assisting Lara in the mission to rebuild confidence within the West Indian ranks is proving a more difficult one.

A 5-0 whitewash by the South Africans in their 1998-99 Test series has further questioned the spirit within a camp that was in disarray before they even stepped foot in Africa. Lara maintains that he and Hooper will get it right and take the boys from the Caribbean back to the top of the game. There will be no better place for the pair to achieve that than in England this summer.

THE STATS

Full name: Carl Llewellyn Hooper

Born: December 15, 1966 in Georgetown, Guyana

Role: Right-hand bat, right-arm off-spinner

Represents: Guyana, Kent, West Indies

Test debut: For West Indies against India at Bombay, Second Test, 1987-88.

One-day international debut: For West Indies against New Zealand at Dunedin, 1986-87.

Finest hour: Taking five for 26 against Sri Lanka at St Vincent in 1996-97.

Extras: Hooper has bagged more than 260 first class catches in his career.

NOW THAT'S A FACT

●Hooper first toured for the West Indies in 1987-88 when the team travelled to India.

●He withdrew from the 1995-96 tour to Australia and the World Cup through illness.

●The middle-order bat was replaced by Zimbabwe's Paul Strang when he was unavailable as Kent's overseas player in 1997.

●He scored 236 not out for Kent against Glamorgan at Canterbury in 1993.

●'Hoops' topped Kent's Championship batting averages in 1998 with 1,215 runs at an average of 45. He scored six centuries and one 50.

●He was reinstated as West Indies' vice-captain on November 9, 1998 after a contract dispute before West Indies' tour to South Africa.

●Carl lives in Telford with his English wife and daughter. He plans to work in real estate after retirement from the game.

●He scored 49 runs in 56 balls for West Indies in the final of the Wills International Tournament in Bangladesh on November 1, 1998.

●In 1998, Wisden Cricket Monthly readers voted him to bat at number four, behind Mark Taylor, Jacques Kallis and Mark Waugh, in their 'World 2nd XI' team.

●He was an Axa Equity & Law Award (Sunday League) winner in 1993 for scoring the most runs.

THE THINGS THEY SAY
HOOPER ON

❝I suffered through my shot selection but that's the way I play and I can't change.❞ On why he averaged barely 30 in his first 86 Test innings.

ON HOOPER

❝Hooper's assurance and strokeplay afford his batsmanship a veneer of rare nobility.❞ Stephen Thorpe, Sunday Times cricket writer before the West Indies tour to England in 1995.

VASBERT DRAKES
Born 5.8.69 ... **right-hand bat** ... right-arm fast medium

Talented all-rounder from Barbados. One-day specialist, called into West Indies' touring squad in England in 1995 when Winston Benjamin was sent home early for disciplinary reasons. Sussex's overseas player in 1996, he made a one-day international appearance against Australia in the 1994-95 series.

OTTIS GIBSON
Born 16.3.69 ... **right-hand bat** ... right-arm fast medium

Dangerous one-day specialist with capacity to hit crowd pleasing sixes. Played for Glamorgan in 1994 and did so well he gained selection for the West Indies' 1995 England tour. Made his Barbados debut in 1990-91 and has spent time playing for Farnworth in the Bolton League and Border in South Africa.

RIDLEY JACOBS
Born 26.11.67 ... **left-hand bat** ... wicket-keeper

Dangerous one-day batsman given his debut in second limited-overs international against England at Bridgetown on April 1, 1998 and scored a vital undefeated 28 in a one-wicket win. That secured the Antiguan his place for next three one-dayers. Toured South Africa in 1998-99.

CLAYTON LAMBERT
Born 10.2.62 ... **left-hand bat**

A full seven years after making his West Indies debut, he returned to the Test scene to gain his second cap in the Fifth Test against England at Kensington Oval, Bridgetown in March 1998.

His first call up for his country was as dramatic as his second. He was playing for Blackhall in the North Yorkshire and South Durham League when opening batsman Gordon Greenidge suffered a knee injury during the Texaco Trophy series at the beginning of West Indies' 1991 tour to England and Lambert was called in as replacement.

His Test debut coincided with Viv Richards' last appearance as captain when the Guyanan replaced the injured Gus Logie for the Fifth Cornhill Test at The Oval.

Lambert scored 39 and 14 before returning to Guyana for domestic regional cricket without regaining Test recognition until his shock recall several years later.

He made a much better fist of his sensational return, scoring 55 and 29 as the anchor foil for the more flamboyant Philo Wallace. He scored 104 in the next Test in Antigua, sharing an opening stand of 167 with Wallace in the first innings as the West Indies romped to a convincing victory by an innings and 52 runs.

A series average of 62.67 guaranteed his permanent return from Test exile and he was selected for the Test tour to South Africa in 1998-99.

NIXON McLEAN
Born 28.7.73 ... **right-arm fast**

Played four Tests against England in 1997-98 and dismissed Alec Stewart, Ben Hollioake and Graeme Hick cheaply in the Fourth one-day international at St Vincent, his birthplace. Made a major impact on the English county scene with Hampshire last year, becoming his side's leading Championship wicket-taker with 62 victims in his first season. His early career was blunted by pulled muscles and groin strains but he seems to overcome those problems now and is one of the new breed of West Indian quickies.

JUNIOR MURRAY
Born 20.1.68 ... **right-hand bat** ... wicket-keeper

Shares the gloves with Courtney Browne in the Test side after becoming the first Grenadian to play for West Indies, taking over from David Williams on the 1992-93 tour of Australia. Has scored some valuable Test runs in the lower order, including an 88-ball century against New Zealand in 1994-95. Not selected for 1997-98 tour of Pakistan and played only one Test against England later that winter but fought back to win a place on the South African tour in 1998-99. Fallen behind Ridley Jacobs in the pecking order though.

DINANATH RAMNARINE
Born 4.6.75 ... **right-arm leg-spin**

The Trinadad-born spinner has brought welcome variety to the West Indies' attack as their Test selectors ring the changes to discover a new winning combination to find success through the millennium.

An aggressive bowler, his rapid progress has restricted the opportunities extended to his rival Rajindra Dhanraj.

Ramnarine bowls with the minimum of fuss and the maximum commitment, giving batsmen little time to relax between one delivery and the next.

He made a major breakthrough at Test level on England's tour to the Caribbean in 1997-98, making his international debut at Georgetown, Guyana in February 1998.

And he celebrated his call up by making Graham Thorpe his first scalp, going on to claim the wickets of Jack Russell and Angus Fraser to finish with a bowling analysis of three for 26 from 17 overs.

Surprisingly, he was omitted from the next Test in Barbados but returned for the Sixth Test in Antigua where his spin wizardry claimed Thorpe again.

He finished with the very impressive figures of four for 29 in England's first innings as the West Indies stormed to victory by an innings and 52 runs.

His retention for the tour to South Africa in 1998-99 was inevitable and although he returned home early because of injury without playing a Test, there is genuine hope that, at last, West Indies have found a spinner who could become good enough to be rated alongside the great Lance Gibbs.

FRANKLYN ROSE
Born 1.2.72 ... **right-arm fast**

Made a sensational Test debut at Kingston, Jamaica in March 1997 by taking six for 100 in India's first innings, including the prized scalps of Tendulkar,

Ganguly and Azharuddin. Played all five Tests, taking 18 wickets in the series. Selected for only one Test on England's tour in 1997-98 but gained valuable experience as Northants' overseas star in 1998, taking 50 Championship wickets. Chosen for the West Indies tour to South Africa in 1998-99. Cuts ball away off seam with nasty bouncer his shock weapon.

PHIL SIMMONS
Born 18.4.63 ... **right-hand bat** ... right-arm medium

A one-day expert with experience of two World Cups, Simmons has made more than 20 Test appearances for the West Indies side without establishing himself as a regular in five-day international cricket over the past 10 years or so.

The feeling persists in his native Trinidad that he is often discriminated against by the West Indies Test selectors. But he excels at the limited-over version of the game with well over 100 appearances for his country in one-day internationals.

Toured England for the first time in 1988 and needed a life-saving operation on that trip after fracturing his skull ducking into a short delivery in the match against Gloucestershire.

He never quite produced the runs his early career form promised but over the years has managed to play his full part with some outstanding performances with bat and ball as a two-in-one performer in one-day cricket.

He crowned a remarkable debut in England for Leicestershire in 1994 by scoring 261 against Northamptonshire and was a major factor in the county winning the Championship for only the second time in their history in 1996.

Simmons averaged 56.54 with the bat in first-class matches that summer and took 56 wickets, being named as one of the prestigious Wisden Cricketers of the Year for 97.

He was not quite so effective with bat and ball at Grace Road last year as Leicestershire lifted the crown for the second time in three years and he was also part of the West Indies one-day squad that trounced England 4-1 in the Caribbean at the start of last year.

PHILO WALLACE
Born 2.8.70 ... **right-hand bat**

All the extravagant forecasts made about the Barbadian on his arrival in the West Indies one-day international side at the age of 21 came to fruition when his aggressive batting put England to the sword on their 1997-98 tour to the Caribbean.

He celebrated his call up for the Fifth Test on his home ground at Kensington Oval by scoring 45 and 61 with some electrifying strokeplay that, on occasions, left England's bowlers and fielders hanging their heads.

For two days, Mike Atherton's team had been in charge but on the fourth evening Wallace and Clayton Lambert launched a violent attack on England's bowlers and scored 71 in 19 overs.

The two openers repeated the dose in the next Test in Antigua, ending the second day with an unbroken stand of 126.

Wallace went on to score 92 in 182 minutes with a six and 11 fours. He had faced 134 deliveries and looked set to complete a maiden Test century when Dean Headley forced him to play on.

His success against England confirmed his selection for the West Indies tour to South Africa in 1998-99 but he failed miserably there. The hope is that this crowd-pleasing batsman can show some stickability to convince selectors that he can score runs on a consistent basis at the highest level. And they won't come any higher in the one-day game than this summer's World Cup.

COURTNEY WALSH
Born 30.10.62 ... **right-arm fast**

More than 100 Test appearances, more than 300 Test victims. No wonder Courtney Walsh is rated one of West Indies' greatest ever players in international cricket.

His acrimonious departure from Gloucestershire - announced in December 1998 — does nothing to diminish the massive contribution he has made to the game since breaking into the awesome West Indies Test team of 1984-85.

He first served notice of his potential by taking 10-43 in Jamaican schools cricket in 1979. He was one of the prestigious Wisden's Five Cricketers of the Year in 1987 and took a hat-trick against Australia on the West Indies' 1988-89 tour.

Walsh took over the captaincy of West Indies from Richie Richardson for the Test series in India and New Zealand in 1994-95 and took full control in 1995-96 after West Indies' tour to Australia.

He was replaced as captain by Brian Lara for the series against England in 1997-98, and became West Indies' record wicket-taker when he broke Malcolm Marshall's haul of 376 victims, against South Africa in 1998-99.

Born in Kingston, Jamaica, he has forged a lethal bowling partnership with Curtly Ambrose over the past decade. At first he was rated no more than a willing workhorse but as his career gathered momentum, so did his reputation for destroying some of the world's best batting line-ups as he and Ambrose ruled the international scene.

No overseas player has given more commitment to his adopted English county than the 6ft 5½in Jamaican and he will be badly missed in Bristol where he became one of Gloucestershire's favourite adopted sons.

STUART WILLIAMS
Born 12.8.69 ... **right-hand bat**

Forcing opener whose Test debut against England in Antigua in 1993-94 was overshadowed by Brian Lara's world record 375. Lovely timer of the ball with fluent strokes, especially through the off-side. Born in Nevis, he has never quite established himself in the Test team because of lack of consistency and poor footwork against swinging delivery.

❶ TO WATCH **DARREN GANGA**
Born 14.1.79 ... **right-hand bat**

Not since Brian Lara reeled off seven centuries in one season for Fatima College, Port-of-Spain, at the age of 15, has a youngster from Trinidad sent pulses racing quite like Darren Ganga.

And at a time when the West Indies batting is in some disarray with places up for grabs, this gifted batsman is on the threshold of an outstanding future.

Skipper Lara clearly rates him highly, hence his shock selection for the West Indies tour party to South Africa in autumn 1998 at the age of 19.

Before the squad left, Lara observed: "When he returns from the tour, even if he hasn't played a Test, I'm sure he will be a better batsman, one we can look to in the future."

Ganga gained a firm foothold in the big time by scoring 138 — his maiden century in competition cricket — against Barbados in April 1998, two months after scoring 68 against a Jamaican attack which included Courtney Walsh and Franklyn Rose.

He also made 41 against England, a performance which prompted the England captain Mike Atherton to describe him as the best young batsman in the West Indies.

Lara has fought for Ganga's inclusion in the Trinidad side even when form sometimes deserted him on rare occasions in his formative years.

At a time when young sportsmen in the Caribbean are chasing the $US by turning to American basketball rather than the game on which their fathers were bred, here is a player whose technique, temperament and run-making ability is almost guaranteed to succeed if he stays free from injury.

He averaged only a modest 20.15 after nine first-class matches since his debut in 1996-97 and did little for the West Indies team competing in the Youth World Cup in South Africa in January 1998 or in the regional Under-19 Championships held in Trinidad last July.

But with youthful rivals Leon Garrick, Wavel Hinds, Floyd Reifer and Ramnaresh Sarwan all failing to advance their Test claims on the West Indies 'A' tour to South Africa in late 1997, Ganga leapfrogged the talented pack to become a surprise selection for the 16-man squad chosen to represent West Indies on the full tour to South Africa in 1998-99.

Lara assesses his batting prodigy thus: "He's a well-organised player, very mature for his age and has a great future. Certainly one of the brightest young prospects we have in the Caribbean."

WISDEN WORLD CUP VERDICT
They surely can't play as badly again as they did in South Africa, and Brian Lara could win a couple of matches off his own bat ... but most of the other batsmen don't look tight enough to stay in for long if the ball's moving about. Expect a couple of great days — and too many lazy days for them to reach the semi-finals.

PART THREE: MEMORIES

WORLD CUP 1975

The first World Cup, hosted by England, had humble cottage-cricket-industry beginnings. Eight countries participated in that tournament, a direct spin-off from the popularity and potential of the new one-day limited-overs game that had been introduced successfully to the English county domestic scene.

For years cricket enthusiasts all over the world had been left to judge for themselves who qualified as the unofficial world champion Test-playing country. No one could produce contrary evidence to doubt the assertion that England (1932), Australia (1948), West Indies (1950) and South Africa (1970) were world champions of their respective eras.

Now, here was a tournament designed specifically to produce the first official world champion cricket country.

Freeze-frame, slow-mo, split-screen, stump cameras and 'third umpires' sitting in the pavilion with instant video playback resources at their elbow were merely futuristic dreams in the minds of eccentric hi-tech boffins when that first World Cup tournament — covered only intermittently by a BBC outside broadcast unit — grossed receipts which paid the cricket authorities little more than £200,000.

It was the year in which Margaret Thatcher became Tory leader; President Nixon's aides were sentenced for the Watergate cover-up; a Channel Tunnel project was abandoned by the British government; 'Bye Bye Baby', 'Sailing' and 'I Can't Give You Anything' topped the hit parade; and *One Flew Over The Cuckoo's Nest* was a hit movie for Jack Nicholson.

Six Test-playing countries, plus East Africa and Sri Lanka, participated in the first World Cup. South Africa were unable to compete because of their apartheid regime.

The teams were divided into two groups of four and the top two in each group would then meet in a knockout semi-final round. Each match would consist of 60 overs per side — the same number used in England's popular Gillette Cup competition.

England's major Test grounds at Lord's, Edgbaston, Headingley and Old Trafford were used to stage the first four matches.

The game between Australia and Pakistan, at Headingley, was a sell-out. Australia, who battled through to the final, reached 278 for seven, with Ross Edwards making 80 not out. Elite Pakistan batsmen Sadiq,

Zaheer and Mushtaq perished cheaply but Majid Khan hit 65 and Asif Iqbal and Wasim Raja carried the score to 181 for four off 41 overs before Dennis Lillee (five for 34) returned to demolish the tail and carry Australia to victory.

Two months later Headingley was in the headlines again — front page headlines. Yorkshire groundsman George Cawthray removed the covers that had protected his World Cup strip to discover that vandals, leading a campaign to overturn a jail sentence for armed robbery imposed on a man named George Davis, had caused irreparable damage to the Test Match pitch, causing the Ashes match to be abandoned.

Dennis Amiss, now the chief executive at Warwickshire, scored 137 in a 202-run victory for England against India, at Lord's, and tournament minnows East Africa and Sri Lanka fell to New Zealand, inspired by Glenn Turner's unbeaten 171, and West Indies.

The crowds were absorbed by the cut-and-thrust of the cricket in the opening group round and by the time Sri Lanka moved to the threshold of victory over the mighty Aussies in the second round of matches, they were positively hooked.

Australia's fast bowler Jeff Thomson was cast as the villain of the hour when his cold-blooded barrage of short and full pitched deliveries forced potential Sri Lankan match-winners Wettimuny and Mendis to retire hurt for treatment at London's St.Thomas's Hospital when both were well established. Australia won by 52 runs and the real prospect of a giantkilling act was lost.

Meanwhile, Keith Fletcher, later to become England coach, led his side to victory over New Zealand with a brilliant innings of 131 and India proved there was no room for sentiment by crushing East Africa by 10 wickets with 30.1 overs to spare.

Pakistan pace bowler Sarfraz Nawaz (four for 44) blew away West Indies' powerful batting line-up only to see his victory hopes dashed by tail-enders Deryck Murray and Andy Roberts in a 64-run 10th wicket stand to win the game as World Cup 75 ebbed and flowed to the delight of large crowds.

The clash between Australia and West Indies was the pick of the third stage battles. West Indies spearhead Andy Roberts restricted Australia to a total of 192 on an Oval pitch favouring pace but when Lillee and Thomson, the world's most famed warhead, went to work, they seemed to be firing rubber bullets. Alvin Kallicharran hit Lillee for 35 off 10 deliveries and the 'calypso-kings' sped to victory.

Unfortunately for England, the 'George Davis' supporters were not around when Mike Denness' team were inserted on a damp, substandard Headingley pitch in the semi-final match against Australia. They were bowled out for 93 in 36.2 overs, with Gary Gilmour celebrating figures of six for 14. Then Gilmour and Doug Walters led Australia to victory with a 55-run stand after they had been reduced to 39 for six.

The other semi-final between New Zealand and West Indies, at The Oval, was another disappointing game. The Kiwis crawled to 158 in 52.2 overs and Gordon Greenidge and Kallicharran scored half-centuries to steer their team into the first final with almost 20 overs to spare.

Lord's was at its loveliest for the first World Cup final between Australia and West Indies on Saturday, 21st June when 26,000 spectators swept into English cricket's headquarters on a scorching summer's day to watch Clive Lloyd lead his men to victory.

Asked to bat, West Indies were in trouble at 50 for three, before Rohan Kanhai, 55, and Lloyd, who scored a century off 82 balls, carried the innings to a respectable total of 291.

There were solid contributions from Ian Chappell (62) and Alan Turner (40) but Keith Boyce's four wickets, aided by five run-outs, left Australia 17 runs short with the Lord's clock showing 8.42pm at the end.

Lloyd, named Man of the Match, received the Prudential Assurance-sponsored trophy from Prince Philip as the West Indies' jubilant supporters blew horns, bashed tin cans together and danced for joy on the outfield beneath the famous Lord's balcony. The first World Cup was their's.

ENGLAND v AUSTRALIA

Semi-Final at Headingley on 18th June. Australia won by four wickets. Toss: Australia.

ENGLAND

D.L.Amiss lbw b Gilmour	2
B.Wood b Gilmour	6
K.W.R.Fletcher lbw b Gilmour	8
A.W.Greig c Marsh b Gilmour	7
F.C.Hayes lbw b Gilmour	4
*M.H.Denness b Walker	27
†A.P.E.Knott lbw b Gilmour	0
C.M.Old c G.S.Chappell b Walker	0
J.A.Snow c Marsh b Lillee	2
G.G.Arnold not out	18
P.Lever lbw b Walker	5
L-b 5, w 7, n-b 2	14
TOTAL (36.2 overs)	93

AUSTRALIA

A.Turner lbw b Arnold	7
R.B.McCosker b Old	15
*I.M.Chappell lbw b Snow	2
G.S.Chappell lbw b Snow	4
K.D.Walters not out	20
R.Edwards b Old	0
†R.W.Marsh b Old	5
G.J.Gilmour not out	28
M.H.N.Walker	
D.K.Lillee	
J.R.Thomson	
B 1, l-b 6, n-b 6	13
TOTAL (28.4 overs; 6 wickets)	94

BOWLING: Lillee 9-3-26-1; Gilmour 12-6-14-6; Walker 9.2-3-22-3; Thomson 6-0-17-0.

BOWLING: Arnold 7.4-2-15-1; Snow 12-0-30-2; Old 7-2-29-3; Lever 2-0-7-0.

FALL OF WICKETS

1/2 2/11 3/26 4/33 5/35 6/36 7/37 8/52 9/73 10/93

FALL OF WICKETS

1/17 2/24 3/32 4/32 5/32 6/39

WEST INDIES v NEW ZEALAND

Semi-Final at The Oval on 18th June. West Indies won by five wickets. Toss: West Indies.

NEW ZEALAND

*G.M.Turner c Kanhai b Roberts	36
J.F.M.Morrison lbw b Julien	5
G.P.Howarth c Murray b Roberts	51
J.M.Parker b Lloyd	3
B.F.Hastings not out	24
†K.J.Wadsworth c Lloyd b Julien	11
B.J.McKechnie lbw b Julien	1
D.R.Hadlee c Holder b Julien	0
B.L.Cairns b Holder	10
H.J.Howarth b Holder	0
R.O.Collinge b Holder	2
B 1, l-b 5, w 2, n-b 7	15
TOTAL (52.2 overs)	158

BOWLING: Julien 12-5-27-4; Roberts 11-3-18-2; Holder 8.2-0-30-3; Boyce 9-0-31-0; Lloyd 12-1-37-1.

FALL OF WICKETS
1/8 2/98 3/106 4/106 5/125 6/133 7/139 8/155 9/155 10/158

WEST INDIES

R.C.Fredericks c Hastings b Hadlee	6
C.G.Greenidge lbw b Collinge	55
A.I.Kallicharran c and b Collinge	72
I.V.A.Richards lbw b Collinge	5
R.B.Kanhai not out	12
*C.H.Lloyd c Hastings b McKechnie	3
B.D.Julien not out	4
†D.L.Murray	
K.D.Boyce	
V.A.Holder	
A.M.E.Roberts	
L-b 1, n-b 1	2
TOTAL (40.1 overs; 5 wickets)	159

BOWLING: Collinge 12-4-28-3; Hadlee 10-0-54-1; Cairns 6.1-2-23-0; McKechnie 8-0-37-1; H.J.Howarth 4-0-15-0.

FALL OF WICKETS
1/8 2/133 3/139 4/142 5/151

AUSTRALIA v WEST INDIES

Final at Lord's, on 21st June. West Indies won by 17 runs. Toss: Australia.

WEST INDIES

R.C.Fredericks hit wicket b Lillee	7
C.G.Greenidge c Marsh b Thomson	13
A.I.Kallicharran c Marsh b Gilmour	12
R.B.Kanhai b Gilmour	55
*C.H.Lloyd c Marsh b Gilmour	102
I.V.A.Richards b Gilmour	5
K.D.Boyce c G.S.Chappell b Thomson	34
B.D.Julien not out	26
†D.L.Murray c and b Gilmour	14
V.A.Holder not out	6
A.M.E.Roberts	
L-b 6, n-b 11	17
TOTAL (60 overs; 8 wickets)	291

BOWLING: Lillee 12-1-55-1; Gilmour 12-2-48-5; Thomson 12-1-44-2; Walker 12-1-71-0; G.S.Chappell 7-0-33-0; Walters 5-0-23-0.

FALL OF WICKETS
1/12 2/27 3/50 4/199 5/206 6/209 7/261 8/285

AUSTRALIA

A.Turner run out	40
R.B.McCosker c Kallicharran b Boyce	7
*I.M.Chappell run out	62
G.S.Chappell run out	15
K.D.Walters b Lloyd	35
†R.W.Marsh b Boyce	11
R.Edwards c Fredericks b Boyce	28
G.J.Gilmour c Kanhai b Boyce	14
M.H.N.Walker run out	7
J.R.Thomson run out	21
D.K.Lillee not out	16
B 2, l-b 9, n-b 7	18
TOTAL (58.4 overs)	274

BOWLING: Julien 12-0-58-0; Roberts 11-1-45-0; Boyce 12-0-50-4; Holder 11.4-1-65-0; Lloyd 12-1-38-1.

FALL OF WICKETS
1/25 2/81 3/115 4/162 5/170 6/195 7/221 8/231 9/233 10/274

LEGEND **CLIVE LLOYD**
WEST INDIES

Clive Lloyd carved his name in the World Cup's 'Hall of Fame' by leading the West Indies to triumph in the first two tournaments held in England. In his prime the power of his batting was awesome and he was the world's best cover fieldsman.

But he is remembered best for taking charge of the West Indies and building them into the finest team in the world, highlighted by their 17-run victory over Australia in the 1975 World Cup and 92-run triumph over England four years later, again at Lord's.

A left-handed batsman, he helped pioneer the use of heavier bats, hitting the ball with incredible power off the middle of willow weighing 3lbs, and, to the consternation of leading batsmen worldwide, the employment of not two, not three, but four fast bowlers.

His brilliant man management brought the best out of every player and he was as popular as an overseas recruit for Lancashire as he was back in his native Guyana.

Born on August 31, 1944, he is the fourth highest Test run-maker of all time for the West Indies, behind Viv Richards, Garfield Sobers and Gordon Greenidge. He had scored 7,515 runs in 110 Tests at an average of 46.67 when he played for the West Indies for the last time in 1984-85.

Nineteen innings ended in scores of 100 or more, 14 of those when he held the added responsibility of captaincy, and several when his team were in trouble.

Lloyd, a cousin of Lance Gibbs, began his career with British Guiana in 1963-64. He missed the 1966 England tour but subsequently toured here 11 times in all, six of them as captain.

Statistics bothered others more than him. He has probably forgotten that he played 58 innings before recording his first duck. He equalled the fastest double century when, playing for West Indies against Glamorgan in 1976, he took 80 minutes for the first hundred and forty for the second.

He captained West Indies in 74 Tests from 1974-75, winning 36. Of the 18 Test rubbers in that time, he lost just two against Australia in 1975-76 and New Zealand in 1979-80.

Lloyd played in 219 first-class matches for Lancashire between 1968-86, hitting 30 centuries and scoring 12,764 runs for an average of 44.94. He also played in 268 one-day matches for the county, averaging 41.24.

He skippered the side to numerous one-day triumphs, especially in the Gillette Cup, after becoming captain in 1981 and clocked up 1000 runs in a season for Lancashire no less than 10 times.

But did he ever play better than in that 1975 World Cup final? The scoreboard at Lord's was showing West Indies in trouble at 50 for three, when he emerged from the pavilion to score a magnificent 102 out of 291 for eight and set a target beyond the scope of Australia's batsmen — and with it clinched the Man of the Match award.

And no one in the cricket world deserved the honour of lifting the first World Cup more than him.

WORLD CUP 1979

Bad weather disrupted the second World Cup to such an extent that the total attendance fell from 160,000 four years earlier to a depressing total of 132,000.

But gate receipts were up to £359,700, almost double the £188,000 yield of the first World Cup, and only one match, a Group B encounter between West Indies and Sri Lanka, at The Oval, was abandoned without a ball being bowled.

Prudential Assurance raised their sponsorship to £250,000 and the format of matches for the eight competing countries was the same as for the first tournament.

Canada replaced East Africa to sweep such colourful new names as Mauricette, Baksh, Javed and Patel into the cricketing limelight and the umpires were told to deal more harshly with wide deliveries and bouncers.

The England-Australia clash at Lord's on 9th June was the pick of the first round group matches. Mike Brearley asked Australia to bat on a dull, grey morning and by the time the first wicket fell, the scoreboard read 56 runs from 21 overs.

Brearley, the master tactician, surprised the capacity crowd by asking Geoff Boycott to bowl, a move that gained reward when he removed Andrew Hilditch and Kim Hughes. Then followed four run-outs and England were given a 160-run target for victory.

Boycott and Derek Randall perished with only five runs scored in reply, but Brearley and Graham Gooch helped England to a six-wicket win by making respective scores of 44 and 53.

West Indies, showing much the same form that had made them world champions four years earlier, destroyed India when Gordon Greenidge and Desmond Haynes, the world's two best openers, shared a match-winning partnership of 138, and by the time his team had scored 194 for victory, Greenidge was 106 not out.

Poor old Canada received a similar hiding on their first appearance, at Headingley, against Pakistan. Deciding to bat against an attack containing Imran Khan, Sarfraz Nawaz and Mudassar Nazar, they crawled to 139 for nine in 60 overs.

Pakistan took just 40.1 overs to reach their target for the loss of Majid and Zaheer's wickets. Sadiq made 57 not out and Haroon Rashid 37.

The New Zealand-Sri Lanka game was another mismatch. Sri Lanka scored a disappointing 189 before Glenn Turner (83 not out) and Geoff Howarth (63 not out) set up the kill.

Bad weather badly damaged the second round group matches with England becoming involved in a bizarre encounter with Canada, at wet, windy and miserable Old Trafford.

No play was possible on the scheduled opening day but when the Canadians batted on the second they were shot out for just 45, the lowest total ever in a one-day international, by Bob Willis (four for 11) and Chris Old (four for eight). Brearley went for a duck and Randall five but Boycott and Gooch steered England home in just 13.5 overs.

The match was significant for two other reasons. The aggregate number of 91 runs was the lowest on record at that level, while the actual playing time of three hours and 35 minutes became the shortest completed international match in England.

At Trent Bridge, Pakistan beat Australia by 89 runs on another rain interrupted day, forcing the game into a second day. Majid and Asif Iqbal scored half-centuries to bolster the Pakistan innings of 286 for seven, and on the second day Australia never drew close to their target, despite Andrew Hilditch's impressive innings of 72.

Meanwhile, New Zealand were polishing-off the under-achieving India at Headingley by eight wickets. They bowled out the Indians for 182 and reached their target thanks largely to an opening stand of 100 between John Wright, now coach at Kent, and Bruce Edgar, the latter taking the Man of the Match award for his unbeaten 84.

Sri Lanka made history in the third round of games when they demonstrated the same winning form against India that would one day carry them to victory in a World Cup final.

Their 47-run win was the first time a non-Test playing country had won a match in the World Cup. Batting first and without their captain Anura Tennekoon, they scored 238 for five in 60 overs. In reply, India's Sunil Gavaskar and Anshuman Gaekwad shared a 60-run opening stand, but the middle order batsmen were spun to distraction by Sri Lanka's leg-spinner Somachandra de Silva, and the victory margin of 47 runs left the telex office in Colombo almost as overworked that June night as it became 17 years later after Arjuna Ranatunga's team swept to World Cup triumph.

The semi-finals were played in brilliant sunshine and New Zealand came close to causing a tournament upset by so nearly beating England, at Old Trafford. Gooch, who scored 71, and Brearley with 53 led England to a modest score of 221 for eight in 60 overs against an accurate New Zealand attack spearheaded by Richard Hadlee.

Eight of New Zealand's first nine batsmen made double figures with John Wright making a top score 69 but Mike Hendrick added three more scalps to the four he had taken in the previous match against Pakistan and England scraped a victory by nine runs.

Most of West Indies' top order batsmen made runs when they piled-up 293 for six in the second semi-final, at The Oval. Greenidge and Haynes shared a 132-run opening stand, but at 208 for four in reply, Pakistan had victory snatched from their grasp by fast bowler Colin Croft, who took three wickets in 12 balls to turn the match.

England were without the injured Bob Willis when a beautiful sunny day welcomed the teams and a capacity crowd at Lord's on June 23.

The game was one-sided from the moment Viv Richards took control after Mike Brearley had invited the West Indies to bat. He scored a match-winning 138 not out — the highest score in a World Cup final — and shared a 139-run partnership with Collis King that consumed only 21 overs and 77 minutes.

Brearley (64) and Boycott (57) put on 129 for England's first wicket before Joel Garner ripped out the middle-order to finish with figures of five for 38 as England collapsed to 194 all out.

On any other day, the giant Garner would have taken the Man of the Match award. But the adjudicator had eyes only for Richards at the end, his three sixes and 11 fours still a vivid memory for all those who attended.

ENGLAND v NEW ZEALAND

Semi-Final at Old Trafford on 20th June. England won by nine runs. Toss: New Zealand.

ENGLAND

*J.M.Brearley c Lees b Coney	53
G.Boycott c Howarth b Hadlee	2
W.Larkins c Coney b McKechnie	7
G.A.Gooch b McKechnie	71
D.I.Gower run out	1
I.T.Botham lbw b Cairns	21
D.W.Randall not out	42
C.M.Old c Lees b Troup	0
†R.W.Taylor run out	12
R.G.D.Willis not out	1
M.Hendrick	
L-b 8, w 3	11
TOTAL (60 overs; 8 wickets)	221

BOWLING: Hadlee 12-4-32-1; Troup 12-1-38-1; Cairns 12-2-47-1; Coney 12-0-47-1; McKechnie 12-1-46-2.

FALL OF WICKETS

1/13 2/38 3/96 4/98 5/145 6/177 7/178 8/219

NEW ZEALAND

J.G.Wright run out	69
B.A.Edgar lbw b Old	17
G.P.Howarth lbw b Boycott	7
J.V.Coney lbw b Hendrick	11
G.M.Turner lbw b Willis	30
*M.G.Burgess run out	10
R.J.Hadlee b Botham	15
†W.K.Lees b Hendrick	23
B.L.Cairns c Brearley b Hendrick	14
B.J.McKechnie not out	4
G.B.Troup not out	3
B 5, w4	9
TOTAL (60 overs; 9 wickets)	212

BOWLING: Botham 12-3-42-1; Hendrick 12-0-55-3; Old 12-1-33-1; Boycott 9-1-24-1; Gooch 3-1-8-0; Willis 12-1-41-1.

FALL OF WICKETS

1/47 2/58 3/104 4/112 5/132 6/162 7/180 8/195 9/208

WEST INDIES v PAKISTAN

Semi-Final at The Oval on 20th June. West Indies won by 43 runs. Toss: Pakistan.

WEST INDIES

C.G.Greenidge c Wasim b Asif	73
D.L.Haynes c and b Asif	65
I.V.A.Richards b Asif	42
*C.H.Lloyd c Mudassar b Asif	37
C.L.King c sub (Wasim Raja) b Sarfraz	34
A.I.Kallicharran b Imran	11
A.M.E.Roberts not out	7
J.Garner not out	1
†D.L.Murray	
M.A.Holding	
C.E.H.Croft	
B 1, l-b 17, w 1, n-b 4	23
TOTAL (60 overs; 6 wickets)	293

BOWLING: Imran Khan 9-1-43-1; Sarfraz Nawaz 12-1-71-1; Sikander Bakht 6-1-24-0; Mudassar Nazar 10-0-50-0; Majid Khan 12-2-26-0; Asif Iqbal 11-0-56-4.

FALL OF WICKETS

1/132 2/165 3/233 4/236 5/285 6/285

PAKISTAN

Majid Khan c Kallicharran b Croft	81
Sadiq Mohammed c Murray b Holding	2
Zaheer Abbas c Murray b Croft	93
Haroon Rashid run out	15
Javed Miandad lbw b Croft	0
*Asif Iqbal c Holding b Richards	17
Mudassar Nazar c Kallicharran b Richards	2
Imran Khan c and b Richards	6
Sarfraz Nawaz c Haynes b Roberts	12
†Wasim Bari c Murray b Roberts	9
Sikander Bakht not out	1
L-b 9, w 2, n-b 1	12
TOTAL (56.2 overs)	250

BOWLING: Roberts 9.2-2-41-2; Holding 9-1-28-1; Croft 11-0-29-3; Garner 12-1-47-0; King 7-0-41-0; Richards 8-0-52-3.

FALL OF WICKETS

1/10 2/176 3/187 4/187 5/208 6/220 7/221 8/228 9/246 10/250

ENGLAND v WEST INDIES

Final at Lord's on 23rd June. West Indies won by 92 runs. Toss: England.

WEST INDIES

C.G.Greenidge run out	9
D.L.Haynes c Hendrick b Old	20
I.V.A.Richards not out	138
A.I.Kallicharran b Hendrick	4
*C.H.Lloyd c and b Old	13
C.L.King c Randall b Edmonds	86
†D.L.Murray c Gower b Edmonds	5
A.M.E.Roberts c Brearley b Hendrick	0
J.Garner c Taylor b Botham	0
M.A.Holding b Botham	0
C.E.H.Croft not out	0
B 1, l-b 10	11
TOTAL (60 overs; 9 wickets)	286

BOWLING: Botham 12-2-44-2; Hendrick 12-2-50-2; Old 12-0-55-2; Boycott 6-0-38-0; Edmonds 12-2-40-2; Gooch 4-0-27-0; Larkins 2-0-21-0.

FALL OF WICKETS

1/22 2/36 3/55 4/99 5/238 6/252 7/258 8/260 9/272

ENGLAND

*J.M.Brearley c King b Holding	64
G.Boycott c Kallicharran b Holding	57
D.W.Randall b Croft	15
G.A.Gooch b Garner	32
D.I.Gower b Garner	0
I.T.Botham c Richards b Croft	4
W.Larkins b Garner	0
P.H.Edmonds not out	5
C.M.Old b Garner	0
†R.W.Taylor c Murray b Garner	0
M.Hendrick b Croft	0
L-b 12, w 2, n-b 3	17
TOTAL (51 overs)	194

BOWLING: Roberts 9-2-33-0; Holding 8-1-16-2; Croft 10-1-42-3; Garner 11-0-38-5; Richards 10-0-35-0; King 3-0-13-0.

FALL OF WICKETS

1/129 2/135 3/183 4/183 5/186 6/186 7/192 8/192 9/194 10/194

LEGEND **VIV RICHARDS**
<u>WEST INDIES</u>

Viv Richards scored more runs and played in more Test Matches than any West Indian cricketer in history.

The hero of West Indies' 1979 World Cup triumph over England at Lord's, he completed an outstanding international career with a batting average of 50.23 in Tests.

He made 121 Test appearances for the West Indies, scoring 8,540 runs, ahead of Sir Garfield Sobers' aggregate of 8,032, Gordon Greenidge's 7,558 and Clive Lloyd's 7,515. Only Sobers (26) scored more centuries than the 24 hundreds Richards made for his country.

In 1976, he scored more runs in a calendar year than any batsman ever. He made seven centuries, scoring 1,710 runs in 11 Tests with an average of 90.00. Trailing in his wake are Sunil Gavaskar (India), 1,555 in 1979; Gundappa Viswanath (India), 1,388 in 1979; Bobby Simpson (Australia), 1,381 in 1964; and Dennis Amiss (England), 1,379 in 1974. Brian Lara is the only other West Indian in the 'Top Ten' chart, placed ninth for his 1,222 in 1995.

Born in Antigua on March 7, 1952, Richards was a brilliant, attacking right-handed batsman. Apart from his phenomenal scoring at Test level, he also scored 6,721 runs in limited-overs internationals.

He retired from international cricket in 1991 having led the West Indies 50 times.

Viv is remembered almost as fondly for his stirring batting deeds for Somerset from 1974 than for his exploits in the world's great Test arenas.

He and Ian Botham played an intrinsic part in Somerset's glory years when they won all the one-day trophies, with his highest score for them being a magnificent 322 against Warwickshire in 1985.

He was released by Somerset in 1986 at the end of an acrimonious season but Taunton's loss was Glamorgan's gain when he re-emerged to make his debut for them in 1990, playing two seasons at the Cardiff club, 1990 and 92, and leading them to the Sunday League title before retirement.

When he departed the scene at Cardiff, he had scored 36,212 runs in first-class cricket at an average of 49.40. Statistics show he scored on average a century every seven innings and made a 50 every five.

A natural athlete, he must be almost unique in the fact that he played World Cup football as well as World Cup cricket, and picked up the Man of the Match award in the 1979 Final after an innings that still that burns brightly in the memory of great performances.

West Indies were in trouble against England when Richards launched a counter-attack with Collis King. They put on 139 for the fifth wicket in 77 minutes with Richards taking a back seat as powerful all-rounder King set about the English attack from his first ball.

Viv completed his hundred shortly after King's dismissal and went on to make 138 in just under three and a half hours, hitting three sixes into the huge crowd and eleven fours as the Lord's watched an exhibition of batting from a master craftsman.

The legend of 'King Viv' was born that June 23rd day at Lord's.

WORLD CUP 1983

The third World Cup, hosted for the third and last time by England before they would be invited to stage the 1999 tournament, became big business.

Prudential Assurance raised their sponsorship to £500,000; gate receipts rose to £1,195,712 and the surplus, distributed to full and associate members of the ICC, was in excess of £1 million, this being over and above the prior payments of £53,900 to each of the seven full member countries and one of £30,200 to emerging Zimbabwe.

The number of matches was substantially increased. Each team in the two groups of four were asked to play six matches instead of three. Zimbabwe replaced Canada, the weather was better than it had been for the previous tournament, and World Cup 83 began in sensational fashion with Zimbabwe celebrating an astonishing 13-run win against Australia.

Zimbabwe's captain, Duncan Fletcher, rescued his team from a poor start after Dennis Lillee had dismissed Paterson to become the first bowler to take 100 wickets in one-day internationals. Fletcher was unbeaten on 69 as Zimbabwe made 239 for six in 60 overs.

A few hours later the Zimbabwe captain was the toast of Trent Bridge, receiving the Man of the Match award for destroying Australia's top and middle order to bowl his side to a famous giantkilling victory. He finished with four for 42.

India pulled-off another surprise by beating the West Indies at Old Trafford. Yashpal Sharma scored 89 of India's 262 for eight, a total quite beyond West Indies, despite gallant attempts by tailenders Andy Roberts (37 not out) and Joel Garner (37) to challenge their score as the mighty West Indies lost for the first time in Prudential Cup matches.

By the second round of matches West Indies had recovered their poise with a 101 run win against Australia, at Headingley. Fast bowler Winston Davis, now a paraplegic confined to hospital and home in the West Midlands after a serious fall, took seven for 51 to bowl out the Aussies for 151 in reply to West Indies' score of 252 for nine. Those figures are still a World Cup record to this day.

England, who had beaten New Zealand on the World Cup's opening day, overcame Sri Lanka at Taunton, with David Gower celebrating a brilliant innings of 130 and New Zealand's Richard Hadlee bowled Pakistan to defeat at Edgbaston.

Australia, beaten by Zimbabwe and West Indies in their first two matches, trounced India by 162 runs with the lesser known Chappell brother, Trevor, contributing 110 to a massive total of 320 for nine in 60 overs. India were dismissed for 158.

David Gower was again in fine form for England's match against New Zealand, scoring an unbeaten 92 with help from Lancashire's Graeme Fowler (69) but despite Bob Willis' four wickets, Richard Hadlee's spirited resistance at the end helped steer the Kiwis to a two-wicket victory in the final over.

England comfortably won their group with five wins and that New Zealand reversal their only blip.

New Zealand themselves failed to qualify for the semi-finals, missing out to Pakistan on runs-per-over, both teams having accumulated 12 points from three wins. A three-wicket defeat by the increasingly confident Sri Lanka was their undoing, at Derby, where Ashantha de Mel's five for 32 did the damage.

West Indies swept all before them in Group B. They were beaten only once in six group matches, by India, who joined them in the semi-finals.

But Zimbabwe nearly produced another sensation against India, at Tunbridge Wells. Choosing to bat, India were five wickets down for 17 and seven down for 78 when Kapil Dev, batting at number six, played one of the greatest one-day international innings of all time. He added an unbroken 126 for the ninth wicket with Syed Kirmani and went on to score 175 not out with six sixes and 16 fours.

Gallant Zimbabwe were 32 runs short of their target at the end and their second 'Goliath and David' slaying of the tournament was denied.

England were firm favourites to take advantage of India's lightweight attack in the Old Trafford semi-final. Graeme Fowler and Chris Tavaré got into the thirties, Allan Lamb scored 29 and Graham Dilley gave the tail a wag but 213 was hardly expected to bother India's powerful batting line-up and they duly reached their target for the loss of only four wickets.

The other semi-final between tournament favourites West Indies and Pakistan, at The Oval, was another contest made one-sided by Viv Richards' brilliance with the bat.

Mohsin Khan had given Pakistan hope with an innings of 70 out of a total score of 184 for eight. For once, Gordon Greenidge and Desmond Haynes were parted early before Richards plundered 80 not out to steer them into their third successive final.

Another huge crowd at Lord's, another sunny day, and another major upset at the end of a roller-coaster tournament. India, the big underdogs, prevented West Indies making it a hat-trick of World Cup triumphs.

Clive Lloyd asked India to bat; Andy Roberts, Joel Garner, Malcolm Marshall and Michael Holding bowled well to restrict their opponents to a total of 183; and everyone assembled at Lord's checked their watches for an early exit.

But opener Greenidge failed again and when Madan Lal dismissed Haynes, Richards and Larry Gomes, the huge crowd began to shuffle uneasily in their seats following their premature dismissal of India's chances.

Lloyd went cheaply and brave resistance by Jeffrey Dujon and Malcolm Marshall was not enough to prevent Man of the Match Mohinder Amarnath from blowing away the tail to establish victory by 43 runs in India's finest hour.

There were some fat-cat punters celebrating their luck that night of June 25, 1983. They had backed outsiders India to win the tournament at 66-1!

ENGLAND v INDIA

Semi-Final at Old Trafford on 22nd June, 1983. India won by six wickets. Toss: England.

ENGLAND

G.Fowler b Binny	33
C.J.Tavare c Kirmani b Binny	32
D.I.Gower c Kirmani b Amarnath	17
A.J.Lamb run out	29
M.W.Gatting b Amarnath	18
I.T.Botham b Azad	6
†I.J.Gould run out	13
V.J.Marks b Kapil Dev	8
G.R.Dilley not out	20
P.J.W.Allott c Patil b Kapil Dev	8
*R.G.D.Willis b Kapil Dev	0
B 1, l-b 17, w 7, n-b 4	29
TOTAL (60 overs)	213

BOWLING: Kapil Dev 11-1-35-3; Sandhu 8-1-36-0; Binny 12-1-43-2; Madan Lal 5-0-15-0; Azad 12-1-28-1; Amarnath 12-1-27-2.

FALL OF WICKETS
1/69 2/84 3/107 4/141 5/150 6/160 7/175 8/177 9/202 10/213

INDIA

S.M.Gavaskar c Gould b Allott	25
K.Srikkanth c Willis b Botham	19
M.Amarnath run out	46
Yashpal Sharma c Allott b Willis	61
S.M.Patil not out	51
*Kapil Dev not out	1
K.Azad	
R.M.H.Binny	
Madan Lal	
†S.M.H.Kirmani	
B.S.Sandhu	
B 5, l-b 6, w 1, n-b 2	14
TOTAL (54.4 overs; 4 wickets)	217

BOWLING: Willis 10.4-2-42-1; Dilley 11-0-43-0; Allott 10-3-40-1; Botham 11-4-40-1; Marks 12-1-38-0.

FALL OF WICKETS
1/46 2/50 3/142 4/205

PAKISTAN v WEST INDIES

Semi-Final at The Oval on 22nd June, 1983. West Indies won by eight wickets.
Toss: West Indies.

PAKISTAN

Mohsin Khan b Roberts		70
Mudassar Nazar c and b Garner		11
Ijaz Faqih c Dujon b Holding		5
Zaheer Abbas b Gomes		30
*Imran Khan c Dujon b Marshall		17
Wasim Raja lbw b Marshall		0
Shahid Mahboob c Richards b Marshall		6
Sarfraz Nawaz c Holding b Roberts		3
Abdul Qadir not out		10
†Wasim Bari not out		4
Rashid Khan		
B 6, l-b 13, w 4, n-b 5		28
TOTAL (60 overs; 8 wickets)		184

BOWLING: Roberts 12-3-25-2; Garner 12-1-31-1; Marshall 12-2-28-3; Holding 12-1-25-1; Gomes 7-0-29-1; Richards 5-0-18-0.

FALL OF WICKETS

1/23 2/34 3/88 4/139 5/139 6/159 7/164 8/171

WEST INDIES

C.G.Greenidge lbw b Rashid		17
D.L.Haynes b Qadir		29
I.V.A.Richards not out		80
H.A.Gomes not out		50
*C.H.Lloyd		
S.F.A.F Bacchus		
†P.J.L.Dujon		
M.D.Marshall		
A.M.E.Roberts		
J.Garner		
M.A.Holding		
B 2, l-b 6, w 4		12
TOTAL (48.4 overs; 2 wickets)		188

BOWLING: Rashid Khan 12-2-32-1; Sarfraz Nawaz 8-0-23-0; Abdul Qadir 11-1-42-1; Shahid Mahboob 11-1-43-0; Wasim Raja 1-0-9-0; Zaheer Abbas 4.4-1-24-0; Mohsin Khan 1-0-3-0.

FALL OF WICKETS

1/34 2/56

WEST INDIES v INDIA

Final at Lord's on 25th June. India won by 43 runs. Toss: West Indies.

INDIA

S.M.Gavaskar c Dujon b Roberts		2
K.Srikkanth lbw b Marshall		38
M.Amarnath b Holding		26
Yashpal Sharma c sub (A.L.Logie) b Gomes		11
S.M.Patil c Gomes b Garner		27
*Kapil Dev c Holding b Gomes		15
K.Azad c Garner b Roberts		0
R.M.H.Binny c Garner b Roberts		2
Madan Lal b Marshall		17
†S.M.H.Kirmani b Holding		14
B.S.Sandhu not out		11
B 5, l-b 5, w 9, n-b 1		20
TOTAL (54.4 overs)		183

BOWLING: Roberts 10-3-32-3; Garner 12-4-24-1; Marshall 11-1-24-2; Holding 9.4-2-26-2; Gomes 11-1-49-2; Richards 1-0-8-0.

FALL OF WICKETS

1/2 2/59 3/90 4/92 5/110 6/111 7/130 8/153 9/161 10/183

WEST INDIES

C.G.Greenidge b Sandhu		1
D.L.Haynes c Binny b Madan Lal		13
I.V.A.Richards c Kapil Dev b Madan Lal		33
*C.H.Lloyd c Kapil Dev b Binny		8
H.A.Gomes c Gavaskar b Madan Lal		5
S.F.A.F.Bacchus c Kirmani b Sandhu		8
†P.J.L.Dujon b Amarnath		25
M.D.Marshall c Gavaskar b Amarnath		18
A.M.E.Roberts lbw b Kapil Dev		4
J.Garner not out		5
M.A.Holding lbw b Amarnath		6
L-b 4, w 10		14
TOTAL (52 overs)		140

BOWLING: Kapil Dev 11-4-21-1; Sandhu 9-1-32-2; Madan Lal 12-2-31-3; Binny 10-1-23-1; Amarnath 7-0-12-3; Azad 3-0-7-0.

FALL OF WICKETS

1/5 2/50 3/57 4/66 5/66 6/76 7/119 8/124 9/126 10/140

LEGEND **KAPIL DEV**
INDIA

One spectacular innings in the 1983 World Cup raised Kapil Dev's image to superstar level.

He produced it against Zimbabwe on a difficult batting pitch at Tunbridge Wells. India, who had chosen to bat, were four wickets down for just nine runs and staring a nightmare defeat squarely in the face when their captain Kapil walked to the crease.

No-one absorbed in the contest at that stage could have foreseen then that a week later India would be winning the tournament.

Kapil shared an unbroken stand for the ninth-wicket of 126 in 16 overs with Syed Kirmani while his captain slaughtered the bowling with six sixes and 16 fours to reach 175 not out, beating the previous highest score for the tournament, Glenn Turner's magnificent 171 not out for New Zealand against East Africa in 1975.

Four days later his pace bowling unhinged England in the semi-final at Manchester, leaving India to score 214 for victory, a target they managed for the loss of only four wickets.

A magnificent catch by Kapil over his shoulder, running back towards the mid-wicket boundary got rid of danger batsman Viv Richards in the final, and India went on to cause a major tournament shock by beating favourites West Indies.

Born in Chandigarh on January 6, 1959, Kapil is the greatest all-rounder India has ever produced. A punishing right-handed batsman, blessed with the ability to bat a long innings and then take the new ball and hurt the opposition with equal effect.

When he retired from Test cricket in 1993-94, only four Indian batsmen, Sunil Gavaskar, Dilip Vengsarkar, Mohammad Azharuddin and Gundappa Viswanath had scored more Test runs. He played 131 Tests from 1978-79, scoring 5,248 runs at an average of 31.05.

His bowling record was more impressive, carrying him to the top of the all-time Test list of major wicket-takers with 434 victims, ahead of Richard Hadlee's 431.

He made his Test debut against India's fiercest rivals Pakistan in 1978-79, and in his 25th Test, with Pakistan again the opponents, he completed 1,000 runs and 100 wickets.

At 21 years 27 days, he was the youngest cricketer to perform the 'double' in Test history.

In his first Test as India's captain in 1982-83, he completed 2,000 Test runs and in the next match he became the youngest player to complete the 'double' of 2,000 Test runs and 200 Test wickets.

He played in the 1987 and 1992 World Cups, and stayed just long enough to overhaul Richard Hadlee's Test wicket record in the 1993-94 series against Sri Lanka, the last of a brilliant career.

On his retirement, Kapil moved into the world of cricket media and also played a role in the development of the Indian youngsters as the search for the next 'Kapil Dev' began.

WORLD CUP 1987

The fourth World Cup, sponsored by Reliance, was more widely watched, more closely fought and more colourful than any of the first three tournaments hosted by England.

The experiment of holding an oriental World Cup was acknowledged to have been a success even if the geographical implications of two host countries staging the 27 matches at 21 venues in India and Pakistan was generally considered a flawed concept.

For successive matches, the Sri Lankans were shunted from Peshawar, in the North-West Frontier Province of Pakistan, to Kanpur in central India, back to Faisalabad, then across the border again to Pune; two-day journeys every time, with hours spent in transit lounges at airports waiting for flights not always running to time.

The extra workload represented an extension of the tournament from 17 to 32 days, with Group A matches played in India and all but three of the Group B games held in Pakistan.

The same eight countries that played in 1983 assembled again and the number of overs per innings was curtailed from 60 to 50.

Australia and World Cup holders India fought a nailbiting match, at Madras, resulting in victory for Allan Border's team by a single run.

A memorable example of fine sportsmanship from Kapil Dev proved the deciding factor in this cliffhanging contest. Australia argued that one of two sixes struck by Dean Jones in his innings of 39 from 35 balls had been signalled four when, in fact, it had cleared the boundary. Kapil concurred, so did the match adjudicator, Australia's innings, boosted by a magnificent innings of 110 by Geoff Marsh, was increased by two runs to 270 for six, a target beyond India, bowled out for 269!

The Hyderabad crowd were treated to a similarly close match the following day when New Zealand swept to a three-run win against Zimbabwe. The Kiwis made 242 for seven and Zimbabwe needed just six runs from the final over after David Houghton's dismissal for 141. They lost their last wicket four runs short of victory with two balls left.

The tournament's capacity to produce almost fictional results continued at Indore where New Zealand needed victory over Australia to give themselves a chance to challenge for the semi-finals.

Postponed for a day because of heavy rain, the game was curtailed to 30 overs per side. David Boon's 87 from 96 balls laid the foundations and Dean Jones, 52 in 48 balls, carried Australia to 199 for four in 30 overs, leaving New Zealand to score at more than six runs per over.

John Wright and Ken Rutherford shared an opening stand of 83 to open the door and Martin Crowe added 58 from 48 balls to smash it wide-open. New Zealand needed seven runs with four wickets left when the final over began. They lost three wickets and were 196 for nine at the close, four runs short of victory.

India and Australia continued to dominate Group A to move into the semi-finals with five wins a piece in their six matches.

In Pakistan, the host nation fought another gripping contest with Sri Lanka before emerging as winners by just 15 runs. Javed Miandad scored his fifth one-day international century to reach 4,000 runs in his 120th one-day match to leave Sri Lanka chasing a formidable 268 to win in 50 overs.

Sri Lanka's exciting young opening batsman Roshan Mahanama — these days batting well down the order — made a courageous attempt to reach the target but with his dismissal they fell behind the required run-rate to finish on 252 in reply.

A well-fought battle in Gujranwala gave England a two-wicket win over the West Indies, Allan Lamb scoring 67 not out, but England came unstuck against Abdul Qadir whose spin steered Pakistan to victory by 18 runs at Rawalpindi.

Meanwhile, Viv Richards was producing the highest individual score of 181 from 125 balls in a World Cup innings against Sri Lanka, at Karachi. The lads from Colombo were dispatched for 360 for the loss of four wickets, the highest in a one-day international. Defeat, by 191 runs, was inevitable.

Pakistan beat West Indies, and England again in Karachi, Qadir's leg-spin doing the damage in harness with Imran Khan.

England toppled the West Indies in Jaipur by 34 runs on a day when no-one could score a century but Graham Gooch and Richie Richardson both made 90s. Chasing England's 269 for five, West Indies began the 41st over needing 65 with six wickets in hand. In 8.1 overs they lost them for 30 runs.

England beat Sri Lanka to secure a place in the semi-finals alongside Australia, India and Pakistan.

At Lahore, Australia were always too strong for Pakistan. Batting first, the Aussies reached 267 for eight off 50 overs, David Boon top scoring with 65. Pakistan were never in the hunt against Craig McDermott's brilliant pace bowling, taking five for 44, and they were all out for 249.

At Bombay, India regretted asking England to bat when opener Graham Gooch scored 115 and skipper Mike Gatting 56 off 62 balls to see their team to a total of 254 for six. Phil DeFreitas rattled Sunil

Gavaskar's off-stump early in India's innings and they never looked like mounting a challenge once dangerman Mohammad Azharuddin had departed, defeated by 35 runs.

In the final, in front of an estimated 70,000 crowd at Eden Gardens, Calcutta, Australia chose to bat first and made 253 for five. At 135 for two in reply, England were on course to win their first World Cup.

Then catastrophe. Mike Gatting forgot his responsibilities and was dismissed attempting to reverse sweep Allan Border's first delivery. Allan Lamb, who scored 45, did his best to shore up the innings but England's batsmen fell behind the clock and were seven runs short of the Aussie total in a game never as close as the final result really suggests.

Captain Border lifted the trophy and David Boon was declared Man of the Match for a knock of 75 that had shaped Australia's innings and their ultimate destiny.

AUSTRALIA v PAKISTAN

Semi-Final at Gaddafi Stadium, Lahore, on 4th November. Australia won by 18 runs.
Toss: Australia.

AUSTRALIA

G.R.Marsh run out	31
D.C.Boon st Miandad b Salim Malik	65
D.M.Jones b Tausif	38
*A.R.Border run out	18
M.R.J.Veletta b Imran	48
S.R.Waugh not out	32
S.P.O'Donnell run out	0
†G.C.Dyer b Imran	0
C.J.McDermott b Imran	1
T.B.A.May not out	0
B.A.Reid	
B 1, l-b 19, w 13, n-b 1	34
TOTAL (50 overs; 8 wickets)	267

BOWLING: Imran Khan 10-1-36-3; Salim Jaffer 6-0-57-0; Wasim Akram 10-0-54-0; Abdul Qadir 10-0-39-0; Tausif Ahmed 10-1-39-1; Salim Malik 4-0-22-1.

FALL OF WICKETS

1/73 2/155 3/155 4/215 5/236 6/236 7/241 8/249

PAKISTAN

Ramiz Raja run out	1
Mansoor Akhtar b McDermott	9
Salim Malik c McDermott b Waugh	25
Javed Miandad b Reid	70
*Imran Khan c Dyer b Border	58
Wasim Akram b McDermott	20
Ijaz Ahmed c Jones b Reid	8
†Salim Yousuf c Dyer b McDermott	21
Abdul Qadir not out	20
Salim Jaffer c Dyer b McDermott	0
Tausif Ahmed c Dyer b McDermott	1
L-b 6, w 10	16
TOTAL (49 overs)	249

BOWLING: McDermott 10-0-44-5; Reid 10-2-41-2; Waugh 9-1-51-1; O'Donnell 10-1-45-0; May 6-0-36-0; Border 4-0-26-1.

FALL OF WICKETS

1/2 2/37 3/38 4/150 5/177 6/192 7/212 8/236 9/247 10/249

INDIA v ENGLAND

Semi-Final at Wankhede Stadium, Bombay, on 5th November, 1987. England won by 35 runs. Toss: India.

ENGLAND		
G.A.Gooch c Srikkanth b Maninder		115
R.T.Robinson st More b Maninder		13
C.W.J.Athey c More b Sharma		4
*M.W.Gatting b Maninder		56
A.J.Lamb not out		32
J.E.Emburey lbw b Kapil Dev		6
P.A.J.DeFreitas b Kapil Dev		7
†P.R.Downton not out		1
N.A.Foster		
G.C.Small		
E.E.Hemmings		
B 1, l-b 18, w 1		20
TOTAL (50 overs; 6 wickets)		254

INDIA		
K.Srikkanth b Foster		31
S.M.Gavaskar b DeFreitas		4
N.S.Sidhu c Athey b Foster		22
M.Azharuddin lbw b Hemmings		64
C.S.Pandit lbw b Foster		24
*Kapil Dev c Gatting b Hemmings		30
R.J.Shastri c Downton b Hemmings		21
†K.S.More c and b Emburey		0
M.Prabhakar c Downton b Small		4
C.Sharma c Lamb b Hemmings		0
Maninder Singh not out		0
B 1, l-b 9, w 6, n-b 3		19
TOTAL (45.3 overs)		219

BOWLING: Kapil Dev 10-1-38-2; Prabhakar 9-1-40-0; Maninder 10-0-54-3; Sharma 9-0-41-1; Shastri 10-0-49-0; Azharuddin 2-0-13-0.

BOWLING: DeFreitas 7-0-37-1; Small 6-0-22-1; Emburey 10-1-35-1; Foster 10-0-47-3; Hemmings 9.3-1-52-4; Gooch 3-0-16-0.

FALL OF WICKETS

1/40 2/79 3/196 4/203 5/219 6/231

FALL OF WICKETS

1/7 2/58 3/73 4/121 5/168 6/204 7/205 8/218 9/219 10/219

AUSTRALIA v ENGLAND

Final at Eden Gardens, Calcutta on 8th November. Australia won by seven runs. Toss: Australia.

AUSTRALIA		
D.C.Boon c Downton b Hemmings		75
G.R.Marsh b Foster		24
D.M.Jones c Athey b Hemmings		33
C.J.McDermott b Gooch		14
*A.R.Border run out		31
M.R.J.Veletta not out		45
S.R.Waugh not out		5
S.P.O'Donnell		
†G.C.Dyer		
T.B.A.May		
B.A.Reid		
B 1, l-b 13, w 5, n-b 7		26
TOTAL (50 overs; 5 wickets)		253

ENGLAND		
G.A.Gooch lbw b O'Donnell		35
R.T.Robinson lbw b McDermott		0
C.W.J.Athey run out		58
*M.W.Gatting c Dyer b Border		41
A.J.Lamb b Waugh		45
†P.R.Downton c O'Donnell b Border		9
J.E.Emburey run out		10
P.A.J.DeFreitas c Reid b Waugh		17
N.A.Foster not out		7
G.C.Small not out		3
E.E.Hemmings		
B 1, l-b 14, w 2, n-b 4		21
TOTAL (50 overs; 8 wickets)		246

BOWLING: DeFreitas 6-1-34-0; Small 6-0-33-0; Foster 10-0-38-1; Hemmings 10-1-48-2; Emburey 10-0-44-0; Gooch 8-1-42-1.

BOWLING: McDermott 10-1-51-1; Reid 10-0-43-0; Waugh 9-0-37-2; O'Donnell 10-1-35-1; May 4-0-27-0; Border 7-0-38-2.

FALL OF WICKETS

1/75 2/151 3/166 4/168 5/241

FALL OF WICKETS

1/1 2/66 3/135 4/170 5/188 6/218 7/220 8/235

LEGEND **GRAHAM GOOCH**
ENGLAND

If Graham Gooch was playing in the 1999 World Cup tournament this summer, you could almost guarantee that England would not win the prestigious tournament.

No player could have tried harder to win cricket's ultimate one-day prize for his country than Gooch, arguably the greatest batsman England has produced since the War.

He played in three World Cup finals, against West Indies, at Lord's, in 1979; against Australia, at Calcutta, in 1987; and against Pakistan, at Melbourne, in 1992, and on each of those memorable occasions he finished up with a loser's medal.

He was never more cruelly denied than in the 1987 tournament when he scored 471 runs at an average of 58.88, only to be cheated of the prize he so thoroughly deserved.

The Essex bat scored 47 and 92 in two matches against West Indies; 21 and 16 against Pakistan; 84 and 61 against Sri Lanka; 115 in the semi-final against India; and 35 in the final against Australia.

Standing tall beneath that famous white batting helmet, Gooch tops the list of English Test run-getters with 8,900 in 118 Tests at an average of 42.58. David Gower is second with 8,231, averaging 44.25; Geoff Boycott third with 8,114 at 47.72; and Colin Cowdrey fourth with 7,624 at 44.06.

In the calendar year of 1990 he scored an incredible 1,264 runs in nine Tests, which included his score of 333 against India, at Lord's, the highest score by an England captain.

Gooch scored more runs in the Sunday League and the Benson and Hedges Cup than anyone and he was the mainstay of Essex's phenomenal success from 1979-92.

He is now an England selector and much admired by the England Cricket Board but it was not ever thus. He launched his Test career with a 'pair' against Australia in 1975 and he would have played more than the 118 Tests he achieved had he not chosen to go on a rebel tour to South Africa.

He became a fitness fanatic, running upstairs rather than taking lifts, road-running when other England players were still in bed, training with his beloved West Ham during the long, winter months to maintain his fitness level. And his agility for a big man enabled him to pull-off some sensational catches at slip.

He saved one of his finest knocks for the semi-final of the 1987 World Cup. With the hostile home fans baying for English wickets as they anticipated a second successive Indian appearance in the final, Gooch led from the front, slowly silencing the crowd as he masterminded England's innings with a brilliant knock of 115.

It was a performance that illustrated all of Gooch's varying talents and guided England into the final.

Born in Leytonstone on July 23, 1953, the former England skipper is best remembered for his courage under fire from fast bowlers. He not only survived, he saw them off — and in style!

WORLD CUP 1992

The 1992 World Cup, sponsored by Benson and Hedges, was again shared by two countries – Australia and New Zealand – but this time the huge airlift needed to fly the nine competing teams vast distances worked smoothly and efficiently.

It served as the catalyst for a new era of cooperation between the administrators of two countries: David Richards, the Australian cricket board's chief executive, and his New Zealand counterpart, Graham Dowling.

After examining the World Cup's history, the World Cup Committee presented a bid based on the two original ICC objectives: first, to widen interest in the game throughout the world; and second, to help smaller cricket countries with their development programmes and coaching.

Each of the 18 associate members of the ICC received a guarantee of £40,000, while £100,000 was provided for joint sponsorship of the 1990 ICC Trophy. In addition, the eight full member countries received a guarantee of £150,000 each.

Before a ball was bowled, over $10 million of expenditure was committed. Without the sponsorship of the Benson and Hedges Company, television support from the National Nine Network in Australia and Television New Zealand, and the income from international TV and radio generated by the committee's agent, CSI Ltd, the World Cup bid for that year would not have been made.

Richards and Dowling spoke of 'unbelievable' man-hours spent on a tournament which drew attendances in the two countries totalling 620,401 spectators, as well as a television audience in 25 countries.

Total spectator involvement was put at a billion people – and the modern World Cup came of age!

This was a media World Cup with 742 accreditations for print, radio and television. This was the World Cup of the replica playing kit explosion. It was the first to be played in coloured clothing and a watershed in the promotion of cricket 'pyjamas' in retail sports shops.

The easy ride to the knockout stages forecast for favourites Australia received a jolt in the first match, when New Zealand beat them by 37 runs. Martin Crowe made 100 not out in a total of 248 for six. David Boon scored exactly 100 but Australia were bowled to a 37-run defeat.

It was the beginning of a spectacular run by the New Zealanders. At one stage their group qualifying table read: played seven, won seven. An undefeated 119 by Ramiz Raja helped ease them to a seven-wicket defeat against Pakistan, at Christchurch, but by then they were guaranteed a place in the semi-finals.

Australia crashed to a nine-wicket defeat against South Africa, at Sydney, their second successive hiding. The Aussies held an inquest, the Springboks read messages of congratulations from African National Congress leader Nelson Mandela and South Africa's President F.W. de Klerk.

"This is the greatest moment in South African cricket history," declared United Cricket Board of South Africa chief executive Ali Bacher.

England also stormed impressively into the semi-finals after a closely fought battle with India in their opening game, a day-nighter, at Perth.

With an over to go, India needed 11 to win. However, the last of four run-outs, by Ian Botham, settled the result after Robin Smith's 91 and a half-century by Graham Gooch had dominated England's innings of 236 for nine, with India finishing on 227 all out in reply.

En-route to the semis, rain deprived England of the emphatic victory they anticipated after dismissing Pakistan for 74 at Adelaide. Derek Pringle celebrated figures of three for eight and there were two wickets apiece for Phil DeFreitas, Gladstone Small and Ian Botham.

The 'rain rule' was applied, England reached 24 for one in eight overs but play was abandoned and the points shared.

South Africa became the third team to book a semi-final place when they beat India in their last qualifying match but the last semi-final place went to the wire, leaving the statisticians to decode the cypher. West Indies could have it by beating Australia; Australia could have it by beating West Indies; but only if Pakistan lost, and Pakistan, who had started disastrously, could have it by beating New Zealand, provided Australia beat the West Indies.

Pakistan beat New Zealand by seven wickets, West Indies lost to the Aussies and the format for the semi-finals finally read: New Zealand versus Pakistan; England versus South Africa.

Pakistan reached their first World Cup final by defeating the previously invincible New Zealand for the second time in four days. But victory appeared to have eluded Imran Khan's side when they needed 123 from only 15 overs at 8.2. Cometh the moment, cometh Inzamam-ul-Haq to play one of the great World Cup innings. He scored 60 from 37 balls to share a partnership of 87 in 10 overs with Javed Miandad, who had anchored the innings. At the close, Pakistan were 264 for six in reply to New Zealand's 262 for seven.

The closing minutes of the other semi-final left England, the winners, embarrassed, the losers, South Africa, disconsolate, and the crowd plain furious.

The 'rain rule' was applied again in this match at Sydney. With 10.10pm fixed for the finish of the day-night match, South Africa had reached 231 for six in reply to England's 252 for six with 13 balls remaining when a downpour interrupted play.

When the players returned, the umpires decreed there was time for only seven balls but, as under the rules the lowest-scoring over of England's innings was discarded, the target was not reduced.

However, before play could begin, there was another stoppage, reducing the time allowed to only one ball. This time the target was reduced by one run to 21, and that was that.

Just under 90,000 spectators packed into the MCG for the World Cup final, which saw Pakistan win their first World Cup.

Batting first, Imran (72), Javed (58) and Inzamam (42) wore down the England attack to reach 249-6 after 50 overs.

England's pursuit of five an over started badly when Ian Botham was surprised to be adjudged caught behind. Allan Lamb and Neil Fairbrother added 72 in 14 overs but Man of the Match Wasim Akram returned to take two vital middle-order wickets and Pakistan swept to victory by 22 runs.

NEW ZEALAND v PAKISTAN

Semi-Final at Eden Park, Auckland on 21st March. Pakistan won by four wickets. Toss: New Zealand.

NEW ZEALAND		PAKISTAN	
M.J.Greatbatch b Aqib	17	Aamir Sohail c Jones b Patel	14
J.G.Wright c Ramiz b Mushtaq	13	Ramiz Raja c Morrison b Watson	44
A.H.Jones lbw b Mushtaq	21	*Imran Khan c Larsen b Harris	44
*M.D.Crowe run out	91	Javed Miandad not out	57
K.R.Rutherford c Moin b Wasim	50	Salim Malik c sub (R.T.Latham) b Larsen	1
C.Z.Harris st Moin b Iqbal	13	Inzamam-ul-Haq run out	60
†I.D.S.Smith not out	18	Wasim Akram b Watson	9
D.N.Patel lbw b Wasim	8	†Moin Khan not out	20
G.R.Larsen not out	8	Mushtaq Ahmed	
D.K.Morrison		Iqbal Sikander	
W.Watson		Aqib Javed	
L-b 11, w 8, n-b 4	23	B 4, l-b 10, w 1	15
TOTAL (50 overs; 7 wickets)	262	TOTAL (49 overs; 6 wickets)	264

BOWLING: Wasim Akram 10-1-40-2; Aqib Javed 10-2-45-1; Mushtaq Ahmed10-0-40-2; Imran Khan 10-0-59-0; Iqbal Sikander 9-0-56-1; Aamir Sohail 1-0-11-0.

BOWLING: Patel 10-1-50-1; Morrison 9-0-55-0; Watson 10-2-39-2; Larsen 10-1-34-1; Harris 10-0-72-1.

FALL OF WICKETS
1/35 2/39 3/87 4/194 5/214 6/221 7/244

FALL OF WICKETS
1/30 2/84 3/134 4/140 5/227 6/238

ENGLAND v SOUTH AFRICA

Semi-Final at Sydney Cricket Ground on 22nd March. England won by 19 runs (revised target). Toss: South Africa.

ENGLAND

*G.A.Gooch c Richardson b Donald	2
I.T.Botham b Pringle	21
†A.J.Stewart c Richardson b McMillan	33
G.A.Hick c Rhodes b Snell	83
N.H.Fairbrother b Pringle	28
A.J.Lamb c Richardson b Donald	19
C.C.Lewis not out	18
D.A.Reeve not out	25
P.A.J.DeFreitas	
G.C.Small	
R.K.Illingworth	
B 1, l-b 7, w 9, n-b 6	23
TOTAL (45 overs; 6 wickets)	252

BOWLING: Donald 10-0-69-2; Pringle 9-2-36-2; Snell 8-0-52-1; McMillan 9-0-47-1; Kuiper 5-0-26-0; Cronje 4-0-14-0.

FALL OF WICKETS

1/20 2/39 3/110 4/183 5/187 6/221

SOUTH AFRICA

*K.C.Wessels c Lewis b Botham	17
A.C.Hudson lbw b Illingworth	46
P.N.Kirsten b DeFreitas	11
A.P.Kuiper b Illingworth	36
W.J.Cronje c Hick b Small	24
J.N.Rhodes c Lewis b Small	43
B.M.McMillan not out	21
†D.J.Richardson not out	13
R.P.Snell	
M.W.Pringle	
A.A.Donald	
L-b 17, w 4	21
TOTAL (43 overs; 6 wickets)	232

BOWLING: Botham 10-0-52-1; Lewis 5-0-38-0; DeFreitas 8-1-28-1; Illingworth 10-1-46-2; Small 10-1-51-2.

FALL OF WICKETS

1/26 2/61 3/90 4/131 5/176 6/206

ENGLAND v PAKISTAN

Final at Melbourne Cricket Ground on 25th March. Pakistan won by 22 runs. Toss: Pakistan.

PAKISTAN

Aamir Sohail c Stewart b Pringle	4
Ramiz Raja lbw b Pringle	8
*Imran Khan c Illingworth b Botham	72
Javed Miandad c Botham b Illingworth	58
Inzamam-ul-Haq b Pringle	42
Wasim Akram run out	33
Salim Malik not out	0
Ijaz Ahmed	
†Moin Khan	
Mushtaq Ahmed	
Aqib Javed	
L-b 19, w 6, n-b 7	32
TOTAL (50 overs; 6 wickets)	249

BOWLING: Pringle 10-2-22-3; Lewis 10-2-52-0; Botham 7-0-42-1; DeFreitas 10-1-42-0; Illingworth 10-0-50-1; Reeve 3-0-22-0.

FALL OF WICKETS

1/20 2/24 3/163 4/197 5/249 6/249

ENGLAND

*G.A.Gooch c Aqib b Mushtaq	29
I.T.Botham c Moin b Wasim	0
†A.J.Stewart c Moin b Aqib	7
G.A.Hick lbw b Mushtaq	17
N.H.Fairbrother c Moin b Aqib	62
A.J.Lamb b Wasim	31
C.C.Lewis b Wasim	0
D.A.Reeve c Ramiz b Mushtaq	15
D.R.Pringle not out	18
P.A.J.DeFreitas run out	10
R.K.Illingworth c Ramiz b Imran	14
L-b 5, w 13, n-b 6	24
TOTAL (49.2 overs)	227

BOWLING: Wasim Akram 10-0-49-3; Aqib Javed 10-2-27-2; Mushtaq Ahmed 10-1-41-3; Ijaz Ahmed 3-0-13-0; Imran Khan 6.2-0-43-1; Aamir Sohail 10-0-49-0.

FALL OF WICKETS

1/6 2/21 3/59 4/69 5/141 6/141 7/180 8/183 9/208 10/227

LEGEND **IMRAN KHAN**
PAKISTAN

The 'Lion of Lahore' led his erratically brilliant Pakistan team to their first World Cup final triumph against England before a 87,182-strong audience jammed into the Melbourne Cricket Ground in 1992.

Clutching the trophy after beating a weary England team, he said: "This is the most fulfilling and satisfying cricket moment of my life."

He made the highest score of the match (72) and took the final England wicket to see Pakistan home by 22 runs.

It was the final crowning moment to a glittering career for one of the greatest all-rounders in cricket history.

Born in Lahore, on November 25, 1952, he played county cricket in England from 1971-88 but did not play domestic cricket in his own country after 1980-81.

His talents were clear from the moment he joined Worcestershire in 1971 and won a Blue at Oxford in 1973. He left New Road in 1976 and the following season played for Sussex, a county he served with distinction until 1988.

But it was on the international scene that Imran's career was to flourish.

He made his Test debut in 1971 but did not fully establish himself until 1976-77. In three series that season against New Zealand, Australia, and the West Indies, he took 57 wickets.

In 1981-82 he became his country's leading wicket-taker, ahead of Fazal Mahmood. He celebrated that feat by taking eight for 58 at Lahore against Sri Lanka, his best Test figures, and, for good measure, six for 58 in the second innings.

Imran was made Pakistan captain for the 1982 tour to England. He took 21 wickets in the series and returned home to mastermind 3-0 defeats of Australia and India. He took 53 wickets in the two series at 13.75.

He was Pakistan's sixth highest run-getter in history when he retired after the 1992 World Cup, scoring 3,807 runs in 88 Tests at an average of 37.69.

Of his contemporaries, only Kapil Dev (434), Richard Hadlee (431), Ian Botham (383) and Malcolm Marshall (376) took more Test wickets than Imran's 362, costing only 22.81 apiece.

He is one of only four cricketers – the others are Ian Botham, Richard Hadlee and Kapil Dev – to achieve 3,000 runs and 300 wickets in Tests.

Pakistan's triumph in 1992 was as much down to his motivational skills as it was the obvious talent that made up his squad.

A dreadful start in their group games had left his side staring a first round exit but Imran called for the individual talents of his side to be gelled together as one solid unit.

His famous speech where he likened his side to 'cornered tigers' inspired his team-mates and drove them on to their finest hour.

Imran is now a respected ambassador for his country, raising funds for a cancer hospital in Lahore he built after his mother's death in 1985, and is married to rich heiress Jemima Goldsmith.

WORLD CUP 1996

The Wills World Cup, hosted by India, Pakistan and Sri Lanka, was all about competing television networks fighting to win a market share, regional and international politics, poorly conceived format and logistics, crowd disorder, and a money-making philosophy given priority over the fundamentals of organising a global sporting occasion.

It was markedly at odds with the 1987 World Cup, also co-hosted by India and Pakistan and widely judged, according to Wisden Cricketers' Almanack, to be an 'organisational triumph'.

Another major factor in the promotion of this sixth World Cup was ICC's decision to hand over all responsibility for the tournament to the World Cup committee, Pilcom.

The opening ceremony was attended by 12 competing countries, a welcome increase of three from the previous World Cup. More than 100,000 attended the event but it flopped badly. The laser show was a disaster, the compere was embarrassing, and sections of the Calcuttan government called for Pilcom convenor, Jagmohan Dalmiya, the current president of ICC, to be brought to task on a charge of 'wasting public money'.

The logistical chaos of the tournament stemmed largely from the unrealistic decision to spread the tournament to virtually every corner of the vast Indian sub-continent.

Internal airlines' schedules failed to cope, and the whole mess was compounded by a bomb blast in Colombo, leading to Australia and the West Indies refusing to play their scheduled group games there.

Thankfully, cricket was the winner! The great game came to the rescue in the nick of time to foil some critics seemingly more interested in rubbishing the tournament than enjoying the action.

Twenty-one years after Sri Lanka had almost shyly entered the first World Cup came the greatest moment in their history.

They were more or less guaranteed a place in the quarter-finals after Australia and the West Indies forfeited their matches against Sri Lanka, refusing to travel there after a terrorist bomb killed 80 people in the capital, Colombo.

But Sri Lanka, who were given the points for a win, clearly earned their progress to the last eight, beating Zimbabwe, India and Kenya, against whom they created all sorts of records in the process.

Their 398 for five in 50 overs of mayhem at Kandy was a world record for a one-day international. Star of the moment was Aravinda de Silva, who scored his country's maiden World Cup century and went on to hit 145, a Sri Lankan record in all limited-overs internationals.

In reply, Steve Tikolo was yorked on 96, four runs short of Kenya's first century at senior level, and on any other day, Kenya's reply of 254 for seven would have been cause for celebration.

But they had their day on February 29 when they pulled-off the biggest upset in World Cup history, beating the mighty West Indies by 73 runs at Pune.

Kenya's captain Maurice Odumbe had good reason to believe a total of 166 was a no-contest score against a batting line-up featuring: Brian Lara, Richie Richardson, Shivnarine Chanderpaul and Jimmy Adams. How wrong that assessment of Kenya's prospects proved to be!

'West Indies 93 all out, Kenya win by 73 runs' sent the world's communications networks crazy for a few hours as another purple passage of cricket history was written.

Meanwhile, South Africa were winning all five Group B matches to join England, Sri Lanka, India, Pakistan, New Zealand, Australia and West Indies in the quarter-finals.

Never beaten before the semi-final stage in five previous World Cups, England sank without trace against Sri Lanka, at Faisalabad. Sanath Jayasuriya played one of the great one-day innings of World Cup history to clinch the Man of the Match award and relieve England of their World Cup 96 ambitions.

He scored 82 off 44 balls, showing unmerciful disdain for the bowling of Phil DeFreitas and Richard Illingworth as Sri Lanka charged past England's 235 for eight score for the loss of five wickets.

The India-Pakistan clash was decidedly turbulent — and a thriller.

Navjot Sidhu was seven runs short of his century when deceived by Mushtaq's flipper, before Ajay Jadeja raised the run-rate with 45 to steer India to 287 for eight in 50 overs.

Saeed Anwar and Aamir Sohail gave Pakistan's reply a blistering start with scores of 48 and 55 respectively as the scoreboard showed 113 for two from the first 15 overs. But gradually Pakistan fell behind the clock and Javed Miandad's run-out signalled the end of Pakistan's reign as World Cup holders and the end of the little man's illustrious career.

Favourites South Africa caught the backlash of West Indies' defeat by Kenya with Brian Lara's century in a total of 264 for eight too much for the Springboks, beaten by 19 runs.

The Waugh twins steered Australia into the last four against New Zealand, Mark becoming the first batsman to score three hundreds in one World Cup.

A riot ended the first semi-final between India and Sri Lanka at Calcutta. Enraged by India's collapse of seven wickets for 22 in reply to Sri Lanka's 251 for eight, some home supporters hurled bottles onto the outfield and set fire to seating. Referee Clive Lloyd took the teams off the field for a cooling off period, attempted a restart, and then awarded the game to Sri Lanka with India needing an impossible 132 from 15.5 overs, with only two wickets standing.

Mark Taylor claimed West Indies had won 95 per cent of the semi-final against his Australian team, at Mohali. Yet they lost by five runs!

Australia's total of 207 for eight relied on half-centuries from Stuart Law and Michael Bevan. At 165 for two, West Indies needed 43 runs from the last nine overs. Shivnarine Chanderpaul was heading for a century and Richie Richardson was a playing a captain's knock on his last appearance as skipper. Chanderpaul missed his century; Shane Warne took three for six; and Richardson was stranded on 49 not out as his side crashed to 202 all out.

The final between Australia and Sri Lanka will be remembered always for Aravinda de Silva's unbeaten 107, an innings that won him the Man of the Match award in a stunning seven-wicket win . It was the first time in six attempts that a side batting second had won a World Cup final.

ENGLAND v SRI LANKA
Quarter-Final at Iqbal Stadium, Faisalabad on 9th March. Sri Lanka won by five wickets.
Toss: England.

ENGLAND			SRI LANKA		
R.A.Smith run out		25	S.T.Jayasuriya st Russell b Reeve		82
*M.A.Atherton c Kaluwitharana b Vaas		22	†R.S.Kaluwitharana b Illingworth		8
G.A.Hick c Ranatunga b Muralitharan		8	A.P.Gurusinha run out		45
G.P.Thorpe b Dharmasena		14	P.A. De Silva c Smith b Hick		31
P.A.J.DeFreitas lbw b Jayasuriya		67	*A.Ranatunga lbw b Gough		25
A.J.Stewart b Muralitharan		17	H.P.Tillekeratne not out		19
†R.C.Russell b Dharmasena		9	R.S.Mahanama not out		22
D.A.Reeve b Jayasuriya		35	H.D.P.K.Dharmasena		
D.Gough not out		26	W.P.U.C.J.Vaas		
P.J.Martin not out		0	M.Muralitharan		
R.K.Illingworth			G.P.Wickremasinghe		
L-b 8, w 4		12	L-b 1, w 2, n-b 1		4
TOTAL (50 overs; 8 wickets)		235	TOTAL (40.4 overs; 5 wickets)		236

BOWLING: Wickremasinghe 7-0-43-0; Vaas 8-1-29-1; Muralitharan 10-1-37-2; Dharmasena 10-0-30-2; Jayasuriya 9-0-46-2; De Silva 6-0-42-0.

FALL OF WICKETS
1/31 2/58 3/66 4/94 5/145 6/171 7/173 8/235

BOWLING: Martin 9-1-41-0; Illingworth 10-1-72-1; Gough 10-1-36-1; DeFreitas 3.4-0-38-0; Reeve 4-1-14-1; Hick 4-0-34-1.

FALL OF WICKETS
1/12 2/113 3/165 4/194 5/198

INDIA v PAKISTAN

Quarter-Finals at Chinnaswamy Stadium, Bangalore, on 9th March. India won by 39 runs.
Toss: India.

INDIA

N.S.Sidhu b Mushtaq	93
S.R.Tendulkar b Rehman	31
S.V.Manjrekar c Miandad b Aamir Sohail	20
*M.Azharuddin c Rashid b Waqar	27
V.G.Kambli b Mushtaq	24
A.Jadeja c Aamir b Waqar	45
†N.R.Mongia run out	3
A.Kumble c Miandad b Aqib	10
J.Srinath not out	12
B.K.V.Prasad not out	0
S.L.V.Raju	
L-b 3, w 15, n-b 4	22
TOTAL (50 overs; 8 wickets)	287

BOWLING: Waqar Younis 10-1-67-2; Aqib Javed 10-2-67-1; Ata-ur-Rehman 10-0-40-1; Mushtaq Ahmed 10-0-56-2; Aamir Sohail 5-0-29-1; Salim Malik 5-0-25-0.

FALL OF WICKETS
1/90 2/138 3/168 4/200 5/226 6/236 7/260 8/279

PAKISTAN

*Aamir Sohail b Prasad	55
Saeed Anwar c Kumble b Srinath	48
Ijaz Ahmed c Srinath b Prasad	12
Inzamam-ul-Haq c Mongia b Prasad	12
Salim Malik lbw b Kumble	38
Javed Miandad run out	38
†Rashid Latif st Mongia b Raju	26
Mushtaq Ahmed c and b Kumble	0
Waqar Younis not out	4
Ata-ur-Rehman lbw b Kumble	0
Aqib Javed not out	6
B 1, l-b 3, w 5	9
TOTAL (49 overs; 9 wickets)	248

BOWLING: Srinath 9-0-61-1; Prasad 10-0-45-3; Kumble 10-0-48-3; Raju 10-0-46-1; Tendulkar 5-0-25-0; Jadeja 5-0-19-0.

FALL OF WICKETS
1/84 2/113 3/122 4/132 5/184 6/231 7/232 8/239 9/239

SOUTH AFRICA v WEST INDIES

Quarter-Finals at National Stadium, Karachi, on 11th March. West Indies won by 19 runs.
Toss: West Indies.

WEST INDIES

S.Chanderpaul c Cullinan b McMillan	56
†C.O.Browne c Cullinan b Matthews	26
B.C.Lara c Pollock b Symcox	111
*R.B.Richardson c Kirsten b Symcox	10
R.A.Harper lbw b McMillan	9
R.I.C.Holder run out	5
K.L.T.Arthurton c Hudson b Adams	1
J.C.Adams not out	13
I.R.Bishop b Adams	17
C.E.L.Ambrose not out	0
C.A.Walsh	
B 2, l-b 11, w 2, n-b 1	16
TOTAL (50 overs; 8 wickets)	264

BOWLING: Pollock 9-0-46-0; Matthews 10-0-42-1; Cronje 3-0-17-0; McMillan 10-1-37-2; Symcox 10-0-64-2; Adams 8-0-45-2.

FALL OF WICKETS
1/42 2/180 3/210 4/214 5/227 6/230 7/230 8/254

SOUTH AFRICA

A.C.Hudson c Walsh b Adams	54
G.Kirsten hit wicket b Ambrose	3
D.J.Cullinan c Bishop b Adams	69
*W.J.Cronje c Arthurton b Adams	40
J.N.Rhodes c Adams b Harper	13
B.M.McMillan lbw b Harper	6
S.M.Pollock c Adams b Harper	6
†S.J.Palframan c and b Harper	1
P.L.Symcox c Harper b Arthurton	24
C.R.Matthews not out	8
P.R.Adams b Walsh	10
B 1, l-b 4, w 2, n-b 4	11
TOTAL (49.3 overs)	245

BOWLING: Ambrose 10-0-29-1; Walsh 8.3-0-51-1; Bishop 5-0-31-0; Harper 10-0-47-4; Adams 10-0-53-3; Arthurton 6-0-29-1.

FALL OF WICKETS
1/21 2/118 3/140 4/186 5/196 6/196 7/198 8/227 9/228 10/245

AUSTRALIA v NEW ZEALAND

Quarter-Final at M.A.Chidambaram Stadium, Madras, on 11th March. Australia won by six wickets. Toss: New Zealand.

NEW ZEALAND

C.M.Spearman c Healy b Reiffel	12
N.J.Astle c Healy b Fleming	1
*†L.K.Germon c Fleming b McGrath	89
S.P.Fleming c S.R.Waugh b McGrath	8
C.Z.Harris c Reiffel b Warne	130
R.G.Twose b Bevan	4
C.L.Cairns c Reiffel b M.E.Waugh	4
A.C.Parore lbw b Warne	11
S.A.Thomson run out	11
D.N.Patel not out	3
D.J.Nash	
L-b 6, w 3, n-b 4	13
TOTAL (50 overs; 9 wickets)	286

BOWLING: Reiffel 4-0-38-1; Fleming 5-1-20-1; McGrath 9-2-50-2; M.E.Waugh 8-0-43-1; Warne 10-0-52-2; Bevan 10-0-52-1; S.R.Waugh 4-0-25-0.

FALL OF WICKETS
1/15 2/16 3/44 4/212 5/227 6/240 7/259 8/282 9/286

AUSTRALIA

*M.A.Taylor c Germon b Patel	10
M.E.Waugh c Parore b Nash	110
R.T.Ponting c sub (R.J.Kennedy) b. Thomson	31
S.K.Warne lbw b Astle	24
S.R.Waugh not out	59
S.G.Law not out	42
M.G.Bevan	
†I.A.Healy	
P.R.Reiffel	
D.W.Fleming	
G.D.McGrath	
B 1, l-b 6, w 3, n-b 3	13
TOTAL (47.5 overs; 4 wickets)	289

BOWLING: Nash 9-1-44-1; Patel 8-0-45-1; Cairns 6.5-0-51-0; Harris 10-0-41-0; Thomson 8-0-57-1; Astle 3-0-21-1; Twose 3-0-23-0.

FALL OF WICKETS
1/19 2/84 3/127 4/213

SRI LANKA v INDIA

Semi-Finals at Eden Gardens, Calcutta, on 13th March. Sri Lanka won by default. Toss: India.

SRI LANKA

S.T.Jayasuriya c Prasad b Srinath	1
†R.S.Kaluwitharana c Manjrekar b Srinath	0
A.P.Gurusinha c Kumble b Srinath	1
P.A.de Silva b Kumble	66
R.S.Mahanama retired hurt	58
*A.Ranatunga lbw b Tendulkar	35
H.P.Tillekeratne c Tendulkar b Prasad	32
H.D.P.K.Dharmasena b Tendulkar	9
W.P.U.C.J.Vaas run out	23
G.P.Wickremasinghe not out	4
M.Muralitharan not out	5
B 1, l-b 10, w 4, n-b 2	17
TOTAL (50 overs; 8 wickets)	251

BOWLING: Srinath 7-1-34-3; Kumble 10-0-51-1; Prasad 8-0-50-1; Kapoor 10-0-40-0; Jadeja 5-0-31-0; Tendulkar 10-1-34-2.

FALL OF WICKETS
1/1 2/1 3/35 4/85 5/168 6/206 7/236 8/244

INDIA

S.R.Tendulkar st Kaluwitharana b Jayasuriya	65
N.S.Sidhu c Jayasuriya b Vaas	3
S.V.Manjrekar b Jayasuriya	25
*M.Azharuddin c and b Dharmasena	0
V.G.Kambli not out	10
J.Srinath run out	6
A.Jadeja b Jayasuriya	0
†N.R.Mongia c Jayasuriya b De Silva	1
A.R.Kapoor c De Silva b Muralitharan	0
A.Kumble not out	
B.K.V.Prasad	
L-b 5, w 5	10
TOTAL (34.1 overs; 8 wickets)	120

BOWLING: Wickremasinghe 5-0-24-0; Vaas 6-1-23-1; Muralitharan 7-1-0-29-1; Dharmasena 7-0-24-1; Jayasuriya 7-1-12-3; De Silva 2-0-3-1.

FALL OF WICKETS
1/8 2/98 3/99 4/101 5/110 6/115 7/120 8/120

AUSTRALIA v WEST INDIES

Semi-Final at Punjab CA Stadium, Mohali, Chandigarh, on 14th March. Australia won by
five runs. Toss: Australia.

AUSTRALIA

M.E.Waugh lbw b Ambrose		0
*M.A.Taylor b Bishop		1
R.T.Ponting lbw b Ambrose		0
S.R.Waugh b Bishop		3
S.G.Law run out		72
M.G.Bevan c Richardson b Harper		69
†I.A.Healy run out		31
P.R.Reiffel run out		7
S.K.Warne not out		6
D.W.Fleming		
G.D.McGrath		
L-b 11, w 5, n-b 2		18
TOTAL (50 overs; 8 wickets)		207

BOWLING: Ambrose 10-1-26-2; Bishop 10-1-35-2; Walsh 10-1-33-0; Gibson 2-0-13-0; Harper 9-0-47-1; Adams 9-0-42-0.

FALL OF WICKETS

1/0 2/7 3/8 4/15 5/153 6/171 7/186 8/207

WEST INDIES

S.Chanderpaul c Fleming b McGrath		80
†C.O.Browne c and b Warne		10
B.C.Lara b S.R.Waugh		45
*R.B.Richardson not out		49
R.A.Harper lbw b McGrath		2
O.D.Gibson c Healy b Warne		1
J.C.Adams lbw b Warne		2
K.L.T.Arthurton c Healy b Fleming		0
I.R.Bishop lbw b Warne		3
C.E.L.Ambrose run out		2
C.A.Walsh b Fleming		0
L-b 4, w 2, n-b 2		8
TOTAL (49.3 overs)		202

BOWLING: McGrath 10-2-30-2; Fleming 8.3-0-48-2; Warne 9-0-36-4, M.E.Waugh 4-0-16-0; S.R.Waugh 7-0-30-1; Reiffel 5-0-13-0; Bevan 4-1-12-0; Law 2-0-13-0.

FALL OF WICKETS

1/25 2/93 3/165 4/173 5/178 6/183 7/187 8/194 9/202 10/202

AUSTRALIA v SRI LANKA

Final at Gaddafi Stadium, Lahore, on 17th March. Sri Lanka won by seven wickets. Toss: Sri Lanka.

AUSTRALIA

*M.A.Taylor c Jayasuriya b De Silva		74
M.E.Waugh c Jayasuriya b Vaas		12
R.T.Ponting b De Silva		45
S.R.Waugh c De Silva b Dharmasena		13
S.K.Warne st Kaluwitharana b Muralitharan		2
S.G.Law c De Silva b Jayasuriya		22
M.G.Bevan not out		36
†I.A.Healy b De Silva		2
P.R.Reiffel not out		13
D.W.Fleming		
G.D.McGrath		
L-b 10, w 11, n-b 1		22
TOTAL (50 overs; 7 wickets)		241

BOWLING: Wickremasinghe 7-0-38-0; Vaas 6-1-30-1; Muralitharan 10-0-31-1; Dharmasena 10-0-47-1; Jayasuriya 8-0-43-1; De Silva 9-0-42-3.

FALL OF WICKETS

1/36 2/137 3/152 4/156 5/170 6/202 7/205

SRI LANKA

S.T.Jayasuriya run out		9
†R.S.Kaluwitharana c Bevan b Fleming		6
A.P.Gurusinha b Reiffel		65
P.A.de Silva not out		107
*A.Ranatunga not out		47
H.P.Tillekeratne		
R.S.Mahanama		
H.D.P.K.Dharmasena		
W.P.U.C.J.Vaas		
G.P.Wickremasinghe		
M.Muralitharan		
B 1, l-b 4, w 5, n-b 1		11
TOTAL (46.2 overs; 3 wickets)		245

BOWLING: McGrath 8.2-1-28-0; Fleming 6-0-43-1; Warne 10-0-58-0; Reiffel 10-0-49-1; M.E.Waugh 6-0-35-0; S.R.Waugh 3-0-15-0; Bevan 3-0-12-0.

FALL OF WICKETS

1/12 2/23 3/148

LEGEND **ARAVINDA DE SILVA**
SRI LANKA

Two innings at the 1996 World Cup propelled Aravinda de Silva's career to legendary proportions back home in Colombo.

They saw little Sri Lanka, so often denied opportunity in the higher spheres of international cricket, achieve the impossible dream of reaching their first World Cup final — and winning it!

Arguably, he is the most exciting batsman in world cricket. Right-handed, wristy, quick-footed, a little rotund, he plays cricket with the sort of freedom you expect to see in a knockabout match on a beach with the tide coming in.

Mention Calcutta and Lahore, the two great cricket centres belonging to India and Pakistan, and you think of Aravinda, as well as cricketers from those two countries.

He wrote his own chapter in the history of those famous grounds when the 1996 World Cup adjudicators awarded him Man of the Match awards in the semi-final and the final of that tournament.

Sri Lanka were in desperate trouble against India in the semi when, batting first, they lost three quick wickets. But Aravinda, showing total disdain for India's attack despite its early success, hit 22 off Prasad's first two overs and went on to make 66 from 47 balls.

In reply, India collapsed, the crowd rioted, and although Sri Lanka were awarded the match by default after the disturbance, Aravinda emerged with his reputation enhanced.

By the end of the end of World Cup 96, he was a legend. He scored an undefeated 107 to steer Sri Lanka past Australia's total of 241 for seven for the loss of only three wickets. It was only the third century in a World Cup final, following knocks from Clive Lloyd and Viv Richards respectively, and the massed ranks of spectators rose to acclaim one of the great innings of one-day international history.

He made his Test debut in 1984 at Lord's and captained Sri Lanka on their 1991 England tour. He made his highest Test score of 267 against New Zealand in 1990-91 and after playing 74 Tests was Sri Lanka's record run-getter with 5129 at 43.10, ahead of Sri Lanka's current captain Arjuna Ranatunga who stands at 4596 with an average of 35.35.

He played for Kent in 1995, illuminating the scene wherever he batted, never better demonstrated than at Lord's in the Benson and Hedges Cup Final that season. He made 112 against Lancashire, one of the finest innings ever seen in a one-day domestic final.

He scored 1,781 first-class runs, averaging 59.36, for Kent before slipping back home to prepare himself for the World Cup.

If Sri Lanka make the 1999 World Cup final, it must be worth a few pounds of anyone's money to place a wager on Aravinda de Silva making a challenge for his second Man of the Match award in successive finals.

No one has more love of the big occasion, nor a temperament better suited to the demands of a Lord's final.

INDEX